The world we live in is a cople
with access to dazzling advan ards
of living. On the other, we 1 , wars,
rampant criminality, inequali , poverty and lack of access to
some of the most basic human needs. Rupen Das, in a sweeping analysis that
encompasses a thorough study of the Old and New Testaments, as well as the
history of the early church, shows in a clear, compelling and fresh way God's
concern for the poor and why, for us Christians, there is no alternative but to
bear witnesses of our Lord Jesus by showing compassion to those in need. It
is the most comprehensive book I have seen about this ever so relevant topic.
I wholeheartedly recommend it.

Marcos Amado
Director for Latin America –Lausanne Movement;
Director of Martureo – Brazilian Center for Missiological Reflection

Where does caring for the poor belong in the gospel message? Rupen Das
does his best to let the material – early evidence of societies and leaders caring
for the poor, the Old Testament, Jesus and the early church – speak for itself.
While the Christian church is growing in its concern for the poor, this book
is a valuable resource for anyone wanting to understand the firm foundation
for a gospel that embraces salvation, compassion and justice.

Dave Toycen
President and CEO, World Vision Canada

This book could only have been written by someone who serves on the
frontlines of emergency relief and community development projects
around the world. The author's recent experience working in the Middle
East in particular motivated him to consider the themes of compassion
and mission. Rupen Das grounds biblical and theological reflections in the
context of hunger, civil violence, extreme poverty and oppression. The initial
chapters offer an analysis of the biblical understanding of poverty and the
practices of the early fathers. Das then moves on to consider theological
currents and mission movements over the last centuries. He argues that
mission organizations often express a limited grasp of God's compassion
and commitment to restore dignity, justice and meaning to human lives. The

chapters on transformation and witness will be valuable for Christians who minister both in places of affluence and in the marginal areas of the world.

Gordon King
Former director of the Sharing Way,
Canadian Baptist Ministries

Born from the heart of a person passionately committed to the practice of compassion, this book gives a rigorous theological case for why followers of Jesus must live out their faith in acts of service with others. In the process, Rupen Das offers us a wonderful and useful overview of the wide sweep of Christian thought through the ages on this topic. He provides a wonderfully nuanced understanding of the tensions inherent in choosing to create works of compassion. But most of all, he inspires us to be people of compassion, and to know, beyond a shadow of a doubt, that this is God's desire for us.

Brian Craig
Director of Leadership Development,
Canadian Baptists of Ontario and Quebec (CBOQ)

Rupen Das invites us to engage with the issues of society as a way of living out our faith, and his invitation is based on a strong theological conviction – God's Word calls on all disciples to identify with the *pathos* of God – his compassion for lostness and brokenness in the world. Giving fresh insights into the broader biblical narrative of God's work in the world, he sheds light on the social dimensions of the gospel from an evangelical perspective united with a sensitive contextual theology. In this excellent book, he has clarified for us an ethic for working with the poor, something that has been in the Bible all along. Given the urgent need for social transformation, justice and peacebuilding in the world today, this is something that the church can no longer ignore if it wants to remain relevant. And more than relevance, the revival of God's people might well rest on how we regard and respond to the poor in our midst.

Fong Choon Sam
Lecturer in Missions and Dean of Academic Studies,
Baptist Theological Seminary, Singapore

What is the heartbeat of God in our troubled world? What does he care about, delight in, and ask of us as his ambassadors? Rupen Das wrestles with these questions on the front lines of some of the world's most difficult places of poverty, war, and injustice. Through a refreshing historical and theological walk, *Compassion and the Mission of God* will inspire reflection and prayerful action to follow the saints in doing justice, loving mercy, and walking with God. Don't pick this book up if you want to remain comfortable – its insights will pull the blinders off and challenge you to new vistas of thought and practice too often buried and forgotten in our churches today.

Peter Howard
Senior Director, Emergency Response, Food for the Hungry

This book brings together in-depth studies on socioeconomic structures of biblical and early Christian times, contemporary theological discussion, and the author's personal passion around the issues of poverty, injustice and compassion. Being a valuable contribution to the ongoing discussion about the right balance between evangelism and social involvement in Christian ministries, it is not only an excellent theoretical study but also a challenging read to reflect on one's own convictions on Christian responsibility for the poor and marginalized, and ultimately on the nature of God. If the reader will allow the book to shape his/her understanding on Christian mission, the kingdom of God will grow in the world.

Helle Liht
Assistant General Secretary, European Baptist Federation

Rupen Das writes from a wealth of experience in a wide variety of cultures in some of the most challenging situations of the world. This book reverberates with his passion for the work of God. He unpacks the social and historical contexts of biblical teaching on poverty in order to answer the "why" questions – why does the Bible say what it does about poverty and the poor? Why does God care for the poor and why should we in turn? Why is compassion important? He also draws from literature and missions to make this writing a compelling read for those who want to make a sustained and effective difference in a starkly polarized world.

Raj Mannar
Regional Field Director, The Navigators of Canada

Rupen Das writes with insight drawn from deep biblical reflection rooted in significant personal experience of seeking to demonstrate the compassion of Jesus to the poor and marginalized. The book articulates that compassion for the poor is no optional extra for the disciple of Christ, but rather an integral part of life for the one who seeks to follow him in seeing the kingdom of God come on earth. The book not only challenges the individual Christian, but also the church community to engage actively and compassionately in being good news for the poor. In our broken world this is a vital message for us all to hear.

Peter Dunn
Director for Mission, BMS World Mission

Out of necessity I have had to find writers who legitimize the personal undoing that occurs as I work toward embracing and engaging in compassion and the mission of God in our incredibly broken world. Dr Das' book *Compassion and the Mission of God* has given me helpful "tracks" to run on. These tracks are travel-worthy for every serious citizen of the kingdom who longs to be caught up in the work of the kingdom of God with all its promise and real transforming potential yet without sticking one's head in the sand. *Compassion and the Mission of God* alerts the kingdom worker to the religious and secular lenses we each employ with conviction that inevitably take us somewhere in our responses. This path of response is sobering if the place it takes us is not toward compassion in Jesus' name.

Scott MacLean
Mission Facilitator, Emmanuel International Canada

Evangelicals, at least in the North American context, have tended to think of the gospel almost exclusively in terms of personal salvation. Further, that salvation has been defined largely, if not exclusively, in terms of a future entrance into heaven with little or no emphasis on a meaningful participation in ushering in the kingdom of God that Jesus announced, right here and now, and in a way that makes the gospel good news for the poor in a specific economic, sociological and political context, especially one that is hostile to Jesus and Christianity. The "already but not yet tension" has largely been absent from evangelical experience, if not in theology. This book is a much-needed corrective call to both mind and heart.

Sunder Krishnan
Senior Pastor, Rexdale Alliance Church

Today, we live in chaos, crisis, and with challenges. Many people are wondering how to address the multiple faces of increasing poverty and conflicts. In this book Rupen Das has wrestled with these hard questions for about forty years with his academic pens and practical pains from theological, biblical, historical, missiological, and especially sociological perspectives. While easily understood it is also powerful and inspirational. As you read it, you can feel the heartbeat of compassion of God. You will be contagiously caught by God's compassion and hopefully start something small like a mustard seed to reveal the invisible kingdom of God, to bless all nations (Gen 12:1–3), especially for the poor, through the poor and with the poor.

Matthew (Keung-Chul) Jeong
Ambassador of Interserve International

Compassion and the Mission of God

Langham
GLOBAL LIBRARY

Compassion and the Mission of God

Revealing the Invisible Kingdom

Rupen Das

Langham
GLOBAL LIBRARY

© 2015 by Rupen Das

Published 2015 by Langham Global Library
an imprint of Langham Creative Projects

Langham Partnership
PO Box 296, Carlisle, Cumbria CA3 9WZ, UK
www.langham.org

ISBNs:
978-1-78368-114-3 Print
978-1-78368-116-7 Mobi
978-1-78368-115-0 ePub
978-1-78368-117-4 PDF

British Library Cataloguing in Publication Data
A catalogue record for this book is available from the British Library

ISBN: 978-1-78368-114-3

Cover & Book Design: projectluz.com

CONTENTS

Foreword

"The future belongs to those who have nothing to lose."

The words continue to haunt me even though they were spoken almost fifteen years ago. It was just a few short weeks after two planes had been flown into the World Trade Center buildings in New York. I was one of two plenary speakers at the Canadian National Conference of the Salvation Army of Canada. They were words spoken by the other plenary speaker, Mary Jo Leddy, a well-known Catholic theologian and activist for refugees and spokesperson for justice issues. She captured the moment with poignant simplicity. These words are as relevant today as they were when she spoke them – a moment when nominal and unengaged religious activity appeared so feeble in the midst of such utter abandoned and unrestrained commitment.

These are confusing times. The rules appear to have changed and many walk numbly through the days aware of the events taking place around them but gripped with a nagging knot of powerlessness. Others simply ignore it, walking dreamily in the confident belief that these events are simply another episode that does not touch them.

Social media allows people to stream famous people holding signs that say "Bring our girls home" and at the same time portray how empty the words are from the reality of inaction and inability to make it so. Political leaders attempt to convince a world captive to their fears that Islamic State (ISIS) does not represent all Muslims while pretending that political forces from the West have nothing to do with marginalization and tensions that have emerged – as if marginalization, corruption and lack of access for socioeconomic empowerment does not produce anger.

Pundits debate on NewsWorld and CNN the intricacies and nuances around the tensions that have brought us to this point in history. Everyone seems to have an opinion except the followers of Jesus Christ whose Scriptures speak profoundly to the root causes of both individual and systemic evil. Some Christians in the global North prefer to continue to bifurcate the gospel into primary/secondary concerns – where evangelism is primary and the acts of compassion and justice are secondary – an illusion that only can be lived out in a bubble.

How did we as the Christian church arrive at this point in history with the seemingly ineffective ability to live or speak into it? Do we have nothing to say? Have we simply become socially acceptable, culturally pasteurized and mediocre in our Christendom framework of faith?

This is why Leddy's comment about the future is so critical. It calls for a renewed sense of the passionate and intentional faith-commitment that made it possible for first-century Christianity to sweep through the Roman Empire, not with power but with servant love. A commitment that enabled these early followers of Christ to engage and influence the culture from the bottom up with a gospel that was for all people – not simply a spiritual gospel, but a sociopolitical and economic one as well.

We live in violent, chaotic times. A cultural Christianity will neither be sufficient or revolutionary enough to address the resolute commitment of forces shaping history. If Leddy is right, then this is a critical moment in the life of the church – a moment demanding a rediscovery of the radical and revolutionary nature of the Christian faith in all its dimensions.

Rupen Das grapples with this issue in this book. It is not just a scholarly and biblical unpacking of the fullness of God's concern for the poor and the marginalized. It is a call for us to live out a compassionate discipleship that tenaciously holds to the fullness of the good news that we are called to proclaim. It is not theory, but emerges from a life which has sought to put this into practice. He has lived the content of this book. It emerges from his global sensibility from which his faith has been vibrantly formed and for the church that he sees as critical to the mission of God. Rupen knows when Jesus said, "you find life by losing it," he really meant it, and at the same time Rupen realizes the alternative is an impotent faith and an irrelevant church.

Dietrich Bonheoffer in his book *Ethics* wrote: "Who stands fast? Only the person whose final standards are not reason, principles, conscience, freedom, or his virtue, but who is ready to sacrifice all this when he is called to obedient and responsible action in faith and exclusive allegiance to God . . . the responsible person, who tries to make his whole life an answer to that question and call of God." Then he asks the crucial question, "Where are these responsible people?"

We are living in a time that cries out for those kinds of people. It demands a recapturing of a faith that is costly in its discipleship. A church whose leaders believe that producing radical and revolutionary disciples of Jesus Christ is the most important thing they do and as a result, nurture followers of Jesus that live as if "they have nothing to lose." Only these followers will have the courage and the humble sensibilities to speak and live into these times with the fullness of a gospel that is proclaimed in both word and deed.

"Where are the responsible people?" Bonheoffer asked in the context of Nazi Germany. He did so to challenge Christians to live differently in that time. We need to ask the same question today. It is not as simple as succumbing to our fears of terrorism. The real questions are far more complicated and challenging – how do I think and live out my life as a Christian in this fragmented and violent world?

Stanley Hauerwas confirms this when he states that, "the primary task of those who would make Jesus' story theirs is to stand within that world – their world – witnessing to a peaceable kingdom which reflects the right understanding of that very world." Read this book for all that it is – a manifesto of this peaceable kingdom that we have been made part of through Jesus Christ. It is for people who seek to live life with nothing to lose.

Dr Gary V. Nelson
President, Tyndale University College & Seminary
Author of *Borderland Churches* and *Going Global*

Acknowledgements

Books are rarely written in isolation. The people who are a part of one's life experiences have a profound impact on how one perceives and understands the world, the Bible, and one's Christian faith. To understand why God cares for the poor has been a lifelong journey. While there have been numerous people who have seeded thoughts and stimulated insights through their books, personal conversations, and the work they do, three people stand out as having been instrumental along the way. Gordon King, a colleague from World Vision Canada and now at Canadian Baptist Ministries (CBM), and Kalyan Das, a Baptist minister in Oxford, UK have been very good sounding boards and their insights have been more valuable than I can express. Bill Brackney at Acadia Divinity College provided valuable input at critical points of the writing.

I'm grateful to Gary Nelson and Janet Clark at Tyndale University College and Seminary who have provided me an academic home for my writing. Numerous students in my classes in different countries were privy to my thinking and research as it developed. Their feedback helped identify gaps and clarified how I was communicating.

I am very appreciative of Sam Chaise, Terry Smith, Sharlene Craig and the rest of the leadership at Canadian Baptist Ministries who have supported me in the ministries that I am involved in. These ministries are the some of the contexts for the questions and insights in this book.

This book would not have seen the light of day without the patient shepherding of the manuscript through the process by Vivian Doub and the team at Langham. It has been a pleasure working with you.

My parents, Prasanta and Ruby Das, and my grandparents were always models of compassion for the poor as an integral part of their faith. I always sensed that they understood this better than my theology could explain. My deep gratitude to my wife Mamta, for her encouragement and the space she provides for me to think and write. Our children and their spouses share our concern for the poor and broken. I am grateful to our daughter Layla for proofreading various parts of the manuscript and to our son Nishant for providing valuable insights and feedback at various points.

Psalm 115:1, "Not to us, LORD, not to us, but to your name be the glory, because of your love and faithfulness."

Rupen Das
Amsterdam, 2015

1

Introduction

"Faith seeking understanding."[1]
St Anselm of Canterbury (AD 1033–1109)

The members of a small church nestled on the slopes of the Bekaa (valley) in eastern Lebanon, seeing the waves of refugees fleeing the bloodshed and violence in their country, decided to open their doors and help in any way they could. They started with helping a few families and over time this small congregation of sixty adults was providing food aid to seven hundred fifty families (at least 4,500 individuals) on a monthly basis. Besides that, they hosted a weekly medical clinic for the refugees and started a school and child-friendly spaces for the children who have been traumatized by the conflict and lost their childhood.

This was not a program that they subcontracted to paid professionals with training in relief, but was a ministry in which many members of their church selflessly gave of their time as they visited the families and helped in any way they could, both physically and spiritually. They were unashamed of their faith as they shared about the God who is approachable and caring, and as they prayed with those who sought help. There was no conditionality in the assistance provided and no manipulation to get people to believe. Reflecting on all that was happening, the pastor said, "We had been praying for years for revival and nothing happened. But when we as a congregation started helping

---

1. St. Anselm the eleventh-century Benedictine monk and philosopher, who later became the Archbishop of Canterbury is said to have written, *Neque enim quaero intelligere ut credam, sed credo ut intelligam. Nam et hoc credo, quia, nisi credidero, non intelligam.* (Nor do I seek to understand that I may believe, but I believe that I may understand. For this, too, I believe, that, unless I first believe, I shall not understand.). Clement C. J. Webb, ed., *The Devotions of St. Anselm Archbishop of Canterbury* (London: Methuen & Co., 1903), 20.

the desperately poor and needy refugees, and shared the love of God with both hands, in words and in action, revival came and changed our church." They were seeing people from different faiths choosing to follow Christ, prisoners in jail transformed, and dramatic answers to prayer.

While this is not a formula or template of what a church should do that would guarantee certain results, what this church was experiencing was the reality of Isaiah 58:7–9:

> Is it not to share your food with the hungry and to provide the poor wanderer with shelter – when you see the naked, to clothe them, and not to turn away from your own flesh and blood? Then your light will break forth like the dawn, and your healing will quickly appear; then your righteousness will go before you, and the glory of the Lord will be your rear guard. Then you will call, and the Lord will answer; you will cry for help, and he will say: Here am I.

The revival they had sought was God drawing near and his presence becoming real – a foretaste of eternity: "God's dwelling place is now among the people, and he will dwell with them" (Rev 21:3).

Is there a connection between God's people demonstrating compassion and welcoming the poor and broken into their midst and caring for them, and God manifesting his presence? Why does it seem that in so many places in Scripture the poor and those who live on the margins of society are so important to God? Is it his way of communicating something about who he is and what his kingdom is like? Is it possible that something profound changes when people in the name of Christ are willing to step out of their comfort zone and self-centeredness, and put their time, money, reputation, and resources on the line by sacrificially helping those who are broken and poor, and then introducing them to the King of the kingdom of God.

One of the more intriguing passages in the Bible is Galatians 2, which describes the controversy between Paul and Peter in the city of Antioch sometime before AD 49. The disagreement was on whether Gentiles could become followers of Jesus Christ without also keeping the Jewish laws. This was the first major theological conflict among the followers of Christ and almost split the early church. As the two leaders and their followers resolved the issues, the decision was as Paul describes in Galatians 2:9: "They agreed that we should go to the Gentiles, and they to the Jews." The next verse seems almost out of place in light of what precedes it. It would seem to have nothing to do with the theological discussion and is almost an afterthought. Verse 10 states, "All they asked was that we should continue to remember the poor, the very thing I had been eager to do all along."[2]

The idea of compassion and care of the poor was so important to what they believed it meant to be a follower of Christ, they wanted to make sure that as Paul and Barnabas shared the gospel among the Gentiles, that *this* expression of their faith was not lost. While the agreement was that the Gentiles did not have to keep the Jewish laws, the care for the poor was one practice that was to be continued. For the leaders of the early church the care for those on the margins of society was as much at the core of the Christian faith and its expression, as the understanding of God's redemptive act in human history through Jesus Christ, because the acts of compassion in the midst of everyday life demonstrated that God is redeemer.

Caring for those who are not part of the mainstream of society because of their poverty, brokenness and rejection is *a prophetic act.* It physically illustrates more clearly than anything else, God's concern for those who are not part of his kingdom because of the evil that has broken them and the darkness that holds them in bondage. It is a prophetic act also because caring for the poor shows what the kingdom of God is really like – where the weak, the vulnerable and the broken are not discarded but are valued; a place where people, regardless of who they are, find a place. It speaks about the value and worth of each person in the kingdom of God.

While it is easy to accept the fact that God is compassionate and therefore redeemer, it has never been clear as to how the church should live out this truth. The church has often struggled with how it should relate to society and be prophetic within the culture and the community in which it is located. Is its message one of *deliverance from* this world and its problems, as one would rescue people from a burning building, or is it one of *engagement with* the problems and issues of society till there is change? Or is there another alternative?

How the church has related to society has varied through out history. Jürgen Moltmann, the German theologian at the University of Tübingen, describes the struggle between *identity* and *relevance* that the church in every generation and in every country faces. The struggle is for the church to constantly define and protect its identity, which is often defined by its history,

---

2. For a detailed discussion of who the poor referred to in Gal 2:10 could have been, see Bruce Longenecker, *Remember the Poor: Paul, Poverty and the Greco-Roman World* (Grand Rapids: William B. Eerdmans Publishing Co., 2010).

in the midst of competing and changing values in the surrounding culture, and threats from the political context. Unfortunately, this causes the church to be inward looking, thereby loosing its relevance. However, the process of remaining true to what it means to be a people of God and followers of Christ, while engaging with the community and finding ways to be relevant, will change the church.[3]

Bishop Kenneth Cragg, the veteran missionary and scholar, tells the story of Robert Curzon, the English traveler, diplomat and author, looking for ancient manuscripts for British museums. While visiting a monastery in 1849 in the mountains of Lebanon, Curzon writes about a meal with the monks in the candlelit refectory. "I have been quietly dining in a monastery when shouts have been heard and shots have been fired against the stout bulwarks of the outer walls . . . which had but little effect in altering the monotonous cadence in which one of the brotherhood read a homily of St Chrysostom from the pulpit."[4] While there was violence and gunfire outside the high walls of the monastery, it did not affect the life of the monks inside the walls as they continued to live and worship as if nothing had happened. The massive walls kept out the world and its violence to preserve the faith and the faithful.

While it would be easy to be critical of such an isolationist attitude of the church, the reality was of a church trying to be faithful to Christ in the midst of chaos, turbulence and changing times. The Lebanon, Greater Syria, and Palestine of Curzon's time were embroiled with violence and communal strife, as the Ottoman Empire started its death spiral and western powers with arrogance and deceit carved up the region for their own national strategic interests. Bishop Cragg describes the times as being a volatile mix of ". . . liturgies and weapons, traditions and encounters, partisans and aliens, devotions and shouts, walls under siege."[5]

In many ways, they describe the realities of Iraq, Syria, Lebanon, Afghanistan, Egypt, Nigeria, South Sudan, Central Africa, Bosnia and so many other countries in our time. Bishop Cragg, reflecting on Robert Curzon's experience, writes of "Chrysostom[6] of golden tongue, of Antioch and the fourth century," still exhorting his listeners 1,500 years later through

---

3. Jürgen Moltmann, *The Crucified God* (London: SCM Press Ltd., 1974), 3.

4. Quoted in Kenneth Cragg, *The Arab Christian: A History of the Middle East* (Louisville: Westminster John Knox Press, 1991), 204, from Robert Curzon, *Visits to Monasteries in the Levant* (London: John Murray, 1849).

5. Cragg, *The Arab Christian*, 204–205.

6. John Chrysostom was an early church father from the fourth century.

his preserved sermons; listeners whose ancestors had survived the armies and empires of the Persians and Byzantines, Arabs and Turks, Crusaders and Europeans through thousands of years.[7] The church's message had not only been preserved, but also continued to speak to the faithful in the midst of turbulent seasons.

There are times when the church needs to protect itself to survive. But too often the walls keep the world out and prevent the church from influencing society, from being salt and light, and from being a witness for the kingdom of God and the King. This has a huge impact on what the role of the church should be.

Understanding this role starts with the people of God themselves. The church – the people of God – relating to the world is not a program or a strategy, but is a life that is lived out daily demonstrating the reality of Christ and the kingdom of God. John Howard Yoder, the Mennonite theologian and ethicist, wrote about what this community would look like. "The church must be a sample of the kind of humanity within which, for example, economic and racial differences are surmounted. Only then will it have something to say to the society that surrounds it about how those differences must be dealt with. Otherwise preaching to a world a standard of reconciliation that is not its own experience will neither be honest nor effective."[8] It is important that this community is *not just inward looking*, focusing on its own integrity and righteousness, hoping that the world will notice. There needs to be intentional engagement with society and its problems.

The church's disengagement from the world and its problems also has its roots in historical theology, unintentionally through the creeds it formulated. Some of the creeds (such as the Nicene Creed) were never intended to be complete encapsulations of the Christian faith, but were attempts to clarify and articulate specific Christian doctrine in the midst of rival claims.[9] However, over time they ended up defining the core of Christianity and became a "rule of faith" within the churches, with everything else being considered secondary.

---

7. Cragg, *The Arab Christian*, 204.

8. John Howard Yoder, *The Politics of Jesus: Vicit Agnus Noster,* 2nd ed. (Grand Rapids: Eerdmans, 1994), 151.

9. Mark A. Noll, *Turning Points: Decisive Moments in the History of Christianity* (Grand Rapids, Baker Academic, 2000), 47–82, and Alister E. McGrath, *The Christian Theology Reader* (Oxford: Blackwell Publishing, 2001), 10–11. The focus of the Nicene Creed is primarily christological and was meant to affirm the full divinity of Christ in response of the Arian heresy.

The Apostles Creed, on the other hand, evolved as a summary of the major beliefs of the Christian faith. The word "creed," whose root is the Latin term *credo* means, "I believe." Cyril of Jerusalem, speaking about the role of the creeds around AD 350, states: "This synthesis of faith was not made to be agreeable to human opinions, but to present the one teaching of the faith in its totality, in which what is of greatest importance is gathered together from the Scriptures . . . this summary of faith brings together in a few words the entire knowledge of the true religion which is contained in the Old and New [Testaments]."[10]

The faith and belief that the Apostles Creed states is almost entirely focused on the eternal and on the vertical relationship with the triune God. It is silent on what God's people need to believe about the world he created and how to relate to it.

> I believe in God, the Father almighty, creator of heaven and earth. I believe in Jesus Christ, his only Son, our Lord, who was conceived by the Holy Spirit, born of the Virgin Mary, suffered under Pontius Pilate, was crucified, died, and was buried; he descended to the dead. On the third day he rose again; he ascended into heaven, he is seated at the right hand of the Father, and he will come to judge the living and the dead. I believe in the Holy Spirit, the holy catholic church, the communion of saints, the forgiveness of sins, the resurrection of the body, and the life everlasting. Amen.

From the creeds it would seem, as Cyril of Jerusalem would imply, that the summary of faith ("the teaching of the faith in its totality," "the entire knowledge of true religion") has only one dimension to the Christian faith, and that it has no relevance to life in this world. What is missing in the creeds is the kingdom of God and the details and significance of Jesus' earthly life. Christ inaugurated the kingdom, demonstrated its reality through his life and ministry, and taught us to pray expectantly "Thy kingdom come, Thy will be done, on earth just as it is in heaven."

It is the Gospels that teach and demonstrate what the kingdom of God looks like and how we are to relate to it. British theologian now at St Andrews University, N. T. Wright explains, "The great creeds . . . which have shaped and expressed the faith of millions of Christians in both eastern and western

---

10. Cyril of Jerusalem, *Catechesis* V, 12; in *Opera quae supersunt omnia*, ed. W. C. Reischl (Munich: Keck, 1849), 150.

Christianity, simply omit the middle section, the story of Jesus' actual life and the meaning this story conveys . . . The canonical Gospels give us a Jesus whose public career radically mattered as part of his overall accomplishment, which had to do with the kingdom of God. The creeds give us a Jesus whose miraculous birth and saving death, resurrection, and ascension are all we need to know."[11]

The impression from the creeds is not just that the church's relationship with society and its problem are secondary – the impression is that they are simply not an essential part of the Christian faith. Drew University professor Leonard Sweet and writer Frank Viola ask the question, "But how are we to *live our lives* as followers of Christ? . . . "As he is, so are we in the world" (1 John 4:17, NKJV). The Bible doesn't just promise us "eternal life" (John 3:16); it also offers us the gift of life lived through Christ (1 John 4:9). Has the popularity of one verse of Scripture – John 3:16 – and its emphasis on "eternal life" in the future blinded us to what the Bible has to say about life in the now?"[12]

During the last three hundred years, various attempts have been made to articulate again whether God cares for the poor and the broken, and about injustice in society. These then have shaped the various ways the church responds to social need, if at all. The two theological approaches that have been much debated are dispensationalism and postmillennialism with its expression in the Social Gospel. The others that have influenced the debate are Liberation Theology and Post-Colonial Theology. Lately, a post-modernist worldview and an emphasis on human rights are influencing a new generation of Christ followers as they struggle to relate to society. A number of these will be discussed in greater detail in this book with regards to whether the church has a mandate to care for the poor and address the injustice that keeps them in poverty. What has been missing in the various discussions is the question, *why* does God care for the poor and the broken; *why* is he compassionate?

A Personal Journey

During a recent interview, the host asked me why I write material that no one reads. It took me by surprise and was a strange question for me, as I do not

---

11. N. T. Wright, *How God Became King: The Forgotten Story of the Gospels* (New York: Harper Collins Publishers, 2011), 19–20.

12. Leonard Sweet and Frank Viola, *Jesus Manifesto: Restoring the Supremacy and Sovereignty of Jesus Christ* (Nashville: Thomas Nelson, 2010), xxiii.

primarily write for others. Writing helps me uncover and understand reality. So writing for me is a vehicle for my journey. This book is not just an academic exploration of poverty and injustice or a pastoral exhortation to respond to the poor, but has its genesis in my own faith journey in trying to understand *Immanuel*, the God who is with us. If he is with us, then is he concerned for the poor and the broken who are so much part of our communities? More importantly, why would he care? I know that many have traveled along the same road in their journeys and asked similar questions. In many ways there is nothing new in this book, yet it provides fresh clarity on truths we have always known. American writer and philosopher Walker Percy in describing his art states, ". . . you are telling the reader or listener or the viewer something he already knows but which he doesn't quite know that he knows, so that in the act of communication he experiences a recognition, a feeling that he has been there before, a shock of recognition."[13]

With a traditional evangelical[14] and fundamentalist upbringing from the 1950s through to the early 1970s, there was very little that was taught in the churches we attended about the social dimensions of the gospel. The focus was on maintaining the "purity" of the gospel message, and any attempt to contextualize the gospel to specific situations of injustice and poverty, as Liberation Theology was doing in the 1960s, were relegated to the realms of heresy.[15] The evangelical theologian, Carl Henry's prophetic book in 1947, *The Uneasy Conscience of Modern Fundamentalism*, where he mourned the lack of action and the loss of voice within the fundamentalist churches against the social ills of society, was not popular reading in the churches we attended. He wrote, "Fundamentalism is the modern priest and Levite, by-passing suffering humanity."[16]

---

13. Walker Percy, in *Conversations with Walker Percy*, ed. Peggy Whitman Prenshaw (Jackson: University of Mississippi Press, 1985), 24.

14. Gabriel Fackre identifies five classifications for evangelicals: (i) Fundamentalist (stress on biblical inerrancy, sectarian, in defense of doctrine); (ii) Old or Traditional (stress on conversion and personal holiness reminiscent of old German pietism); (iii) New or Neo- (stress on social relevance but not at the expense of personal faith, compassion, intellectual development); (iv) Charismatic and Pentecostal (signs and wonders, power of the Holy Spirit, experience); and (v) Justice and peace (also known as radical evangelicals). In Al Tizon, *Transformation after Lausanne: Radical Evangelical Mission in Global-Local Perspective* (Eugene: Wipf and Stock Publishers, 2008), 3.

15. There were numerous exceptions to this among the evangelical churches – the American Baptists in Central America being one.

16. Carl F. H. Henry, *The Uneasy Conscience of Modern Fundamentalism* (Grand Rapids: William B. Eerdmans Publishing Company, 1947), 2.

In spite of the churches we attended, within my own family I had grandparents and parents who were deeply concerned about the poor and demonstrated the compassion of Christ as an integral part of who they were and what they believed, without ever loosing their zeal to be open about their faith and to worship the living God. My father, because of his work, believed that this world could be a better place.

My journey came to a crisis point, when moving to India for a season I was confronted with pervasive poverty, which I had never noticed as a child. Verses like Matthew 5:42 – "Give to the one who asks you, and do not turn away from the one who wants to borrow from you" – haunted me. I was failing every time I stepped out of our home. How do I deal with the scores of beggars who would crowd around every time I came out of a store? Were they part of a gang? Was a "leader" exploiting the children, and should I give if he was? What good were my few coins for the old man without legs who dragged himself along the filthy pavement or for the leper who reached out with stubs that used to be hands? How do I relate to the family that lived on the pavement in a cardboard shack the size of a large box?

The struggle finally brought me to a breaking point, as I could no longer speak about God's promise of *eternal* life after death if he did not have any relevance or meaning for the billions of poor and oppressed in *this* life. My question was about the character of God. Was the creator God only powerful and demanding, or was he also compassionate, caring and loving? Did the poor, the broken, the marginalized, the displaced and the oppressed really matter to him?

The mission organization I was involved with at the time, was very much focused on seeing individuals experience eternal life and facilitating the movement of the gospel through relational networks. There were other Christian leaders and thinkers struggling with these issues, but their responses did not answer some of the *why* questions I was asking. It was only during the last few decades that I have been able to work through these issues and have a better grasp of both the eternal and temporal dimensions of salvation and the good news about the reign of God.

The Question

Why does it seem that the poor are important to God? If God's mission is to save humanity by forgiving their sin and rebellion through Jesus Christ, why is there so much in the Bible about compassion and care of the poor, the broken, and those who live in the margins of society? Are they just ethical teachings and commands that should define society whenever possible or is compassion fundamental to the Christian faith? Why is God so concerned about a broken world?

Jürgen Moltmann writes about the crucified God. He refers to the Jewish Rabbi Abraham Heschel's concept of the *pathos of God*. This *pathos* is not what he calls "irrational human emotions," but he describes a God who is affected by events, human actions and suffering in history. Moltmann writes, "He is affected by them because he is interested in his creation, his people . . ."[17] This *pathos* is contrasted with the *apatheia* of the gods that Judaism and early Christianity encountered in the religions of the ancient world. *Apatheia* was their inability to feel or be influenced. Centuries later the church encountered Islam, where God is not one who knows suffering and therefore cannot relate to the problem of human suffering. For most people God remains distant and uncaring.

Bruce Fawcett, the President of Crandall University in New Brunswick, Canada, illustrates how and why the poor and vulnerable affect God. He muses that suppose one of your children was severely disabled. While you would love all your children equally, you would have a special concern and love for your disabled child because of his or her inability to function fully in society and because of their dependence on others. This child's disability and his needs would influence all your decisions and you would even write your will keeping this child in mind. The poor, similarly, are unable to function and participate fully in society as God intends all his children to, which is the reason for God's "preferential option for the poor."[18]

The Parable of the Refugee – Understanding How God Felt

Imagine for a moment refugees running away from their homes. They don't have to be Syrian or Iraqi refugees; they could be anyone, anywhere, fleeing devastation. Now picture one of the refugees returning to his devastated home. It does not look like what he had built. All that he had lovingly made is broken, destroyed or missing. Imagine his emotion, seeing the extent

---

17. Moltmann, *The Crucified God*, 270.

18. Personal conversation with Bruce Fawcett. The terms "preferential option for the poor" is a term used extensively by Peruvian theologian and Dominican priest, Gustavo Gutierrez.

to which his home had been destroyed beyond recognition. Everything he had built and made with his own hands and his labor, is now destroyed and unrecognizable.

Now consider how God would have felt entering this world in the person of his Son. This world does not look like what he had created. All he had loving made is broken or destroyed, especially that which he made with his own hands and into whom he breathed his own spirit. This living being is broken and not functioning the way he intended and planned. Imagine God's emotion at seeing the extent to which his creation has been destroyed, and feel the urgency in his mind that this must be put right, ASAP![19]

The evidence of the *pathos* of God, of him being affected by the darkness and evil that has warped his creation, is the incarnation, where God identifies himself as Immanuel – God with us. Because of the incarnation, he understands the depth of human suffering and says, "Come to me, all you who are weary and burdened, and I will give you rest." (Matt 11:28) He answers the prayers of those who cry out to him in desperation. "And I will do whatever you ask in my name, so that the Father may be glorified in the Son. You may ask me for anything in my name, and I will do it" (John 14:13–14).

This astounding offer not only transforms the nature of prayer but also offers insight into the character of God. Prayer then is no longer just worshiping a powerful god out of fear in order to appease him. Neither is prayer a petition to a god asking for mercy and favor, not knowing if he hears, much less answers. When the church members who were providing assistance to the Syrian refugees asked them if they could pray for them, many would comment, "You mean God would hear if I prayed? You mean he cares?" They were surprised that God would be concerned for their pain and struggles. They were encountering a God whose very nature was to "defend the weak and the fatherless; uphold the cause of the poor and the oppressed." He rescues the weak and the needy; delivers them from the hand of the wicked (Ps 82: 2–4).

---

19. Kalyan Das, sermon preached at Botley Baptist Church, Oxford, UK on 12 October 2014.

Compassion was what motivated Jesus in his ministry. The disciple Matthew having observed Jesus firsthand writes in 9:36, "When he saw the crowds, he had compassion on them, because they were harassed and helpless, like sheep without a shepherd." When he healed, it was because he was moved with compassion (Matt 20:34, Mark 1:41, 9:22) When he taught using parables, Jesus spoke about the compassion a father felt towards a rebellious son (Luke 15:20). The Greek word is *splanchnizomai* and literally means, "to be moved in the inward parts." It connotes a strong physical and emotional reaction, "a gut-wrenching response."[20] Unfortunately the word "compassion" has come to mean feeling sorry for someone or a mental attitude of pity at someone's misfortune. The word *splanchnizomai* only occurs in the Gospels and is only used to describe Jesus' reactions. "It is used . . . to describe the attitude of Jesus to people defined as the (multitudes) and the action that ensues from that attitude . . ."[21]

The *pathos* of God is not just a sense of sadness or an intellectual acknowledgement that there is something wrong with the world that he created. For Jesus it was a gut-wrenching reaction as he saw the "lostness" of people, the poor who were victims of injustice, those with crippling diseases and illness, the premature death of the young, and the abuse of the human beings he had created. Compassion is a divine attribute fundamental to God's nature. It defines him.

So, *if* God is so deeply moved and concerned for the poor and those who are broken, then his people need to reflect his values and qualities of compassion, just as they need to reflect his holiness, his love, and his creativity. "As he (Jesus) is, so are we in the world" (1 John 4:17 NKJV).

Putting It Simply – Why Another Book?

Most people find meaning in life as they discover their place within a narrative that they feel explains the world and life for them. In the pluralistic world we live in, there are competing narratives about the meaning of life and about our relationship and obligations to society. Most of these narratives are usually not communicated through a comprehensive philosophical presentation, but through the exploits of heroes and role models, through

---

20. D. Preman Niles, *From East and West: Rethinking Christian Mission* (St Louis: Chalice Press, 2004), 79.

21. Ibid., 79.

parables, stories and folk wisdom, through advertisements, commercials and TV sitcoms, and occasionally through religious education. They are the tools and vehicles through which ideas and values are communicated. Philosopher Nassim Nicholas Taleb, author of *The Black Swan: The Impact of the Highly Improbable* writes, "Metaphors and stories are far more potent (alas) than ideas; they are easier to remember and more fun to read . . . Ideas come and go, stories stay."[22]

While narratives have their limitations because they tend to simplify reality rather than explain its complexity, narratives are important and powerful because they are able to embody ideas within real contexts, thereby giving meaning to events in history and in life. Canadian sociologist at the University of Calgary, Arthur Frank, writes about how stories influence and shape human behavior:

> Stories animate human life; that is their work. Stories work with people, for people, and always stories work *on* people, affecting what people are able to see as real, as possible, and as worth doing or best avoided. . . . Human life depends on the stories we tell: the sense of self that those stories impart, the relationships constructed around shared stories, and the sense of purpose that stories both purpose and foreclose.[23]

Unfortunately narratives are viewed as an inferior form of communicating truth in our technological age. Professor of homiletics, Paul Borden, writes:

> Our literate technological culture has convinced us that truth cannot be communicated [through stories]. Stories may be used to illustrate truth but not communicate it . . . While analytical and logical presentations are sometimes required and beneficial, the assumption behind such presentations is often one of disdain for narrative as the means for communicating major ideas . . . However, more people in culture are influenced, not by papers and books by philosophers, ethicists or commentators, but by the artistic communication of their ideas in the media . . . In

22. Nassim Nicholas Taleb, *The Black Swan: The Impact of the Highly Improbable* (New York: Random House Trade Paperbacks, 2010), xxxi.

23. Arthur W. Frank, *Letting Stories Breathe: A Socio-Narratology* (Chicago: The University of Chicago Press, 2010), 3.

other words, it is the stories and ideas taught by stories that influence people . . ."[24]

Is it any surprise that narratives and stories are a major form of communication in the Bible?[25]

When it comes to the narrative of the Bible as a whole, there are different understandings of what the larger narrative of the Bible is. Some focus on the issue of justice and the theme of God liberating people from social and economic bondage. Others focus on a God who blesses, heals and prospers. Yet others focus on the eternal dimensions, specifically life after death. Many focus on the love of God, and God wanting to fulfill us and make us everything that we were intended to be, in the process freeing us from our psychological bondages. The biblical narrative is often understood as having four parts: creation, fall, redemption and new creation. Craig G. Bartholomew and Michael W. Goheen offer the biblical narrative as a six-act drama: creation, fall, redemption started with Israel, redemption accomplished in Christ, the church, and the final consummation.[26]

Is there a larger narrative about a creator God redeeming not just human beings but all of creation; where history and time have a purpose – "to bring unity to all things in heaven and on earth under Christ" (Eph 1:10) – and that there will come a time when it will be said, "The kingdom of the world has become the kingdom of our Lord and of his Messiah, and he will reign for ever and ever" (Rev 11:15)? Is not the biblical narrative about the eternal King who is the Creator and about his kingdom? The issues of justice and liberation, redemption, blessings, the love of God, hope, eternal life and wholeness in this life, are all realities of the kingdom of God and not separate narratives. It is critical to understand this, because the narrative provides the context for the truth to be understood and then communicated. American theologian Alan E. Lewis wrote, "narrative is now being tested as theology's

---

24. Paul Borden, "Is There Really One Big Idea in That Story?," in *The Big Idea of Biblical Preaching*, ed. Keith Willhite and Scott M. Gibson (Grand Rapids: Baker Books, 1998), 68.

25. For example, Klyne Snodgrass estimates that more than one-third of the teaching material recorded in the synoptic Gospels are parables. Klyne Snodgrass, *Stories with Intent: A Comprehensive Guide to the Parables of Jesus* (Grand Rapids: Eerdmans, 2009), 22.

26. Craig G. Bartholomew and Michael W. Goheen, *The Drama of Scripture: Finding Our Place in the Biblical Story* (Grand Rapids: Baker Academics, 2004), *passim*.

starting point, in response to which, and in reflection upon which, concepts, doctrine, and prescriptions for action may subsequently be constructed."[27]

In the midst of the discussion of the biblical narrative, it is important to remember who the Narrator is, even as he speaks through the limitations and individuality of the human writers. The biblical narrative is not only unique in that it addresses the issues of evil and injustice, but is all the more astounding as it gives meaning to an absolutely magnificent, incredibly beautiful and terrifying universe. It is the story of a creator, of love spurned, redemption and second chances. It describes justice and judgment, and the intriguing possibility of forgiveness. It is a story of an eternal kingdom and its King. This narrative is not a fairy tale or a Russian novel grappling with the existential questions about life and society. Instead, it is the history of time. Brian Wicker writes, "The claim to be able to tell such a story amounts to the claim to be in the position of God."[28]

The Annales School is a style of historiography developed by twentieth-century French historian Fernand Braudel and others that studies long-term social history referred to as *la longe duree*. Rather than focusing on "episodic events or the public deeds of Great Men"[29] they pioneered an approach that looked at the influence of geography, material culture and the psychology of the period on history. William Dever, professor of Near Eastern archeology at the University of Arizona, writes: "They looked rather at history as the result of cultural adaptation to the 'deeper swells' of changing natural conditions over the millennia."[30] Too often the study of Scripture has focused on narrow and specific issues, or on individuals and heroes without understanding the larger narrative of God's work, as well as the history and the context of the Bible. *This book will revisit some of the biblical narratives to try and*

---

27. Alan E. Lewis, *Between Cross and Resurrection: A Theology of Holy Saturday* (Grand Rapids: William B. Eerdmans Publishing Company, 2001). 10. Lewis writes about the impact of narrative theology. "On the surface at least, this is, therefore, an inauspicious, even perilous, moment for theologians of many varieties and all confessions to agree that it is precisely the genre of the story, or narrative, upon which they should concentrate their analysis of how truth is conveyed, and with which they should begin their attempts at communication . . . 'Stories' have recently emerged in much theology as the very means by which the truth of God is understandably received and effectively passed on by the community of faith." Ibid., 10.

28. Brian Wicker, *The Story-Shaped World: Fiction and Metaphysics: Some Variations on a Theme* (Notre Dame: University Press, 1975), 101.

29. William A. Dever, *Who Were the Early Israelites and Where Did They Come From?* (Grand Rapids: William B. Eerdmans Publishing Company, 2003), 133.

30. Ibid., 113.

understand where the poor and the broken fit within the economy of God and why. Understanding this will provide the basis for a theology of compassion.

Over the past several decades there has been a lot of work done on the social, historical and economic contexts of the Old and New Testaments, and that of the early church. These provide the context for the teaching on care for the poor. They explain *why* certain laws were given and *why* Jesus said what he did about the rich and those in power. These are beginning to answer the question: *Why* does the Bible say what it does about poverty and the poor? The second purpose for this book is to draw this material together from the diverse sources into one place to answer the question about compassion: *Why* does God care for the poor, and as a result, *why* should we? *Why* is compassion important? By drawing this material together, I have allowed different voices to be heard rather than my interpretation of what I think they are saying. Christian social responsibility is not a new topic and there are excellent books and other material exploring this issue from both biblical and ethical perspectives.

Much of the discussion in missions on strategies for missions, on evangelism, church planting, social justice, and on being a missional church have focused on the details of how ministry and missions should be done, and as to what rightfully constitutes mission. Somewhere in there the larger question of why God even cares, is lost. How does God see the world and what does he desire for it?

My background in community development and disaster relief provided an urgency to try and understand how to integrate my practice with my faith. The questions I write about are from the messiness of the trenches of being in places of conflict or disasters where society had collapsed, and where grueling poverty and gross injustice challenged my understanding of life and the goodness of God. Being a person with a very strong pragmatic streak, American theologian and philosopher Francis Shaffer's question, "How should we then live?" has become a constant refrain in the recesses of my conscience. The final purpose of this book is to explore the question: Does what I do in the ministries of compassion, social justice and transformation have any relevance to the mission of God?

2

Issues That Frame the Discussion on Compassion

The issues of the poor, of poverty, of compassion and of the church's response are not neutral topics and it is difficult to conduct a rational discourse on them – at least in the western world. Many western evangelicals have, until recently, responded to the needs of the poor with acts of compassion, while others within different streams of Christianity have not been satisfied by mere acts of compassions but sought social transformation and justice in their quest to seek the kingdom of God.

However, a more thorough reading of the Scriptures reveals that poverty is not just a sociological phenomenon that Christians are asked to address. In the teachings of Jesus and in the writings of the Old Testament prophets, there are moral imperatives and spiritual dimensions of poverty and how we are to treat the poor. Most people in the developed or "northern countries" live in social contexts where the acquiring and possession of wealth is a result of hard work and does not have any moral connotations. Hard work, rooted in the Protestant work ethic,[1] is valued; the basic principle being that hard work results in prosperity. This in turn provides security, honor, and social and economic privileges.[2] Because of this cherished value of hard work, most do not understand the role of unjust social and political systems that enslave people in poverty. They also have a hard time understanding the teachings of

---

1. Max Weber coined the phrase in 1901 in his book *The Protestant Ethic and the Spirit of Capitalism* (New York: Scribner). Martin Luther transformed the prevailing Catholic concept of good works to work being an obligation and duty that had positive benefits for both the individual and society. While it is a multidisciplinary concept that encompasses economics, sociology and history, in a theological paradigm hard work and frugality resulting in prosperity was a consequence of one's salvation.

2. I am grateful to Gordon King for these insights.

Jesus, where it seems that wealth is often portrayed as evil and that the poor have special favor with God.[3]

There are four foundational issues that influence the different perspectives on whether compassion is a fundamental biblical value and whether the church should respond to poverty and other social issues. These are (1) how is Scripture read and understood, (2) can theology be contextual, (3) the exact nature of the mission of the church, and (4) how one views the poor.

Reading the Bible: The Lenses through Which the Bible Is Read

The first problem is a hermeneutical[4] question and the issue of translation on how one reads, understands and applies the Scriptures. This is the starting point to try and understand if God cares for the poor.

Each theological approach – whether the Social Gospel, Liberation Theology, Post-Colonial Theology, or an Evangelical Dispensational Theology – claims to use the Bible to understand the world and justify their points of view. The relevance of the Christian faith to issues like poverty and injustice is handled using either proof texts[5] from Scripture or by imposing a theological framework (like dispensationalism, postmillennialism, or Liberation Theology) onto Scripture.

Using proof texts ignores the context and the sweep of Scripture, and usually puts an end to any questions or discussion to try to understand the reasons and implications of what is said in Scripture. On the other hand, imposing a theological framework onto Scripture can limit or distort the breadth of the biblical narrative. As a result, one reads Scripture through a specific theological lens rather than understanding the breadth of Scripture as it was written in its historical context. What is lost, as well, is the mosaic of authors throughout the Bible with their different styles that somehow together communicate the work of God and his mission.

It is important to note that each theological orientation has its own theory and principles of interpreting the biblical text. While there are a range of evangelical perspectives, fundamentalists over the past century

---

3. See Richards and O'Brien on how Westerners read the Scriptures. Randolph E. Richards and Brandon J. O'Brien, *Misreading Scripture with Western Eyes:Removing Cultural Blinders to Better Understand the Bible* (Downers Grove: IVP Books, 2012).

4. Hermeneutics is the theory and principles of interpreting texts. Biblical hermeneutics is the study of the principles of interpreting the books of the Bible.

5. Proof texting is the practice of using texts in isolation of their context to prove a point.

have viewed the Bible as God's eternal Word. For them, the difference of the contexts of the Old and New Testament from that of the present is not an issue. Context has little effect on how the Bible is read. Walter Houston, at Mansfield College, Oxford University, writes that they see the Bible, "not [as] a series of documents arising from and reflecting the interests and beliefs of people within a particular ancient society, but as words spoken from above and beyond them, certainly speaking to them, but equally speaking to us."[6] So if it is God's word, it is to be obeyed unquestioningly. It must be studied and mastered but not critiqued.

Others approach the Bible differently. More recent scholars such as David Pleins, professor of Religious Studies at Santa Clara University, struggle with the ethics and social vision of the Hebrew Bible and its relevance to today's society. He writes, "In a sense, in the Bible's struggles we will see our own. In its wrestling with divergent theological perspectives and diverse ritual practices, we can hear our own civic debates. In its people's struggle for survival, autonomy, and liberation, we can see enduring political aspirations. In its conflicting voices, we find encouragement to add to its provoking of the conscience of the postmodern polis."[7] But the past is more than just a mirror. The Bible is rooted in time and space and Pleins acknowledges the particularity of the biblical contexts, the cultural and historical differences, and sees within it God's engagement with his creation. It is by understanding and critically engaging with these contextual issues that relevance for today's society emerges.

Gustavo Gutiérrez, often perceived as the voice of Liberation Theology, identifies a number of themes that provide the paradigm for understanding God's work of salvation. Central to this paradigm is the story of the exodus, the liberation of Israel, which according him is a political act.[8] For Gutiérrez, all of Scripture is then read and understood through the prism of the exodus. He writes, "The memory of the exodus pervades the pages of the Bible and inspires one to reread often the Old as well as the New Testament."[9] South African theologian, Allan Boesak, speaking from within South Africa's struggle for social and political justice, crystalizes Gutiérrez' thinking on the centrality of the exodus to understanding all of Scripture. He writes,

---

6. Walter Houston, *Contending for Justice* (London: T & T Clark, 2008), 7.

7. J. David Pleins, *The Social Visions of the Hebrew Bible: A Theological Introduction* (Louisville: Westminster John Knox Press, 2001), vi–vii.

8. Gustavo Gutierrez, *A Theology of Liberation* (Maryknoll: Orbis Books, 2009), 88.

9. Ibid., 90.

"Yahweh's liberation is not an isolated happening, a kind of flash-in-the-pan that is here one day and gone the next. It is the movement through history wherein Yahweh has proven himself to be the liberator."[10]

Houston refers to liberation theologian Jose Porfirio Miranda's perspective that a specific moral position needs to be adopted when reading the Bible. He quotes Miranda: "What prevents people from hearing what the Bible is saying is not that they live in a different *cultural* world from the Bible, but that they do not stand *morally* where the Bible stands, on the side of the poor and the oppressed."[11] So the hermeneutics of Liberation Theology are based on specific moral assumptions of justice being at the core of the mission of God, with the exodus event as the foundational act that demonstrates what God intends to do in history.

In each of these cases their hermeneutical starting points are different. All believe in the Bible's relevance for today, but they differ on the grand, overarching narrative of the Bible. This has a profound influence on how God's people should relate to society and whether they should address social issues. The hermeneutics one uses determines the narrative one reads.

According to the narrative method in theology, the process starts with a simple reading of the biblical text to "hear" what the text and the story declare. Alan Lewis describes what should follow:

> Only then shall we proceed to more abstract, conceptual reflection, both historical and contemporary, on the story's meaning – how Christians past and present have thought out what they have heard from the story about God, about ourselves, and about reality, and how, conversely, the story has been or should be able to correct and control the church's thinking. Finally, we shall ask what the story implies for the actual living of life and dying of death by individuals, communities, and the world as a whole.[12]

However, it would be naïve to believe that anyone could read the Scriptures without the lenses of their own culture, gender, social and economic status, life experiences, season of life, political ideology, and value

---

10. A. A. Boesak, *Farewell to Innocence: A Socio-Ethical Study on Black Theology and Black Power* (Maryknoll: Orbis Books, 1977), 17.

11. Jose Porfirio Miranda, *Marx and the Bible: A Critique of the Philosophy of Oppression* (English Translation. London: SCM Press, 1977), xviii.

12. Lewis, *Between Cross and Resurrection,* 11.

system. Trinity Lutheran Seminary professor, Mark Allan Powell, gives an example of life experiences influencing how one reads the Bible. He had his American students read the Luke 15:11–31, the parable of the prodigal son, close their Bibles and then retell the story as faithfully as possible to their student partner. Powell notes that not a single one of his students mentioned the famine in Luke 15:14. Some time later, while teaching in St Petersburg in Russia he asked fifty participants to do the same; forty-two of the fifty mentioned the famine. Why the difference? The Russians remembered or had been told first hand of the Nazi siege of the city during World War II when 670,000 died from starvation. Their experience influenced how they read the Bible. Powell notes that for them, the parable was about God rescuing them from a desperate circumstance. While for the American students, who had never experienced a famine, the parable was about a disobedient son who repents and return to his father, who in turns forgives him.[13]

This is known as *domain specificity*. It means that a person's reactions, mode of thinking and intuition is dependent on the context in which the matter is presented. It is "what evolutionary psychologists call the 'domain' of the object or event . . . We react to a piece of information not on its logical merits, but on the basis of which framework surrounds it, and how it registers with our social-emotional system."[14]

So the poor read the Bible from within their context and life experiences and are attracted to a God who heals, provides for their needs, gives them dignity, and frees them from the economic and social bondages and exploitation that they experience. The non-poor focus primarily on the spiritual dimensions of Scripture. For example, Luke 4:18–19, "The Spirit of the Lord is on me, because he has anointed me to proclaim good news to the poor. He has sent me to proclaim freedom for the prisoners and recovery of sight for the blind, to set the oppressed free, to proclaim the year of the Lord's favor." Traditional evangelical commentary sees in these verses Jesus freeing individuals from sin and demonic oppression, and enabling them to see the truth. This is what they understand the meaning of the year of the Lord's favor or "the acceptable year of the Lord" (the Year of the Jubilee) to be.[15]

---

13. Mark Allan Powell, "The Forgotten Famine: Personal Responsibility in Luke's Parable of 'The Prodigal Son,'" in *Literary Encounters with the Reign of God*, eds. Sharon H. Ringe and H. C. Paul Kim (London: T & T Clark International, 2004), 265–274.

14. Taleb, *The Black Swan*, 53.

15. From Matthew Henry's commentary of Luke 4:18–19, "By Christ, sinners may be loosed from the bonds of guilt, and by his Spirit and grace from the bondage of corruption. He came

So everyone perceives and understands Christ and reads the Scriptures through the lenses of their everyday lives, their memories and the experience of their own culture and history.[16] If they have encountered poverty and suffering in the context where they live, their reaction to it will influence how they read the Bible and their understanding of God. Princeton University theologian Daniel Migliore articulates the need to be aware of one's own context and values. The context determines the theological questions. "Confession of Jesus Christ takes place in particular historical and cultural contexts. Our response to the questions of who we say Jesus Christ is and how he helps us is shaped in important ways by the particular context in which these questions arise."[17]

This is foundational to what British theologian and missiologist Andrew Walls refers to as the "translation principle," of when the gospel, the good news of Jesus Christ, is communicated in different cultures and places. Walls writes: "Incarnation is translation. When God in Christ became man, divinity was translated into humanity . . . The first divine act of translation thus gives rise to a constant succession of new translations. Christian diversity is the necessary product of the incarnation."[18] While this translation includes language and culture, one wonders if it should also include patterns of thought and reasoning, as well as philosophical frameworks and worldviews. While the gospel message is universal, it is contextual in the way it is translated and understood in different societies and socioeconomic groups.[19]

---

by the word of his gospel, to bring light to those that sat in the dark, and by the power of his grace, to give sight to those that were blind. And he preached the acceptable year of the Lord. Let sinners attend to the Savior's invitation when liberty is thus proclaimed. Christ's name was Wonderful; in nothing was he more so than in the word of his grace, and the power that went along with it. We may well wonder that he should speak such words of grace to such graceless wretches as mankind. Some prejudice often furnishes an objection against the humbling doctrine of the cross; and while it is the word of God that stirs up men's enmity, they will blame the conduct or manner of the speaker. The doctrine of God's sovereignty, his right to do his will, provokes proud men. They will not seek his favor in his own way; and are angry when others have the favors they neglect. Still is Jesus rejected by multitudes who hear the same message from his words. While they crucify him afresh by their sins, may we honor him as the Son of God, the Savior of men, and seek to show we do so by our obedience." Matthew Henry, *Matthew Henry's Concise Commentary* (Nashville: Thomas Nelson, 2003).

16. Richards and O'Brien, *Misreading Scripture*.

17. Daniel L. Migliore, *Faith Seeking Understanding: An Introduction to Christian Theology* (Grand Rapids: William B. Eerdmans Publishing Company, 2004), 197.

18. Andrew Walls, *The Missionary Movement in Christian History: Studies in the Transmission of Faith* (Maryknoll: Orbis, 1996), 27–28.

19. For a detailed discussion of this, see these two texts by Lamin Sanneh, *Encountering the West: Christianity and the Global Cultural Process* (London: Orbis Books, 1993), and

One of the drivers for contextualization is the concept of people groups, which is one of the bedrocks of mission strategy today, and is based on socio-cultural, linguistic and political criteria to determine the uniqueness of each group.[20] The more recent work around the culture[21] and psychology[22] of poverty raises the question of whether the poor in a given context are sociologically (and maybe even psychologically) different. Even if they speak the same language and are part of the same ethnic group, they have different worldviews, community history, culture, and life experiences than the communities around them. So the question arising from the translation principle is how do the poor and those living in poverty perceive and encounter the living God and understand that Jesus Christ is indeed good news? Fundamental to this is, how do they read and understand Scripture?[23]

So one's hermeneutics, based on their theological approach, will determine if and how the church addresses the issues of the poor and of poverty. The principle of translation will determine how various communities and individuals, especially the poor, understand (or don't understand) the message of the gospel.

Translating the Message: The Missionary Impact on Culture (London: Orbis Books, 2009).

20. This is based on Rev 7:9 where it says "... a great multitude ... from every nation, tribe, people and language ..." were before the throne of God; the transliteration for the word nation being *ethnos*, meaning ethnic group.

21. Oscar Lewis identifies the term culture of poverty. His descriptions of this culture of poverty have been controversial because of the perceived generalization he makes.

22. Paulo Freire's *Pedagogy of the Oppressed* (New York: The Seabury Press, 1970) was seminal in addressing this issue.

23. Throughout the history of missions tremendous effort has been made to be relevant to the context, whether it was in language, dress, lifestyle, forms of worship and even church design and architecture. The challenge has been to understand the uniqueness of Christ and his work in relationship to the religions of the world. Among the early radical attempts to understand the uniqueness of Christ was Bishop John Nicol Farquhar in India who in 1913 wrote a book entitled "The Crown of Hinduism." He focused on the theology of "fulfillment," in that Christ not only came to fulfill the law and the prophets (Matt 5:17) but also all the world's "higher religions." It is in this sense that Christ is the "crown" of Hinduism. Years later, E. Stanley Jones' efforts in India to use local forms for dialogue (the *satsangh*) to communicate who Christ was, has extended contextualization to evangelism by using a method of communication that was appropriate for a religiously pluralistic society such as India. Don Richardson's pioneering missionary work among the Sawi people of Irian Jaya took the process one step further with the use of local redemptive analogies to explain the redemptive work of Christ using stories, cultural practices and incidents from within their own context. The challenge of contextualization is ensuring that the uniqueness of Christ and his work of redemption is not lost in the process of adapting the message and strategy to a new culture.

The Question of Theology and Context

Understanding the issues of poverty and injustice is not just based on *how* one reads the Scriptures, but also on theology. For a long time theology focused on articulating the core and essence of the Christian faith systematically, often referred to as biblical and systematic theology. It was believed that this constituted a corpus of truth that was not only unchangeable in the way it was articulated but was complete in and of itself. Canadian theologian Douglas John Hall describes that the challenge of relating systematic theology to context is in the very nature of what systematic theology is meant to be. He writes:

> Systematic or dogmatic theology has been slow to learn the lessons of contextuality, especially its place-component, and one cannot avoid the conclusion that a (if not the) predominant reason for this lies in the character of the enterprise as such. The very adjectives *systematic* and *dogmatic* . . . betray a predilection to permanency. It so easily happens that a . . . desire to "see the thing whole," to integrate, to describe connections, to honor the unity of the truth, and so on becomes, in its execution, an exercise in finality.[24]

However, over time theology has moved beyond this to try and understand the relevance of one's faith and spirituality in an increasingly complex and pluralistic world where moral dilemmas are pushing against boundaries that had not previously existed.[25] It is important to hear the different voices as they try to articulate the relationship between theology and context.

Daniel Migliore writes about this process:

> Theology must be *critical reflection* on the community's faith and practice. Theology is not simply reiteration of what has been or is currently believed and practiced by a community of faith . . . when this responsibility for critical reflection is neglected or relegated to a merely ornamental role, the faith of the

---

24. Douglas John Hall, *The Cross in Our Context: Jesus and the Suffering World* (Minneapolis: Fortress Press, 2003), 45.

25. The Gospel and Our Culture Network, http://www.gocn.org/ is "A network to provide *useful research* regarding the encounter between the gospel and our culture, and to encourage *local action* for transformation in the life and witness of the church."

community is invariably threatened by shallowness, arrogance and ossification.[26]

In the 1920s through to the 1950s Karl Barth focused on the attitude that is required, that of repentant humility, as the community of faith seeks to examine itself in the light of revealed truth. "Theology is an act of repentant humility . . . This act exists in the fact that in theology the church seeks again and again to examine itself critically as it asks itself what it means and implies to be a church among men."[27]

Alister McGrath defines the understanding of theology. He writes that Christian theology "is therefore understood to mean the systematic study of the ideas of the Christian faith"[28] which include the issues of sources, of development, of relationships, and of applications.[29] With regards to applications he says, "Christian theology is not just a set of ideas: it is about making possible a new way of seeing ourselves, others, and the world, with implications for the way in which we behave."[30]

So while truth is universal, theology is contextual, because it influences how we live out our faith and spirituality. Most of the basic understandings in systematic theology evolved and crystalized as a result of questions or challenges to the Christian faith during specific periods of history. So in effect, all theology is contextual. For example, John Calvin's *Institutes* are his theological method. Though Martin Luther and Huldrych Zwingli wrote extensively, they never systematized their theology. Calvin's *Institutes* is one of the earliest major systematic presentations of the core of Reformation theology. In retrospect, the *Institutes* are a reflection of Calvin's attempts at developing theology in the context of sixteenth-century Europe, and then applying theology to daily life, specifically in Geneva. For Calvin, theology was not just an academic discipline developed in isolation, but it was developed and applied in context.

---

26. Migliore, *Faith Seeking Understanding,* xv.

27. Karl Barth, *God in Action* (Edinburgh: T. & T. Clark, 1936), 44.

28. Alister E. McGrath, *Christian Theology: An Introduction.* 5th ed. (Chichester: Wiley-Blackwell, 2011), 101.

29. Ibid., 101. The "sources" address the sources on which Christian ideas are based and include the Christian Bible, tradition, reason and experience. "Development" looks at how ideas have evolved over time. This is the field of historical theology. "Relationships" looks at how the various Christian ideas relate to each other – "the interconnected network of ideas."

30. Ibid., 102.

Yale Divinity School theologian, Hans Frei's *Typologies of Christian Theology*[31] describes the spectrum of theological engagement with specific contexts. On one end of the spectrum is theology as a unique academic discipline, which is universal in its content and has no specific relationship with context, if any. On the other end of the spectrum is Christian self-description (different from academic theology). This defines itself solely from Scripture and from Christian experience, which is usually influenced significantly by context and culture.

Hans Frei's colleague at Yale, Richard Niebuhr's taxonomy on Christ and culture elaborates on engagement with context.[32] The understanding of how Christ relates to culture has profound implications on whether Christians and the church believe that social issues should be addressed and whether social transformation is possible. His taxonomy consists of five categories:

- *Christ against Culture* – This is based on 1 John as well as John 2:15–17 and 5:5, where the world is understood as the society that is outside the church. Niebuhr writes, "The counterpart of loyalty to Christ and the brothers is the rejection of cultural society."[33]

- *Christ of Culture* – Christ is seen as the pinnacle of human achievement. Niebuhr writes, "In every culture to which the gospel comes there are men who hail Jesus as the Messiah of their society, the fulfiller of its hopes and aspiration."[34] A pioneer in this thinking was Bishop John Nicol Farquhar in India, whose book in 1913 entitled "The Crown of Hinduism" focused on the theology of "fulfillment," in that Christ not only came to fulfill the law and the prophets (Matt 5:17) but also all the world's "higher religions." It is in this sense that he stated that Christ is the "crown" of Hinduism.

- *Christ above Culture* – In Matthew 22:21 Jesus exhorts his disciples "to render to Caesar the things that are Caesar's, and to God the things that are God's." So according to Niebuhr, there is the realm we live in the midst of culture, and then there is the realm where Christ is, the realm we aspire to. So culture is separate from Christ. Niebuhr writes, "The synthesist alone seems to provide for willing and intelligent cooperation with non-believers in carrying on the

---

31. Hans W. Frei, *Types of Christian Theology*, eds. George Hunsinger and William C. Plancher (New Haven: Yale University Press, 1992).

32. H. Richard Niebuhr, *Christ and Culture* (New York: Harper, 1951).

33. Ibid., 47.

34. Ibid., 83.

work of the world, while yet maintaining the distinctiveness of Christian faith and life."[35]

- *Christ and Culture in Paradox* – The Christian and the world exist in tension. The believer who lives in this duality and tension "knows he belongs to the culture and cannot get out of it, that God indeed sustains him in it and by it."[36] The starting point of dealing with any cultural problem therefore must be the God's act of reconciliation through Christ.

- *Christ the Transformer of Culture* – While there is a profound influence of sin upon the world, Niebuhr recognizes Christ as the Redeemer. Niebuhr agrees with the theology of Augustine who saw Christ as the transformer of culture, the Christ who "redirects, reinvigorates and regenerates that life of man, expressed in all human works."[37]

Baptist theologian and ethicist James McClendon elaborates on the concept of theological engagement with specific contexts further. He writes, "Doctrine is not manufactured by theologians to be marketed by churches and pastors. It is the church that must (and does!) ask questions and seek answers."[38] He states that there are two facts that undergird the development of theology and Christian ethics. The first is that theology is not without hard struggles. This struggle is seen in the interaction between theology held by the church and the world. He states that the theology, the basic points of view of the church and that of the world, are not the same. He writes, "The church's story will not interpret the world to the world's satisfaction."[39] This difference cannot be diminished. He explains, "conspiring to conceal the difference between the church and the world, we may in the short run entice the world, but we will only do so by betraying the world."[40]

The reason theology will always struggle with the world is because there is a moral dimension in theology's interaction with culture. The gospel will always confront the evil in culture and society – anything that is against the very nature of who God is. Veteran missionary and missiologist Paul Heibert

---

35. Ibid., 143.

36. Ibid., 156.

37. Ibid., 209.

38. James McClendon, *Doctrine: Systematic Theology, Vol. II* (Nashville: Abingdon Press, 1994), 24.

39. James McClendon, *Ethics: Systematic Theology, Vol. I* (Nashville: Abingdon Press, 2002), 17.

40. Ibid., 18.

warns that contextualization is not an indiscriminate adopting of culture, customs and values. "The foreignness of the culture we add to the gospel offends and must be eliminated. But the gospel itself offends. It is supposed to offend, and we dare not weaken its offense. The gospel must be contextualized but it must remain prophetic. It must stand in judgment of what is evil in all cultures as well as in all persons."[41]

Therefore attaining the right balance in interacting with the world is a challenge. Mennonite theologian Thomas Finger writes that the church cannot be separated from the world, though, as he states, the Anabaptists have sometimes attempted to do this. Finger writes, "Theology is always in dialogue with its cultural contexts . . . including the academic sphere. Theology tests the church's current beliefs and often revises them through conversations with its culture. Anabaptists should not only celebrate their distinctives but also recognize how preoccupation with distinctives can encourage narrowness, exclusivity and a false sense of superiority."[42]

The second fact McClendon states is that because the church is not one congruent whole, there are divided theologies. He refers to German theologian Friedrich Schleiermacher, whom he considers the father of modern theology, who argued that any given theology must represent and refer to the doctrine of some particular Christian body at some particular time.[43] So the various theological approaches arise from specific contexts at specific times, which may or may not be relevant in other contexts in different periods of history.

Theology needs to be systematic but it also needs to be relevant in each and every context where the church is present. With poverty so pervasive in the global south and growing in the northern countries, the church has to ask the question whether God is concerned for the poor and the issues of social justice. How central is compassion to biblical faith? Contextualization will always result in the gospel standing in judgment of society and therefore there needs to be critical reflection by the church on what God has to say about issues of injustice, social concern, traditions, culture, and values in a specific context. Douglas John Hall points out that a focus on a single systematic and dogmatic theology in its "reluctance to open itself to the great *variety* of worldly contexts . . . has again and again resisted criticism from

---

41. Paul Hiebert, *Anthropological Reflections on Missiological Issues* (Grand Rapids: Baker, 1994), 86.

42. Thomas N. Finger, *Contemporary Anabaptist Theology: Biblical, Historical, Constructive* (Downers Grove: InterVarsity Press, 2004), 96.

43. McClendon, *Ethics,* 18.

the perspectives of those whose worlds were virtually ignored or excluded in the great systems of Christian thought. This is not a mere academic concern, for the excluded ones have not just been individuals, or tiny minorities but whole populations, whole races, whole economic and other groupings."[44] *Any Christian ministry, Christian ethic, or Christian response to social issues, needs to flow out of the understanding of contextual theology.*

The Missiological Question

Two conversations over the past many years helped frame the questions that are at the heart of this book. The first was with a veteran western evangelist and church planter who had lived in the Middle East for a long time and had suffered at the hands of the authorities in various countries because of his faithful work. He stressed that ministries of compassion were only good and had value, if any at all, if they supported the verbal proclamation of the gospel. The priority was to save people for eternity.

A couple of years earlier, in a conversation after one of the many wars that have roiled the Middle East with devastating consequences, an Arab Christian leader said that one of the few ways left for the church in the Middle East to maintain a effective witness in an increasingly hostile Islamic context, was to reach out to the poor and demonstrate the love and compassion of Christ.

These two conversations represent the two bookends of an intense discussion within the larger Christian community about the poor and poverty in the context of the mission and mandate of the church, with many perspectives in-between and some even beyond the bookends. The missiological issue is whether addressing the needs of the poor and issues of justice is a mandate given by God to the church. The question is: What does the mission of God (*missio Dei*) include?

Responding in compassion to human needs, which from a human point of view seems fairly straightforward, has become a complex discussion involving theology, an understanding of missions, eschatology (understanding the events of the end times), and even what one means by "church." Some would concede that compassion is not only good but also necessary, but they would question whether fighting for justice and community transformation are biblical concepts. Archbishop Dom Helder Camara (1909–1999) of Recife, Brazil, once noted, "When I care for the poor they call me a saint; when I

---

44. Hall, *The Cross*, 48.

ask why so many people are poor they call me a communist."[45] Even though significant thinking has been done at the Lausanne conferences (LCWE[46]) and other forums since, deep theological divides remain.

There probably aren't many who would question whether Christians should show compassion towards the poor. It seems a good thing to do, whether one is a Christian or not. The question is not just a missiological one but also one of Christian ethics, whether the church as an organized community of faith (an institution) should also be involved in addressing poverty and issues of justice. The fear is that this would somehow detract from what God has to say about eternity.

Different Perspectives

There are a variety of perspectives within the church on what the content of the gospel is and on how Christians and the church should relate to society. Theologian and social activist Ron Sider identifies four divergent models.[47] The first is the *individualistic evangelical model* where the focus is on personal sin, and the content of the gospel is salvation of the individual and where society is changed when converted individuals are salt and light. The second model is the *radical Anabaptist model* where the main emphasis is on personal sin with some emphasis on social sin. The content of the gospel is the good news of the kingdom and where converted individuals and the example of the church, change society. The third model is *dominant ecumenical model*, where the main emphasis is on both personal and social sin, though more of the emphasis is on the social sins. The content of the gospel is the good news of the kingdom and where society is changed through conversion, life of the church and through restructuring social institutions. The last model is *the secular*, where the emphasis is on the offense against one's neighbor and structural injustice. The content of the gospel is on peace and justice in society, where society is changed by restructuring it.

Expanding on the four divergent models, there are six perspectives as to whether Christians and the church should be involved in addressing social

45. Robert Ellsberg, ed., *Modern Spiritual Masters: Writings on Contemplation and Compassion* (Maryknoll: Orbis Books, 2009), 119.

46. Lausanne Committee for World Evangelization.

47. Ronald J. Sider, *Good News and Good Works: A Theology for the Whole Gospel* (Grand Rapids: Baker Books, 1993), 33–46.

issues.[48] All of them draw from specific readings of Scripture dependent on their theology. While there is overlap between these perspectives, each one highlights a particular emphasis.

1) *A human rights perspective:* For many Christians, compassion is a good thing and is not necessarily a reflection of their faith. It is part of living in this world and being part of a common humanity. Many Christians in the postmodern generation believe that compassion is one of the highest of human values, and is modeled by celebrities like musicians Bob Geldof (the driving force behind Live Aid) and Bono, and actors such as Angelina Jolie, among many others. They do not draw their inspiration from Scripture but root themselves in the concept of human rights and a sense of social responsibility.[49]

2) *Saving souls for eternity:* Quoting Matthew 26:11,[50] some say that Jesus himself said that there would always be the poor in this world, implying that if this was so, then nothing can be done for them. They state that Jesus was prioritizing worship of him over the needs of the poor, though the Deuteronomy passage Jesus quoted from does not imply that at all.[51] For them the focus of ministry is evangelism and the Great Commission. The nineteenth-century American evangelist Dwight L. Moody highlights the urgency of the task when he said, "I look upon this world as a wrecked vessel. God has given me a lifeboat and said to me, 'Moody, save all you can.'"[52]

---

48. This is based on the author's observations and interactions over the past three decades of ministry in a variety of contexts and cultures.

49. Robert Weber writes that younger evangelicals live in constant tension with the world. He summarizes: "The younger evangelicals' presence in the world is clearly a threefold tension. They live in this world and want to be responsible citizens, yet they are not of this world. They are moving away from moral relativism of their postmodern world, seeking to offer a sharp alternative to the dominant culture. In personal and the family and church life, they hope to be an embodied presence, an alternative culture that acts as salt and light, transforming society towards the kingdom ideal." Robert E. Weber, *The Younger Evangelicals: Facing the Challenges of the New World* (Grand Rapids: Baker Books, 2002), 235. The clarity they seek is not necessarily in historical, biblical Christianity.

50. "The poor you will always have with you, but you will not always have me." Cf. Mark 14:7, John 12:8.

51. The cross reference in Deuteronomy 15:11 "There will always be poor people in the land. Therefore I command you to be openhanded toward your brothers and toward the poor and needy in your land," indicates a very different emphasis. Since there will always be poor in the land, God commands generosity towards the poor and the needy.

52. Quoted in David J. Bosch, *Transforming Mission* (New York: Orbis Books, 2008), 318.

What value then is there in providing them food and improving the quality of their lives, if their eternal destiny is not addressed? This group rejects any involvement in social issues. Ron Sider describes this perspective as the individualistic evangelical model. He writes, "What do people who adopt this model care most passionately about? Nothing in the world, not even life itself, they believe, is as important as coming to saving faith in Jesus Christ that leads to eternal life in the presence of the risen Lord."[53]

3) *The primacy of evangelism:* There are some who say that caring for the poor and those in need is important as it provides an opening for evangelism. As their physical needs are met, it provides an opportunity to share the gospel. While they acknowledge that God is concerned about issues of justice and reconciliation, for them the only purpose for addressing social needs is that it opens doors and builds bridges. Providing assistance is a means to an end and the objective is evangelism. Both Billy Graham and John Stott acknowledged the need to address social issues, but were clear that evangelism was the primary mandate of the church. This was articulated in the Lausanne Covenant (1974) where in section 5 (Christian Social Responsibility) it states, "We affirm that evangelism and sociopolitical involvement are both part of our Christian duty" but clarifies this in section 6 (The Church and Evangelism), "In the church's mission of sacrificial service evangelism is primary."[54]

4) *Integral mission:* Since Lausanne 1974, there has been a growing belief that evangelism and addressing social issues are integrally linked. The proclamation of the gospel has social implications and social involvement has evangelistic consequences. The thinking has sought to balance the focus on the *Great Commission* (Matt 28:19–20), to make disciples of all nations, with the *Great Commandment* (Matt 22:36–40), to love God with your total being and your neighbor as yourself. The emphasis is *both* on the last thing that Jesus said – the commission that he gave us – and on the greatest commandment he gave us – to obey. They do not prioritize one

---

53. Sider, *Good News*, 34.

54. The Lausanne Movement, *The Lausanne Covenant*, 2013, http://www.lausanne.org/en/documents/lausanne-covenant.html.

over the other. For them, both comprise two interconnected parts of God's mandate for the church.[55] This is articulated in the Micah Declaration.[56]

5) *Development and transformation:* Since the mid-1800s there has been a strong emphasis on the church being the instrument to bring justice and establish the kingdom of God here on earth. This is to happen by transforming society through every God-given means possible such as education, health programs, food security programming, and technology, among others.[57] David Bosch describes this perspective: "Sin is defined preeminently as *ignorance.* People had only to be *informed* about what was in their own interest. The western mission was the great educator, which would mediate salvation to the unenlightened."[58] The focus is on the improvement of the quality of life rather than of a radical restructuring, which ensured justice. Many Christian community development organizations ascribe to this perspective of transformation of communities and of the world, even if they theologically don't agree with Postmillennial Theology and the Social Gospel.[59] Their focus is on community transformation while only acknowledging in passing

---

55. The expression "integral mission" was first articulated within the Latin American Theological Fraternity (FTL). René C. Padilla and Tetsunano Yamamori, *The Local Church, Agent of Transformation: An Ecclesiology for Integral Mission* (Buenos Aires: Kairos Ediciones, 2004).

56. "Integral missions or holistic transformation is the proclamation and demonstration of the gospel. It is not simply that evangelism and social involvement are to be done alongside each other. Rather, in integral mission our proclamation has social consequences as we call people to love and repentance in all areas of life. And our social involvement has evangelistic consequences as we bear witness to the transforming grace of Jesus Christ. If we ignore the world we betray the Word of God, which sends us out to serve the world. If we ignore the Word of God, we have nothing to bring to the world." Available at http://www.micahnetwork. org/en/integral-mission/micah-declaration.

57. This is discussed in detail in chapter 6. Theologically, the basis of their thinking is *postmillennialism.* This optimistic view has its roots in the Enlightenment with the realization that science and human knowledge could solve the world's problems. This thinking was known as the Social Gospel. The idea was to change the world and bring transformation. This was worked out differently in different contexts.

58. Bosch, *Transforming Mission,* 396.

59. When most Christian development NGOs talk about transformation, they are referring to provision of basic services such as access to education, health care, and microfinance, while also ensuring food security, proper nutrition and viable livelihoods. Most will refer to issues of justice, but their programming does not reflect efforts at addressing unjust social and political structures that perpetuate marginalization of communities.

the fundamental flaw of human nature (sin) and the issue of eternal destiny.[60]

6) *Justice through Christ as Savior, deliverer and liberator:* Many in the majority world, especially in poor and marginalized communities, yearn for a God who is concerned for all aspects of their often crushed and broken lives. They are attracted to a God who draws near (Immanuel), who walks with them and understands their sorrows and pain, because he himself has experienced them. They also know that the causes of their poverty are the unjust structures of society and the injustice perpetuated by those with power. For them, salvation is not just knowing the God who draws near, but also experiencing justice in the society that they live in. The good news for them is that Jesus Christ is Savior, deliverer and liberator. Being poor, they not only cry out to Christ for help, but they look forward to the day when God's kingdom will be established and justice and poverty will be wiped away. They not only yearn for heaven, but also for a just world. The focus of ministry among them is Micah 6:8, "He has shown you, O mortal, what is good. And what does the Lord require of you? To act justly and to love mercy and to walk humbly with your God."

Acknowledging that there are different perspectives is an important step in the discussion on how the church should relate to society and its problems. Each perspective highlights various teachings of Scripture, which need to be understood as a whole.

The Poor

It is hard to imagine that there would be any disagreement among Christians about who the poor are. The challenge is that the poor are viewed only through various economic, social and moral lenses, and not through a biblical lens. The conservative Hindu Brahmin sees the poor as having received their just rewards for sins committed in a previous life. As a result they are not deserving

---

60. Interestingly, the focus and theology of Evangelical Christian development NGOs reflect more closely those of Liberation Theology. "Liberation for modern people, says Gutierrez, is a 'process of transformation' designed to 'satisfy the most fundamental human aspirations – liberty, dignity, the possibility of personal fulfillment for all.'" Pleins, *The Social Visions,* 164.

of assistance. Many people in the West see the poor as people who are lazy with destructive lifestyles, which should not be encouraged. Others see the poor trapped in poverty and marginalization because of a class struggle, with the rich and powerful oppressing the poor. As a result the poor and the masses need to be liberated. The more recent perceptions of the poor are of people who have been denied their human rights. The solutions to poverty hinge on whether the poor are able to claim their rights and move into the mainstreams of society. Most Christians are influenced by the prevailing social and political perceptions of the poor and the cultural understandings of poverty rather than having a biblical perspective.

Each of us have iconic mental images of the poor – the disheveled homeless man who sleeps under the bridge; the family that lives in an urban slum with a stream of sewage outside their door where a road should be; the emaciated farmer trying to eke out a living from a dry and hard land with only hand implements while his malnourished children sit in the shade of his hut; or the family surviving in a run down apartment living off welfare because the husband is unable to find enough work to care for his family. While these images of the poor represent real people, they somehow seem distant because we don't have to interact with them on a daily basis and we can turn off the mental images. Because they are distant, it is easy to judge the poor without understanding their circumstances.

However encountering the poor in person makes us uncomfortable. It is this discomfort that elicits different responses of how one responds to the poor. They make us uncomfortable because it seems that by their presence they make a demand on us to respond to their need. They shake our understanding of what the world should be like. They somehow have the ability to question our worldview, where we believe that hard work has provided all that we have. Our thought is that if they are poor it is because they are lazy and morally corrupt (drug and alcohol addicts, gamblers, etc.). It is then easy to ignore them and pretend that they don't exist or that they are not worthy of assistance because of their moral failures. I am always afraid to ask *why* families and communities live in poverty, because it may raise uncomfortable questions about our culpability and collective actions that have condemned them to destitution.

Are there biblical values which influence how one looks at the poor?

The confusion starts with verses such as Luke 6:20, "Blessed are you who are poor, for yours is the kingdom of God." Do the poor have special favor in the eyes of God? If they do and are blessed, then why empower them to move out of poverty? Is the term "God's preferential option for the poor" from Liberation Theology a valid biblical concept?

When God created all forms of life, he created them "according to their kind" (Gen 1: 21). However, when he created human beings he said, "Let us make man in our image, in our likeness" (Gen 1:26). Human beings are unique in all of creation as only they bear the image of God. Traces of it are still evident in spite of their fallen sinful condition. And because they are created and bear the image of God, human beings are holy (*set apart for service and to worship; belong to God; of divine origin; the root word implies "wholeness"*).

Even though they reflect his triune nature and his character, God as creator remains the *Other*, distinct from his creation. He is the only One who is all powerful, all knowing and present everywhere. He is the only source of life and the giver of life.

When we abuse, ignore, destroy, disfigure, dehumanize, discriminate against, torture and kill human beings, we blaspheme against God (*showing irreverence towards things that are holy*). James 2:9 takes this further and says that if we show favoritism we sin. If we prefer one human being to the other on the basis of wealth, culture, creed, race, nationality, gender, ability or talent we break God's law – we sin. Every person is to be valued and treated as having worth because each person is made in the image of God and nothing less.

So when Mother Teresa said that she saw Christ in the poor or that she saw God in those who have been abandoned, she saw the image of God in the person through the dirt, filth, brokenness and poverty.[61] She saw them as body, soul and spirit reflecting the mystery of the Trinity. Like every other human being, they are someone of value whom God created as the pinnacle of creation. The beggar, in spite of what he looks like, is someone who is holy – someone belonging to God, of divine origin, set apart for service and to worship God. In the person's suffering, one sees what the suffering of Christ would have looked like – Christ who is Creator, the God who is the source of life, who then takes on human form and experiences the suffering and pain of the world. What one sees in the poor is the image of the incarnated Christ, of

---

61. Mother Teresa is supposed to have said every time she pulled a beggar from the gutter that she saw Jesus Christ. "They are Jesus. Everyone is Jesus in a distressing disguise." http://www.suffering.net/servmo-t.htm. She was anchored in Matt 25:35–40. "For I was hungry and you gave me food, I was thirsty and you gave me drink, a stranger and you welcomed me, naked and you clothed me, ill and you cared for me, in prison and you visited me." Then the righteous will answer him and say, "Lord, when did we see you hungry and feed you, or see you thirsty and give you drink?" The king will say to them in reply, "Amen, I say to you, whatever you did to one of these least brothers of mine, you did for me."

a unique human being who is the image and likeness of God, but now marred and disfigured by suffering.

Mother Teresa then wrote what should our response to the poor be.

> We make ourselves live the love of God in prayer and in our work, through a life characterized by the simplicity and humility of the gospel. We do this by . . . loving and serving [Jesus] hidden under the painful guise of the poorest of the poor, whether their poverty is a material poverty or a spiritual one. We do this by recognizing in them (and giving back to them) the image and likeness of God.[62]

Like any other human being, the rich and non-poor are also persons of value, made in the image of God and holy; the difference being that the rich are self-sufficient and often don't have a sense of need. The rich *who don't acknowledge and worship God* exert their independence and control. They rarely understand that they are part of a world and system that God has created. They don't understand what being part of that system means; what it means to need the air to breathe; the need for the land to produce the food so that they can eat. They don't understand the role that each individual plays so that the world could be a place of blessing. Rules and laws don't apply to them. They speak and command and they get what they want. They are able to demand their rights and get them. They determine and set the rules, and these rules ensure that their wealth and position are safeguarded. They seek to control all that they encounter. Their security is in their wealth and power rather than in the God who created all.

With the poor, the abandoned and the vulnerable, all their self-sufficiency has been stripped away. Philip Yancey writes:

> Poor people find themselves in a posture that befits the grace of God. They are needy, dependent, and dissatisfied with life, for that reason they may welcome God's free gift of love. We need the poor to teach us the value of dependence, for unless we learn dependence we will never experience grace. The Beatitudes reveal at once God's "preferential option for the poor" and the poor's "preferential option for God." Underqualified for success in the kingdom of this world, they may turn to God. "Blessed

---

62. Mother Teresa, *In My Own Words,* comp. Jose Luis Gonzalez-Balado (Linguori: Linguori Publications, 1996), 108.

are the desperate" is how one commentator translates "poor in spirit." Human beings do not readily admit desperation. When they do, the kingdom of God draws near.[63]

When they admit that desperation, God draws near and exerts his authority and rule in their lives. Yancey concludes, "The poor, the hungry, the mourners and the oppressed are really blessed. Not because of their miserable states, of course – Jesus spent much of his life trying to remedy these miseries. Rather, they are blessed because of an innate advantage they hold over those more comfortable and self-sufficient."[64]

The poor are not part of the kingdom of God just because they are poor. The poor are sinners like everyone else, desperately in the need of the grace of God. Because they have been stripped of everything, including their dignity, they manipulate and beg to ensure that they survive. However, the poor, because of their poverty are in a place where they are far more open to experiencing the kingdom and wanting to know its King, than those who are not poor. The poor understand the reality of sin. They experience daily the impact of the sin of others – of those who don't care, of those who perpetuate injustice, of those who deliberately exploit the poor and vulnerable to their own advantage. They have very little control over their lives.

However, not all the poor responded to Jesus. In the incident of the ten lepers, only one returned to thank Christ and acknowledge him for who he is. Lepers in first-century Palestine were among the poorest, the most marginalized and despised in society, feared by most because of the grotesque deformities that their disease had inflicted. Luke writes about the ten: "They stood at a distance and called out in a loud voice, Jesus, Master, have pity on us!" (Luke 17:12–13) While all ten in their desperation were seeking the benefits of the kingdom of God, only a few were willing to acknowledge the King, even though they had recognized who he was. Yet Christ does not deny them the healing but is deeply saddened by their attitude. "Was no one found to return and give praise to God except this foreigner?" (Luke 17:18).

The poor themselves are no different than anyone else in the fact that they too are sinful and fall short of God's standards in relationships, in their attitudes, in their actions and in their speech. In speaking about God's preferential option for the poor, there is a great danger of idolizing

---

63. Philip Yancey, *Finding God in Unexpected Places* (London: Authentic Books, 1997), 163–164.
64. Ibid.

the poor and romanticizing poverty, of somehow thinking of them as the noble savage, that there is a certain innocence in who they are and a purity in how they live. Poverty is ugly and there is nothing noble in being poor. So while the poor also need a Savior, their desperation *makes them realize* they need deliverance. Each still faces a choice of whether they will accept the gift that this Savior offers. The difference between the rich and the poor is this realization of desperation. When the rich reach this point of desperation (Na'aman, Hezekiah, Nebuchadnezzar, Nicodemus, the centurion) they then have a "preferential option for God";[65] they are open to God, his kingdom and his rule and authority in their lives. The poor live this desperation daily; the rich only reach it when all they have and all that they are fails them; when they can no longer control what happens to them.

When looking at the poor through a biblical lens, the second thing to realize is that the poor are individuals and not just an anonymous category of those living in poverty. Each of them has a name with their own dreams and struggles. By acknowledging their name they become human, even though they may be vulnerable and in desperate need. Because they have a name, it challenges us to acknowledge their existence.

In the parable of Lazarus and the rich man (Luke 16:19–31) Jesus does something that was culturally radical. The parable is about the rich and poor in first-century Palestine, where the rich were immortalized in lavish burial tombs that honored their name and memory. Going against the cultural norm, Jesus instead honors Lazarus the beggar so that he is remembered by history because he has a name, but leaves the rich man anonymous and thus having no lasting honor. By giving Lazarus a name, Jesus identifies him as a unique individual and not just as one of the poor who made up the masses.

In the parable neither man is a great sinner. The rich man is not condemned for being rich but for not being concerned for the poor. His concern right to the end remains only for his family and never for those who are not part of his social circle. He excludes the outsider as not being worthy of his attention and care.

In the parable the name that Jesus pointedly chooses for the beggar is "Lazarus," which is derived from Hebrew, El'āzār, which means "one whom God has helped." Through that he reveals the heart of God for the poor. The dogs, whose saliva is healing for his sores, care for Lazarus. God's creatures had more compassion for the beggar who was sick and desperately hungry

---

65. Ibid., 164.

than the rich man, who passed Lazarus everyday as he went in and out of his house. Lazarus never complains and never speaks throughout the parable. Culturally he would not have been allowed to speak to the rich. Rather God honors him and speaks for him who has no voice.

One of the persons whose thoughts I have often sought wrote back: "I always despair when we take the focus on people, particularly individuals, and group them into some comfortable statistical or sociological agglomeration. 'The poor' is not a label you put on them. Face-to-face with the poor can be disturbing to us, and so we tend to 'package' them into something we can relate without emotional engagement."[66]

One of the challenges of institutionalizing charity either through the "common chest" (as Martin Luther proposed in the sixteenth century), or through the modern NGO, is that it removes the personal encounter with the person who is poor. It removes the discomfort of not knowing how to relate to the poor, and silences all the uncomfortable questions of why the poor exist, while satisfying one's conscience to be charitable.

How much God values the poor and broken is seen in the fact that he "defend[s] the weak and the fatherless; uphold[s] the cause of the poor and the oppressed." He rescues the weak and the needy; delivers them from the hand of the wicked. (Ps 82:2–4). In light of this, how one sees and understands who the poor are, influences the discussion on whether the church should be involved in addressing social issues that perpetuate poverty.

Filters and Lenses

Filters and lenses change whatever passes through them. The discussion on whether the church has a mandate from God to respond to social issues, especially the needs of the poor, is influenced by the various filters and lenses each of us bring to the conversation. This is inevitable because the filters and lenses either remove distractions or bring life into focus, and this helps us make sense of the world we see and experience. The debate as to what is the mission of God and whether compassion for the poor and social transformation are the responsibility of God's people, cannot be a valuable dialogue unless there is an acknowledgement that our life experiences and social contexts influence how we read and interpret the Bible.

---

66. Email from Rev Kalyan Das.

Because the poor are dependent on others for assistance, the question is whose responsibility is it to help them, if at all. Our politics, our understanding of the role of government, the presence of social and religious institutions in the community, as well as our social theory of how society is structured, all influence the discussion of whether the care for the poor is the responsibility of God's people.

Going back to the Bible with an awareness of these filters and lenses, as well as understanding the biblical contexts that provide insight into why things were said and the social laws given, will be a first step in understanding the mandate of the church with regards to social issues like poverty and injustice.

3

The Biblical Basis to Understand the Poor and Poverty: The Old Testament

There are a variety of ways to approach a biblical study on poverty and compassion. Rather than doing a study of key texts and passages to see what the Bible has to say about the poor and poverty (which has been the most commonly used approach), this study will borrow from a social-scientific and historical approach to Scripture to understand the context of the biblical passages.

A methodology adapted from the life sciences by social scientists is called the General Systems Theory (GST). The basic premise is that all living organisms are highly complex systems comprising of a variety of subsystems. While GST is not totally transferable to the social sciences, there is value in understanding the subsystems and how they relate to each other. Biblical archeologists and biblical scholars who use GST to study communities look at the following "subsystems":

- House-plan and village layout
- Subsistence and economy
- Social structure
- Political organization
- Technology
- Art, ideology, religion
- External relations[1]

Each of these subsystems provides a perspective to understand a community and the larger society. It is this understanding of the biblical

---

1. Dever, *Who Were the Early Israelites*, 102.

context and its history that provides insight as to why the biblical writers and characters say what they do. It is hoped that this will explain why poverty existed in biblical times and provide the context for the teaching on helping the poor and vulnerable, and the exhortations for social justice. Such an approach is key to this book (though each subsystem will not be analyzed), as it will not only provide a biblical analysis for the causes of poverty, but will also contrast how the biblical teaching to care for the poor and vulnerable differed from the values of other societies in the region.

So what is the biblical basis for compassion towards the poor? Until recently many western evangelicals have seen responding to the needs of the poor as an act of compassion based on proof texts from Scripture such as James 1:27, Luke 6:30 and Leviticus 19:15, 33–34.[2] Others have used Micah 6:8 and its emphasis on social justice to address the realities of poverty. However, understanding the contexts of the Old Testament law, Israel's history, Jesus' teaching, and the New Testament churches would begin to provide insights into why Scripture addresses the issues of poverty and care for the poor the way it does.

In trying to understand what the Bible has to say about poverty, one is confronted by a variety of perspectives that at times seem divergent. David Pleins writes, "In the Hebrew Bible we encounter texts that refuse to give only one view about the poor or about social injustice and its causes . . . we confront a document that forces us, by its very diversity of perspectives, to reassess our own views about oppression and political oppression."[3] The Torah or Pentateuch, the first five books of the Hebrew Bible, provide the cornerstone of Jewish social ideals and practice through two distinct modes of theological discourse. *Aggadah* is the first of the two primary components of rabbinic tradition and is the narrative strand that tells the story of the Jewish people. The other component, *halakhah* (usually translated as "Jewish law") is concerned with the legal decisions and the creation of a just society

---

2. James 1:27, "Religion that God our Father accepts as pure and faultless is this: to look after orphans and widows in their distress and to keep oneself from being polluted by the world." Luke 6:30, "Give to everyone who asks you, and if anyone takes what belongs to you, do not demand it back."
Leviticus 19:15, 33–34, "Do not pervert justice; do not show partiality to the poor or favoritism to the great, but judge your neighbor fairly . . . When a foreigner resides among you in your land, do not mistreat them. The foreigner residing among you must be treated as your native-born. Love them as yourself, for you were foreigners in Egypt. I am the Lord your God."
3. Pleins, *The Social Visions*, 21.

under the reign of God.[4] These two modes of theological discourse continue throughout the Old Testament.

Both of these discourses provide differing voices and perspectives on poverty, which at times converge. For example, the writers and compilers of Genesis, Exodus, Samuel-Kings and Chronicles hardly refer to the question of poverty, and neither is vocabulary describing the poor used. Instead the prevailing issue in these narratives is a critique of kingship, monarchic power, and foreign domination, rather than an analysis of the structure and causes of poverty in society.[5] Even in the three cases where there seems to be a critique of the socioeconomic abuses – those of Samuel's critical analysis of kingship (1 Sam 8), Solomon's employment of forced labor (1 Kgs 5:13–18, 9:20), and Ahab usurping Naboth's vineyard (1 Kgs 21) – these were more about royal abuse of power and do not use the vocabulary of poverty. This is in contrast to the Prophets, Proverbs, Job and the legal tradition, where the concern for the poor and issues of injustice stand at the core of their discourse.[6] This chapter explores the legal requirements with regards to the poor and marginalized within the context of the narrative strand.

The Wisdom Literature

The Books of Wisdom[7] have much to say about poverty and wealth. There are three reasons given as to why someone may be poor.

The most common reason for poverty, which is readily understood by the western world, is laziness. Proverbs 10:4 "Lazy hands make for poverty"; Proverbs 20:13 "Do not love sleep or you will grow poor"; Proverbs 21:17 "Whoever loves pleasure will become poor." This is further elaborated in Proverbs 13:18 "Whoever disregards discipline comes to poverty and shame . . ." Leslie Hoppe, Professor of Old Testament Studies at Northwestern University, says that these Proverbs imply that the reader is in control of his own destiny and that there are consequences to their actions.[8] In cultures

---

4. Ibid., 41.

5. David Noel Freedman, "Poor, Poverty," in *The Anchor Bible Dictionary* (New York: Doubleday, 1996), 402.

6. Pleins, *The Social Visions,* 526.

7. These are Job, Psalms, Proverbs, Ecclesiastes, and Song of Songs.

8. Leslie J. Hoppe, *There Shall be No Poor among You: Poverty in the Bible* (Nashville, TN: Abingdon Press, 2004), 106.

and societies with supposedly equal access and opportunities for everyone, poverty is the result of laziness and the lack of personal discipline.

Proverbs was written at a time when Israel was at the zenith of its power and enjoyed tremendous prosperity. Of all the wisdom literature, Proverbs provides a different perspective on poverty. It defines the poor as "lazy, lacking in diligence, morally obtuse, and socially inferior."[9] This is in sharp contrast to the prophetic writings where laziness and moral failure are never mentioned as causes of poverty. Pleins explains that such a perception about the poor was "useful for protecting the [wisdom] creed's views of wealth and status, establishing in this way its own peculiar social ethic."[10] If the socially and politically powerful defined the causes of poverty as being personal moral failure, then there was no need to address the issues of injustice, which may have been the major cause of poverty. Proverbs, written by the elite, ensured that the socioeconomic status quo remained and nothing changed.

However, Proverbs also has a prophetic voice and is in line with the social critique of the prophets. Besides shedding light on human action (failure) and their consequences, it also provides a warning on social injustice.

This is the second reason for poverty. In the Old Testament period and in New Testament Palestine, as in much of the majority world today, the poor are not the lazy. Proverbs 13:23 "An unplowed field produces food for the poor, but injustice sweeps it away." The majority of the poor would probably have enough food and more if they did not have to live within unjust systems, which rob them of their livelihoods and deny them a fair return or income for their work. There is a warning for those who exploit the poor. Proverbs 14:31 "Whoever oppresses the poor shows contempt for their Maker . . ." Proverbs 22:22 pronounces God's judgment, "Do not exploit the poor because they are poor and do not crush the needy in court, for the Lord will take up their case and will exact life for life."[11] Similarly there is commendation for those who are kind. Proverbs 14:31 ". . . but whoever is kind to the needy honors God." Ecclesiastes 5:8–9 states that one should not be surprised by such injustice and denial of rights because this is a reality of the world we live in.

This basic understanding of why people are poor is expanded in the rest of the Bible and additional causes are mentioned. There are at least 245

---

9. Pleins, *The Social Visions*, 474.

10. Ibid., 474.

11. Alternate translation, "and will plunder those who plunder them."

references to the words *poor, poverty* and *lack* in the concordance[12] and these begin to provide insight into some of the types and causes of poverty. However, David Freedman, biblical scholar and general editor of the *Anchor Bible* series, cautions that the context and usage of the words for the poor and poverty, and not necessarily their etymology, is the key in determining their meaning.[13] Moreover the meaning of words may change or evolve over time.

Poverty manifested itself in different ways. In the Old Testament, the realities of the poor varied and the different Hebrew words used for the poor highlight this.[14]

The poor were those who lacked the basics essentials for living and survived mainly on bread and water. In the modern study of poverty these people would be those who live in extreme poverty.

- The poor were those who had been dispossessed of their land and assets through acts of injustice or lack of diligence.
- The poor were those who were frail or weak. These referred to the poor beleaguered peasant farmers.[15] This would have been both a result of and cause of poverty. In community development, this is referred to as the social determinants of health – the social and economic factors that determine poor health. The worse the socioeconomic indicators (i.e. the level of poverty), the worse the health of the individuals.
- The poor were those who were needy or dependent, the "economically or legally distressed; destitute; beggar."[16] David Pleins states that the *'ebyon* were the beggars, as they were not able to be self-sufficient.[17]
- The poor were those who had been oppressed or afflicted. They were the economically poor, oppressed, exploited and suffering. The

---

12. The Hebrew words are *chaser, yarash* or *rush, dal* or *dallal, 'ebyon, 'ani* and *anau, mashor, misken,* and *ras*.

13. Freedman, *Poor,* 402. As an example, Freedman states that *dal* in Proverbs refers to a lazy person, while for the prophets *dal* is an object of exploitation.

14. Jayakumar Christian, *God of the Empty-Handed: Poverty, Power and the Kingdom of God,* (Monrovia, CA: MARC, 1999), 17 and Freedman, *Poor,* 402. Thomas Hanks adds a further dimension to the understanding of poverty when he analyzes the Biblical vocabulary of oppression and its relationship to poverty. Thomas D. Hanks, *God So Loved the Third World: The Biblical Vocabulary of Oppression* (Maryknoll, NY: Orbis Books, 1983), 3–39.

15. Freedman, *Poor,* 402.

16. Ibid., 402.

17. Pleins, *The Social Visions,* 53.

Hebrew word 'ani is sometimes also used to mean humble. During the postexilic period, because of their experience of the exile, most of the population felt that they had joined the ranks of the poor. So poverty, humility and piety were often used synonymously during this period.[18]

The Hebrew words 'ani, 'ebyon and dal are the most commonly used terms for the poor, and identify Israel's disenfranchised who consisted mainly of the widows, the orphans, the resident aliens, and the oppressed.

The third reason for poverty is God's judgment. Speaking specifically to God's people, Moses states that there are times when God punishes with poverty those who transgress his laws (Deut 28:15–46). The basic premise is that those who follow the way of wisdom (i.e. following God's laws) will "live in safety and be at ease, without fear and harm" (Prov 1:33). The implication was that if one suffers or is in poverty (the idea being synonymous, Deut 28:15–48) it is because they have sinned by not following or obeying God's laws, which were meant for their well-being and prosperity.

The book of Job explores this argument further. The basic argument of Job's friends Eliphaz, Bildad, and Zophar is that *if you sin you will suffer* (known as retribution theory).[19] There is truth in this because breaking God's laws has consequences at the physical, social, emotional, spiritual and moral levels. However, the three friends went further and reversed the cause and effect to say that *if you suffer, then you must have sinned*.[20] While sin may cause suffering (or lead to poverty), not all suffering (or experience of poverty) is caused by personal sin and disobedience. Professor of Biblical Studies at Westmont College, Tremper Longman, and former Professor of Old Testament at Westminster Theological Seminary, Raymond Dillard, write: "The book of Job does not begin to explain all the reasons for suffering in the world. It rejects the retribution theory of the three friends as the only explanation of the origin of suffering. Job establishes once and for all that personal sin is not the only reason for suffering in this world."[21] There are

---

18. Ibid., 52, and Freedman, *Poor,* 402.

19. Many religions (especially Islam and Hinduism) teach that suffering and poverty are a result of the wrongs that human beings have done. For them poverty and suffering are indicators of sin and wrongdoing. Echoes of this belief are heard within the Christian church.

20. Tremper Longman III and Raymond B. Dillard, *An Introduction to the Old Testament* (Nottingham: Inter-Varsity Press, 2007), 235.

21. Ibid., 235.

times when suffering and poverty are not easily explained by any social theory or any Christian theology.

So poverty was not only the result of laziness or of personal sin (and God's resulting judgment). As noted in the Books of Wisdom the issue of injustice is a major reason for poverty.

Ancient Israel

Who were the poor in ancient Israel and why were they poor?

The Ancient Near East

The earliest biblical description of the life of the poor is from the period of the Patriarchs (2100–1800 BC) and is found in the book of Job.[22] Job, struggling to understand the cause of his misfortune, sees in the poor a mirror to his own experience, in that the suffering of the poor is not caused by their own sin. Pleins contrasts the book of Job with the standard explanation for poverty found in Proverbs, that poverty is caused by laziness and personal moral failure. Instead he states "poverty is the product of exploitation."[23]

Job indicts the wealthy for their mistreatment of the poor (Job 24:2–14). They rob the poor (even widows and orphans) of their land and their livestock, the only source of livelihood they have (2–3); they physically abuse and terrify them (4); they force the poor to forage for food and gather what little they can from the wastelands to feed their children (5–6); the poor are forced to sleep outside with no clothes and little covering in the drenching rain trying to find what little shelter they can from the rocks (7–8); defenseless infants and children are taken away as collateral for unpaid debts (9); the poor have few clothes, work hard and still go hungry (10); while producing olive oil and wine for the wealthy, the poor suffer from thirst (11); the poor groan under their pain and suffering and no one hears them (12); and at night they are robbed and killed (14).

---

22. There is much debate on the dating of the book of Job. The three commonly used dating are the pre-Moses (before 1500 BC), at the time of Solomon (around 900 BC) or as late as the Babylonian exile or later (600 BC or later).

23. Pleins, *The Social Visions*, 501.

While there is evidence of significant poverty in early antiquity in the Near East, especially among the Phoenicians, Babylonians, and Egyptians,[24] other than Job's description of the poor there is very little that describes the nature and causes of poverty.[25] However, there is a lot of evidence in the various ancient Near Eastern legal codes and wisdom literature of how the poor and vulnerable in society should be taken care of. Professor of Old Testament at Sankt Georgen Seminary in Frankfurt, Germany, Norbert Lohfink writes, "Reality may often have been cruel; nevertheless, in Egypt, in Mesopotamia, among the Hittites and the Canaanites, the care for the poor probably had a higher profile in ethical consciousness than in our modern societies."[26] It was a virtue of the gods, kings and judges, and determined the piety of a ruler.[27]

Professor of Biblical Studies at Liberty University, Richard Patterson writes, "One wonders if it is too much to suggest that it's [the virtue of caring for the poor] early predominance in the Near East might not have been a primeval reflection of God's own self-disclosure as being the Redeemer of the helpless."[28] The creator God, the lawgiver, had written his laws and values onto the hearts of all people (Rom 2:15[29]), even before he gave the law to Moses. The social values inherent in these ancient codes and literature would deeply influence the social contract that Israel as a nation and society would

---

24. Philip Ball, "Few Had Wealth in Ancient Egypt," *Nature: International Weekly Journal of Science* (29 November 2002), accessed 8 December 2012, http://www.nature.com/news/2002/021129/full/news021125-8.html. Ball quoting the work of Egyptian mathematician A. Y. Abul-Magd of Zagazig University and his study of the housing market in 14th-century BC in the city of Akhetaten states there was almost no middle class and the wealth was concentrated in less than 20 percent of the population. The other major cause for poverty in ancient Egypt was the occasional catastrophic decline in the flooding of the Nile, for example, after the reign of Pepy II (Neferkare) ending in 2152 BC when there was widespread famine, poverty and lawlessness.

25. Most studies of society in antiquity based on archeological evidence or manuscripts have focused on the structure of society, religious practices, the type of governance, trade and the economy, and conquests and other military related issues. There is very little on understanding the dynamics of poverty and who the marginalized groups were and why they were marginalized.

26. Norbert Lohfink, "Poverty in the Laws of the Ancient Near East and the Bible," *Theological Studies* 52 (1991): 34.

27. Charles F. Fensham, "Widow, Orphans and the Poor in Ancient Near Eastern Legal and Wisdom Literature," in *Essential Papers on Israel and the Ancient Near East*, ed. Fredreick E. Greenspan (New York: New York University Press, 2000), 176.

28. Richard D. Patterson, "The Widow, Orphan, and the Poor in the Old Testament and the Extra-Biblical Literature," *Bibliotheca Sacra* (July 1973): 233.

29. Rom 2:15 "Since they show that the requirements of the law are written on their hearts, their consciences also bearing witness."

develop. Yet there are some fundamental differences between these ancient legal instruments and literature and the Mosaic law (as will be discussed later).

There seems to have been a general awareness of the need for the king to make sure that the widows, the orphans and the poor received justice and had their needs taken care of. The oldest evidence of this value was in the Mesopotamian region in ancient Sumer in the earliest well-known codes of Urukagina of Lagash (2380–2360 BC),[30] and that of Ur-Nammu (2050 BC),[31] who was the founder of the third dynasty of Ur. Both detailed the protection of the widow, orphan and the poor.[32] The Code of Hammurabi (1795–1750 BC) built on these two earlier codes.[33] The king, as the living representative of the god of justice, the sun god Shamash, was expected to take care of the poor and needy. In the prologue, Hammurabi states that the gods have called him to,

- bring about the rule of righteousness in the land;
- destroy the wicked and the evil-doers;
- so that the strong should not harm the weak.[34]

In the epilogue, Hammurabi clarifies what that means by stating,

- that the strong might not injure the weak,
- in order to protect the widows and orphans.[35]

30. This was the oldest example of a legal code in recorded history. Other later codes were Lipit-Ishtar (1934–1924 BC), Eshnunna (1850 BC), the Hittite Laws (1650 BC), the Middle Assyrian Laws (prior to 1100 BC) and Neo-Babylonian Laws (700 BC). Pleins, *The Social Visions*, 42–43. Urukagina of Lagash exempted the widows and orphans from taxes. He decreed that the rich must use silver when purchasing from the poor, and if the poor does not wish to sell, the powerful man (the rich man or the priest) cannot force him to do so. "The Reforms of Urukagin," World History Project, 2007, accessed 10 December 2012, http://world-history.org/reforms_of_urukagina.htm.

31. Though earlier law-codes existed, such as the Code of Urukagina, Ur-Nammu represents the earliest extant legal text – three centuries older than the Code of Hammurabi. Some historians think that the code should be ascribed to his son Shulgi. Ur-Nammu stated that an orphan was not to be delivered up to the rich man and that the widow was not to be delivered up to the mighty man. Victor H. Matthews and Don C. Benjamin, *Old Testament Parallels: Law and Stories from the Ancient Near East* (Mahwah: Paulist Press, 2006), 101–102.

32. Patterson, "The Widow," 226.

33. There are a lot of parallels between the Code of Hammurabi and the Covenant Code (Exod 21–23), The Holiness Code (Lev 17–26), and the Deuteronomic Code (Deut 12–26). See Matthews and Benjamin, *Old Testament Parallels*, 105–114. Because the Code of Hammurabi predates the Old Testament codes, there is a lot of debate as to the nature and extent of its influence on the Old Testament codes.

34. Paul Halsall, "Code of Hammurabi," March 1998, accessed 9 December 2012, http://www.fordham.edu/halsall/ancient/hamcode.asp#text.

35. Ibid.

In the central region of the Fertile Crescent in Syria-Palestine similar values of compassion were highly regarded, though the legal codes or wisdom literature did not reflect this. Instead these are found in various epics.[36] In Ugarit, the stories of two kings were well known.

In the Aqhat Epic, King Dan'el is described as being compassionate.

> Thereupon Dan'el the Raphaman . . .
> . . . picks himself up
> he sits before the gate . . .
> he judges the cause of the widow(s)
> he adjudicates the case of the fatherless.[37]

In another epic, the mortally ill King Keret[38] is confronted by his son Prince Yassib for failing to behave like a king.

> You did not judge the cause of the widow,
> You did not adjudicate the case of the wretched,
> You did not drive out them that preyed upon the poor;
> You did not feed the orphan before you or the widow behind you.[39]

There were no legal codes in Egypt as the word of the reigning king was regarded as law and no written code could exist alongside it.[40] However, there is much in their wisdom literature on the king being compassionate. In ancient Egypt, a king who was beneficent was supposed to take care of the poor, the widows and orphans. King Merikare, who ruled during the First Intermediate Period (2075 BC), is instructed by his father Khety III, saying, "The good king does not oppress the widow or confiscate the property of the orphans."[41] Similarly King Amenemhat of the Middle Kingdom's twelfth dynasty emphasized concern for the poor and Ramses III (1186–1155 BC) of the twentieth dynasty boasted that he had given special attention to ensure justice for the widow and orphan.[42] Besides these, there is considerable other evidence of the ruler's concern for the poor, the widow and the orphan.[43]

---

36. Fensham, "Widow," 182.

37. Patterson, "The Widow," 227. Also see James B. Pritchard, ed. *Ancient Near Eastern Texts Relating to the Old Testament,* 3rd ed. (Princeton: Princeton University Press, 1969), 149–151.

38. Sometimes identified a "Kirta" in various other manuscripts and inscriptions

39. Patterson, "The Widow," 227.

40. Fensham, "Widow," 180.

41. Patterson, "The Widow," 226.

42. Ibid., 226–227.

43. See a more detailed listing in Fensham, "Widow," 180–182.

In the ancient Near East, the responsibility of the king was to maintain order in his kingdom. This involved administering a judicial system that ensured that the rights of the vulnerable were protected.[44] So the expectation was that the king was to take care of the poor and the vulnerable. Lohfink summaries this: "Thus the king was the center of welfare for the land; it was he who took care of the disadvantaged part of the population. Along with his victorious wars against outside enemies and the shrines he had built for the gods, these social and economic actions were a main topic of royal propaganda."[45] Maybe a few wealthy individuals would have been generous, particularly in Egypt. An inscription by Montuwser, who was a steward of King Amenemhat's successor, Sesostris I, in Egypt reads, "I was a father to the orphans, a helper of the widows."[46] A tomb inscription of the upper classes in Egypt may have included biographical information such as, "I gave bread to the hungry, water to the thirsty, clothing to the naked, and a passage to those who had no ship."[47]

The reason the king had this social and moral responsibility was that in the earlier kingdoms of Ugarit, the king was seen as the adopted son of the god who heads the pantheon of gods. Bernard Levinson, Professor of Classical and Near Eastern Studies at the University of Minnesota, gives the example of Keret (or Kirta), who as monarch, was designated "A scion of El – Son of the Gentle and Holy One."[48] However, by the Ur III period (2112–2004 BC), this would change from the concept of divine adoption to divine appointment, as ". . . divine appointment of the monarch to rule came to be the standard motif of royal legitimation in Babylon and Assyria, whose kings thus ruled under divine aegis."[49] In Egypt, the Pharaohs were reincarnation of the gods. So whether it was divine adoption or appointment, or reincarnation, the king was the representative of the gods and was responsible for the well-

---

44. John H. Walton, *Ancient Near Eastern Thought and the Old Testament* (Grand Rapids: Baker Academics, 2006), 283.

45. Lohfink, "Poverty," 35.

46. Patterson, "The Widow," 227.

47. Lohfink, "Poverty," 34. He also refers to the ancient Egyptian funerary text *Book of the Dead 125* where among the "Negative Confessions" the following are listed "I have not orphaned the orphan of his goods . . . I have not caused affliction; I have not caused hunger."

48. Bernard M. Levinson, "The Reconceptualization of Kingship in Deuteronomy and the Deuteronomistic History's Transformation Torah," *Vetus Testamentum* 51, no. 4 (2001): 512–513. Levinson further writes, "The metaphor of legal adoption to symbolize the close bond between god and king, [is] found in the literature of Ugarit and Israel . . ." (Ibid., 514).

49. Ibid., 514.

being of society and was endowed with divine wisdom[50]. This responsibility rested solely on him. The absolute minimum that was required of him was to ensure the legal protection of the most vulnerable in society. Levinson writes, "Because of the divine endowment of judicial wisdom, a primary duty of the monarch was to administer justice. In particular, he was responsible for ensuring the socially marginalized equal access to legal protection."[51]

Early Israel and the Origins of Social Organization

Any study on the social organization of early Israel has to understand the geographical and historical context from which Israel as a nation emerges. Pleins explains the basis of justice, which was then manipulated to oppress the vulnerable:

> It is not merely quaint, therefore, to know that the Bible arises out of an agriculturally based society; for a compelling theological analysis of the Bible's social ethics, it is imperative to understand the ways ancient Israel's land ownership and distribution may have functioned to oppress large sectors of ancient Israelite society. Only in this way will we, for example, grasp the strength of the prophetic social critique or discern the weakness in ancient Israel's gleaning laws.[52]

The origin of Israel as a society was during the exodus from Egypt and the subsequent wilderness wanderings. It was during this period that Israel's social contract was developed through the giving of the law. The Torah or the Pentateuch weaves the narrative of Israel's story with the principles and laws that together were to form the basis of society and social discourse. Both strands are important to understand, as the narrative partially explains the existence of the laws. During the period of the prophets, the laws provided the lens through which the prophets critiqued society and its narrative.

According to biblical scholar formerly at the Ecole Biblique in East Jerusalem, Roland de Vaux, ancient Israel in the wilderness was a semi-nomadic society and was not divided into social classes.[53] Israelite society,

---

50. Ibid.

51. Ibid.

52. Pleins, *The Social Visions*, 22.

53. Roland de Vaux, *Ancient Israel: Its Life and Institutions* (London: Darton, Longman & Todd, 1965), 68.

as originally structured, was nonhierarchical and decentralized. Missiologist and Dean Emeritus of the School of Intercultural Studies at Fuller Seminary, Arthur Glasser, writes about the value of that. "It protected the social health and economic viability of the lowest unit, not wealth, privilege, or power of any structured hierarchy. Its aim was to preserve the broadly based egalitarian self-sufficiency of each family and protect the weakest, poorest, and most threatened persons in the nation."[54]

What is remarkable is that according to the traditional dating of Exodus, Leviticus and Deuteronomy, at least the Covenant Code (Exod 21–23) and the Deuteronomic Code (Deut 12–26) are given during and towards the end the wilderness sojourn.[55] Even though at the time they were a nonhierarchical and very egalitarian society, the law addressed issues of poverty, social vulnerability and marginalization, and warned about class distinction and the dangers of social polarization when the divide between the rich and the poor deepened. It would seem that God, being aware of the depth of human sinfulness and their propensity towards evil, gave the law before they even entered the land ensuring protection and provision for the weak, the poor and the marginalized of society.

As Israel moved from the desert and wilderness, at the end of the conquest, Joshua instituted the land tenure system. His objective was to prevent any sort of absentee landlord system, where a wealthy landlord would demand a percentage of the produce from the land being worked by tenant farmers. Instead land tenure was to be based on the kinship system with regards to both possession and the use of the land. This ensured the economic viability of all the Israelites.[56] All enjoyed more or less a similar standard of living, with wealth coming from the produce of the land. The ideal that God intended for his people was, "There should be no poor among you" (Deut 15:4). But knowing the reality of sin and greed and its consequences, God states: "There will always be poor people in the land" (Deut 15:11a). This was a statement of fact and of reality rather than of God's ideal. Because of this, he commands,

---

54. Arthur Glasser, *Announcing the Kingdom: The Story of God's Mission in the Bible* (Grand Rapids: Baker Academic, 2003), 117.

55. There is considerable debate about when the various laws and codes were written and by whom. For a more detailed discussion on the dating of the various books and sections see Harold V. Bennett, *Injustice Made Legal: Deuteronomic Law and the Plight of Widows, Strangers and Orphans in Ancient Israel* (Grand Rapids: William B. Eerdmanns Publishing Company, 2002), 6–21. Also see Douglas A. Knight, *Law, Power, and Justice in Ancient Israel* (Louisville: Westminster John Knox Press, 2011), 261.

56. Glasser, *Announcing the Kingdom*, 117.

"Be open handed toward your brothers and toward the poor and needy in the land" (Deut 15:11b).

Possession or non-possession of land during this period would be the major indicator of poverty. The non-possession of land would identify who the vulnerable in society were. These were identified as the slaves, widows, fatherless children, the needy, non-Israelites who had placed themselves under Israel's protection, and the sojourners or "resident aliens." So, while the laws ensured the vulnerable were taken care of, fundamental to everything else, there was to be equitable distribution of the land and a system (the Sabbatical and Jubilee years) to ensure that equity and justice would continue and that generational poverty not be perpetuated.

Though slaves were not regarded as marginalized and were "of the family," they had no civic rights.[57] Because of this, Mosaic law ensured that slave owners treated their slaves justly and properly (Deut 15:12–15). The law protected the slaves from exploitation (Exod 21:2–27; Lev 25:25–55).

Others were similarly protected and provided for through the law. These were the non-Israelites under Israel's protection (Deut 10:19), the sojourners and "resident aliens," also known as *gerim* or *ger* (Lev 19:10; 23:22; Deut 24:19–21; Num 35:15), and widows (Exod 22:22–24; Deut 10:18; 24:17–21). Glasser identified the widows as symbolic of those vulnerable in the community. "Widows were regarded as helpless, needy persons, unable to protect or provide for themselves . . . In a sense widows represent all the disenfranchised persons in society, those who are deprived of reasonable livelihood and need care by others."[58] Lohfink, referring to the context of early Israel and the surrounding cultures, writes: "The fixed word-pair 'widow and orphan' is old. Israel inherited it from its surrounding cultures as a symbolic name for those in need of help."[59]

The foreigners who had settled in the land, also known as resident aliens, were a unique category of the vulnerable. The concept is similar to the practice among ancient Arab nomads, where a *jar* was a refugee or individual who, while seeking protection, had settled in a tribe other than his own. Similarly, the *ger* "is essentially a foreigner who lives more or less permanently in the midst of another community, where he is accepted and enjoys certain rights."[60]

---

57. Ibid., 87.
58. Ibid., 87–88.
59. Lohfink, "Poverty," 34.
60. de Vaux, *Ancient Israel*, 74.

Abraham and Moses were *gerim*. Later when the Israelites settled in the land and saw themselves as "the people of the land" and perceived themselves as the legitimate owners, all the former inhabitants became *gerim*, unless they became slaves or were assimilated into Israelite society through marriage. Immigrants were later added to this group. So while the *gerim* were free men and not slaves, they did not have full civic or political rights. Since most of the land and property was in the hands of the Israelites, the *gerim* worked by hiring out their services. So they were poor and were considered in the same category as the widows, orphans and the other poor, who were protected by the Mosaic law to receive charity and help. Besides the charity, they were entitled to justice (Deut 1:16), they had access to the cities of refuge (Num 35:15), and they were subject to the same penalties as the Israelites (Lev 20:2; 24:16, 22). Some *gerim* did manage to become rich (Lev 25:47; Deut 28:43).[61]

However, settlement on the land changed ancient Israel socially. The basic unit of the society was now no longer the tribe (as during their wilderness sojourn) but the clan (the *mishpahah*). They settled in towns, which were very rarely more than the size of villages. There is also evidence of isolated farmsteads across the land. The municipal law given in Deuteronomy with regards to cities of refuge, unknown murderers, rebellious sons, adultery, and the Levites, formed the basis of social life in these small towns. Over time there was some diversity in the various types of settlements and there were a handful of major town and cities. However, between 80–95 percent of the population lived outside the urban areas in villages averaging 75–150 people per settlement, sometimes even fewer.[62]

Most of the villages were agricultural and usually showed no significant social differences. However, according to Research Fellow in the Centre for Biblical Studies at the University of Manchester, Walter Houston, the towns and cities began to be characterized by social stratification and economic specialization.[63] Douglas Knight, Professor of Hebrew Bible and Jewish Studies at Vanderbilt University, states that there is very little archeological evidence of lower-class residential neighborhoods in Israelite cities till later (about the seventh century BC and the fall of the northern kingdom). There is some limited evidence of neighborhoods of bureaucrats, laborers, artisans

---

61. Ibid., 75.
62. Knight, *Law*, 262.
63. Houston, *Contending for Justice*, 20.

and other defined trades within the cities. The majority of the poor lived outside the walls where archeologists have found traces of built-up areas.[64]

So poverty in the land was either event based (the widow, orphan and those who because of misfortune ended up needy and in poverty) or those who did not belong to the community (foreigner) and as a result did not have the same rights (or obligations). These included the slaves, non-Israelites who had placed themselves under Israel's protection, and the sojourners or "resident aliens." This would have been the same in any ancient Near Eastern society.

Lohfink comments that all the categories designated as poor had one thing in common and that is that they did not possess land. He states that what the law in Deuteronomy seeks to do "is not to add new groups to the poor, but rather to change the structures of society so as to provide support for those groups which, for very different reasons, are not in a position to live off their own land."[65] Knight states that there evolved a culture of concern in the village communities as they all were vulnerable to famine, droughts, and passing armies. So the biblical laws on protection of the widows, orphans, strangers, and the poor mirrored the vulnerabilities of individuals and groups in the community.[66]

This would, however, change as Israel established itself in the land and the very fabric of society changed. There would be new causes for poverty and new groups of poor and disenfranchised.

Was Israel's Social Contract Different?

Was the social contract, defined by the Mosaic law given to Israel, unique and any different from those in other ancient Near Eastern societies, especially in the light of their legal codes and wisdom literature? While many of the ancient Near Eastern codes and biblical legal material are similar, biblical law was not merely "civil law"; they blended religious ritual with social obligation. Pleins writes: "Social well-being is not simply a product of royal or judicial fiat but finds its roots in the community's worship response to Israel's divine sovereign."[67]

---

64. Knight, Law, 75.

65. Lohfink, "Poverty," 44.

66. Knight, Law, 153.

67. Pleins, The Social Visions, 44.

Lohfink makes an interesting observation. Using the Code of Hammurabi as an example (but not limited to it), he states that these ancient codes "make a distant approach to the topic of the problems of the poor. But they never deal directly with the poor or with their rights in society."[68] He identifies the linguistic difference between the prologue[69] and epilogue[70] of each of the codes and the laws themselves. The prologue usually states the religious background and general policy of the king.[71] He says that while the prologue and the epilogue have a major focus on the poor, the laws themselves never mention the poor but only refer to some of the issues that they faced.[72] So it would seem while the concern and intention (as expressed in the prologue and epilogue) was there to assist the poor, the actual means to ensure justice and provide help were never properly defined other than the occasional injunction. John Walton, Professor of Old Testament at Wheaton College, states that the Hammurabi Code did not impose any obligation on society or the courts and that there was no call to obey.[73]

In approaching the Old Testament, Lohfink suggests that in the earliest of the legal codes, the Covenant Code of Exodus 20:22–23:33, the actual means of how to ensure justice for and assistance to the poor were an integral part of the laws and their status was explicitly defined in the second giving of the law in Deuteronomy.[74] The details of the social protection were important as Charles Fensham, former Professor of Semitic Languages at Stellenbosch University, South Africa, writes: "These people [the poor] had no rights,

---

68. Lohfink, "Poverty," 37.

69. A prologue is usually defined as a separate introductory section of a literary piece.

70. An epilogue is usually a section at the end that serves as a comment on or conclusion to what has been stated.

71. Fensham, "Widow," 178.

72. Lohfink, "Poverty," 37. Lohfink specifies the issues of the poor that are mentioned in the various codes. "From the *Code of Eshnunna*: on the right of repurchase of a house sold in financial difficulties (39 A 3). From the *Code of Hammurabi*: on the treatment of a fee when he who holds it is in war captivity or returns from it – somewhat feudal law (27–29); on the death of a person taken as pledge (115–116); on persons who were sold into slavery for debts (117–119); the case of a woman with the *la'bu* disease (148–149); on widows and orphans – more marriage law and law of succession (177). From *Middle Assyrian Laws*: casuistics on widows – more marriage law and law of succession (33–36, 46). From *Neobabylonian Law Fragment* 12–15: a similar prescription. Nevertheless, at the most, only 148–149 of the *Code of Hammurabi* actually approaches the area of the problems of the poor." See also Fensham, "Widow," 178–179.

73. Walton, *Ancient Near Eastern Thought*, 298.

74. There is some critical discussion stating certain elements of this passage were added later. See Lohfink, "Poverty," 38–39 for a brief discussion of this.

no legal personalities, or in some cases restricted rights. They were almost outlaws. Anyone could oppress them without danger that legal connections might endanger his position."[75] While the ancient literature and codes expressed concern for the poor, the Mosaic law explicitly stated how they were to be defended.[76] The biblical law codes provided structured solutions for those who were hungry, the wage laborers, the landless, the debt slave, and the poor.[77]

Second, while there is much that is similar to the Egyptian wisdom texts and prayers, and to the ancient Near Eastern royal ideology of being just and compassionate to the poor in everyday life, in business dealings, and in the court, the part that is new in the Old Testament is the concern for and care of the stranger. The implications of this are not fully fleshed out till Deuteronomy, but a foundation is laid in Exodus in the first giving of the law (the Covenant Code).

While the formulaic language identifying the poor had till then been the "widow and the orphan," how and when did the "stranger" get inserted into that formula? While Lohfink suggests a variety of possible historical and sociological influences,[78] what is clear is that God states his reason for including the stranger in the law. Exodus 3:9 and Deuteronomy 26:7 describe the treatment of the Jews in Egypt as oppression. At the end of the Covenant Code in Exodus 23:9, using the same language, God states, "Do not oppress an alien; you yourselves know how it feels to be aliens, because you were aliens in Egypt." The experience and history of the Jews would give them a fresh and deeper understanding of a new dimension of poverty and exclusion, and as a result would impact the social contract that was beginning to be defined by the Covenant Code of Exodus.[79] The formulaic language identifying the poor had now become the "widow, the orphan and the stranger in the land."

The third distinction is that under the Mosaic law, not only was God concerned about justice (as was the god, Shamash), God identifies himself as the protector of the poor and vulnerable. Shamash, the sun god, is called the judge of heaven and earth and the judge of the gods and men[80], thereby

---

75. Fensham, "Widow," 188.

76. Pleins, *The Social Visions,* 51.

77. Ibid., 525.

78. Lohfink, "Poverty," 40–41.

79. Ibid., 40–42.

80. This was found on the inscription found at Iahdun-Lim of Mari discovered in 1953 (and not on the Code of Hammurabi) and the inscription was dedicated to Shamash.

indicating that the religious and social ethics are closely related. The king was to execute justice and ensure that the strong did not oppress the weak so that Shamash (the god of justice) may rise over the people.[81] There is a more nuanced difference when it came to the Mosaic law. Psalm 82[82] illustrates this distinction. The idea is that Yahweh is the God of justice and there is no other like him. Verses 3–4 are the key, where God challenges the gods to "defend the weak and the fatherless; uphold the cause of the poor and the oppressed. Rescue the weak and the needy; deliver them from the hand of the wicked." The gods fail to accomplish this. The implication is that God is the only One who can truly provide justice and bring deliverance to the poor and vulnerable.[83] Fensham summarizes this: "The important difference between this conception and that of Mesopotamia and Egypt is that the exercising of justice is narrowed down to one God and all the others are excluded."[84]

So God's defense of the poor is an integral part of his character, of who he is. Psalm 68: 5 states, "A father to the fatherless, a defender of widows, is God in his holy dwelling." Deuteronomy 15:9 and 24:15[85] both state that when the poor have been taken advantage of, they may cry out to God against their oppressors, the result being that "you will be guilty of sin." The seriousness of the crime and the severity of the punishment are described by Lohfink. "The connected sanction is that whoever forces the poor to cry will be in the state of *hêt'*."[86] *Hêt'* is not just any sin. As Old Testament scholar at Eberhard Karls University of Tübingen, Klaus Koch has shown, *hêt'* is a sin which

---

81. Fensham, "Widow," 178.

82. Psalm 82:1–8; God presides in the great assembly; he renders judgment among the "gods": "How long will you [plural] defend the unjust and show partiality to the wicked? Defend the weak and the fatherless; uphold the cause of the poor and the oppressed. Rescue the weak and the needy; deliver them from the hand of the wicked. The 'gods' know nothing, they understand nothing. They walk about in darkness; all the foundations of the earth are shaken. I said, 'You are "gods"; you are all sons of the Most High.' But you will die like mere mortals; you will fall like every other ruler." Rise up, O God, judge the earth, for all the nations are your inheritance.

83. Fensham, "Widow," 183–184.

84. Ibid., 184.

85. Deut 15:9 "Be careful not to harbor this wicked thought: 'The seventh year, the year for canceling debts, is near,' so that you do not show ill will toward the needy among your fellow Israelites and give them nothing. They may then appeal to the Lord against you, and you will be found guilty of sin."
Deut 24:15, "Pay them their wages each day before sunset, because they are poor and are counting on it. Otherwise they may cry to the Lord against you, and you will be guilty of sin."

86. Lohfink, "Poverty," 46.

can be expiated only by the death of the sinner."[87] Unlike the ancient gods who heard the cry of the poor and either blessed them or cursed them, God defended the poor and considered their oppressors as having broken his laws. Their condemnation is clear. Deuteronomy 27:19, "Cursed is the man who withholds justice from the alien, the fatherless or the widow." Exodus 22:21–24 is even more explicit. "Do not mistreat or oppress a foreigner, for you were foreigners in Egypt. Do not take advantage of the widow or the fatherless. If you do and they cry out to me, I will certainly hear their cry. My anger will be aroused, and I will kill you with the sword; your wives will become widows and your children fatherless."

The final distinction between Israel's emerging social contract and the ancient legal codes of the Near East, is that responsibility for the care of the poor and the vulnerable shifted from the responsibility of the king and sometimes the wealthy, to the community that received the Mosaic law. The responsibility mentioned in the above verses of Deuteronomy 27:19 and Exodus 22:21–24 are clearly addressed to everyone in the community and not just to the ruler and elites. Systems were put in place to ensure that the widows, the orphans and the foreigners in their midst were taken care of and entitled to justice. Slaves were to be treated humanely. The vulnerable were the responsibility of the community and not just the king.

Fensham summarizes the relationship between social values evident in the legal codes and ancient literature from the region and the Mosaic law. He writes, "The Israelites in later history inherited the concept from their forbearers, some of whom had come from Mesopotamia, some had been captive in Egypt, and others had grown up in the Canaanite world. In the Israelite community this policy was extended through the encouragement of the high ethical religion of Yahweh to become a definite part of their religion."[88] Israel's social contract draws deeply from the values God the lawgiver had already revealed in the surrounding cultures, and its uniqueness is that it raises it to a higher ethical standard that reflects the character of their God.

---

87. Ibid., 46. Lohfink's reference for Klaus Koch is K. Koch, *Theological Dictionary of the Old Testament*, ed. G. Botterweck and H. Ringgren (Grand Rapids: William Eerdmans Publishing Company, 1974) 3:309–320, esp. 315–316.

88. Fensham, "Widow," 198.

Social Change and Consequences

Social and Economic Polarization, Abuse and Poverty

Roland de Vaux notes that between the tenth and eighth century BC a social revolution took place within Israel that would change the very fabric of Jewish society.[89] Houston contends that up to that point, variations in wealth were not significant, and it did not amount to a class system, although some variations can be traced back to the pre-monarchic period. He writes, "They were sufficiently shaped by the egalitarian ethos of traditional society even to make special provision for the destitute in their cities. Nevertheless, profound changes began to develop in society, and gathered strength in the ninth century for Israel and from the eighth in Judah."[90]

As the monarchy grew, there were the court officials, military and civil authorities, who formed a sort of "caste" separate from the people in the villages, who started profiting from their positions and from the favors that were granted to them by the king. Others made profits from their land by hard work or good luck. Over time, realities of business transactions, corrupt judges and officials, and the greed of the wealthy elite destroyed any social equality there was, with some becoming rich while others sank into poverty.[91] De Vaux contends, "The wealth of the day was in fact badly distributed and often ill-gotten."[92] Pleins, quoting German theologian Gerhard Johannes Botterweck, says that the injustice of the economic system that the large landowners set up disadvantaged the small farmers who usually had hardly enough left over after a harvest, but they were then forced to pay rent and taxes on what they produced,[93] thus enriching the landlords at the expense of the small farmers.[94] In addition to this the poor were victims of artificially high

---

89. de Vaux, *Ancient Israel*, 73.

90. Houston, *Contending for Justice*, 49.

91. Ibid., 49.

92. de Vaux, *Ancient Israel*, 73.

93. D. N. Premnath notes that agrarian societies tended to be socially stratified. "In a stratified society, the power and status of individuals dictate the distribution of goods and services, whereas in a less stratified society, the distribution of goods is dependent on need. A stratified society implies a condition where a dominant class of people control and dictate the distribution of goods. The basic concern of the dominant class is how to extract the maximum surplus from the primary producers. It requires a delicate balance between extracting maximum surplus but allowing just enough for the producing class to survive in order to continue production." D. N. Premnath, *Eighth Century Prophets: A Social Analysis* (St Louis: Chalice Press, 2003), 78.

94. Pleins, *The Social Visions*, 371. See Amos 5:11.

prices and extortion.[95] As patronage, hired labor and credit on the security of
the person became part of economic life, by the sixth century BC the abuse
of credit that threatened the peasants with eviction from the land that they
owned became common.

It is important to note, as de Vaux points out, that the poor in ancient
Israel (at least in the early stages) did not constitute a separate social class in
contrast to the rich. They were individuals who were isolated and defenseless.[96]

Of all the prophets, this social evolution is described in detail by Amos
who lived during the first half of the eighth century BC during the reign of
Jeroboam the II (793–753 BC) in Israel and the reign of Uzziah (791–740
BC) in Judah. This provides the context for his messages of divine judgment.
It was a period of unprecedented prosperity in both kingdoms as a result
of military success and territorial expansion. In the process both kingdoms
had accrued great wealth, and a powerful and wealthy upper class of society
had developed.[97] They enjoyed new levels of leisure time and disposable
wealth, and this brought with it open vices (Amos 2:7–8), including alcohol
abuse which had become a problem for the women (4:1). The wealthy could
purchase justice (5:12) while the poor and those less fortunate were reduced to
servitude (2:6–7; 8:6). "The poor and needy were crushed by the powerful."[98]
(2:7; 4:1; 5:11; 8:6)

Research Associate at the University of the Witwatersrand, South Africa,
William Domeris' extensive study of poverty in Israel during the monarchic
period[99] demonstrates the complexity of the causes of poverty in Israel. The
peasants experienced a significant level of deprivation as a result of inadequate
land, poor weather and the collapse of what he calls positive reciprocity,
which is when help and favors are given and returned within a community.
According to Domeris the impact on the poor was compounded as the legal
and economic systems failed, something that the prophets of the time had
much to say about.[100]

---

95. Ibid., 372. See Amos 8:4–6.

96. Vaux, *Ancient Israel*, 74.

97. Longman III and Dillard, *An Introduction*, 423.

98. Ibid., 431–432.

99. This would be the Iron Age II, which would be the 8th and 9th centuries BC.

100. William Domeris, *Touching the Heart of God: The Social Reconstruction of Poverty
among Biblical Peasants* (New York: T&T Clark, 2007).

Injustice and the New Poor

One thing that is clear from the eighth-century prophets is that poverty and injustice were not accidental. As D. N. Premnath, associate professor of Biblical Studies at St. Bernard's School of Theology and Ministry, notes: "They knew exactly what the causes were and who was responsible for it. They did not speak in abstraction. They knew what the oppression/injustice was, and who the oppressors and oppressed were."[101] The prophets, particularly Amos, Micah, Isaiah and Jeremiah, give a description of the poor who emerged during the period of the monarchy. Traditional scholarship has always maintained that the poor mentioned by the prophets were predominantly the peasants in the countryside. Other scholars[102] contend that besides the peasants, the poor also lived in the cities and were often exploited. Houston writes, "With the steady development of urban culture in Judah from the late eighth, and the breakdown of the old kinship networks in the sixth century, it would have become more common for the marginalized people to fail to find succour in their communities: hence, later prophets more frequently show concern for the widow, the fatherless and stranger."[103]

Amos uses the three words *'ebyon, dal* and *'ani* to identify the poor. The first two are either used in the singular or plural forms and the last only in the plural. All three are in the masculine form. This is significant as Phyllis Bird explains later. There has been much discussion on who these three words describe. Some scholars state that the word *dal* translates simply as "peasant." Others argue that *dal* refers to a poor peasant who still possessed some land when compared to *'ebyon* as those who did not own property and made a living as a casual day laborer. *'Ani* referred to either.[104] Houston, refering to Brazilian Old Testament scholar Milton Schwantes' work, says that though there may be differences, Amos uses them interchangably. "They all refer, obviously, to people lacking in material resources and therefore in poverty."[105] Amos also uses the word *saddiq* in 2:6 and 5:12. Normally this word is translated as "righteous." However, in both these passages he uses them in parallel with others words for poor, in particlar *'ebyon* or *'ebyonim*. The passages seem to indicate the *saddiq* as either the innocent or the victims of a miscarriage

---

101. Premnath, *Eighth Century Prophets,* 182.

102. Houston, *Contending for Justice,* 61.

103. Ibid., 63–64.

104. Ibid., 62.

105. Ibid.

of justice. Houston implies from this that they may be morally innocent, meaning that while there may be a legal case against them, the *saddiqs'* only crime is that they are unable to pay their debts.[106] One interesting observation by Houston, "in Amos the trio of the widow and the fatherless and the alien are not mentioned as victims of oppression. The focus is on full citizens, adult males, who are being deprived of their rights."[107]

Phyllis Bird, Associate Professor of Old Testament Interpretation at Garrett-Evangelical Theological Seminary, notes who are the poor and victims of injustice not mentioned by Amos.[108] Other than the word *hanna 'ra* in 2:7, which refers to a victim of oppression, specifically a sexually abused woman (probably a bondservant), the words for "poor" and the word *saddiq* in the Hebrew Bible do not occur in the feminine.[109] This does not mean that the women were not poor. Bird who has written extensively about women and gender issues in the Old Testament writes, "Even where women of the community are clearly suffering from the conditions of poverty . . . the injustice done to the poor by the rich is formulated with males in mind."[110] This may also reflect the patriarchal structure of society. While Amos may not mention women as being poor or marginalized, Micah (2:9) and the other prophets mention women and children (orphans). Bird points out that in only two places in the prophets, Isaiah 10:1–4 and Zechariah 7:10, are women mentioned in the same context as the poor (male).[111] When families were forced, because of debt or extreme poverty, to give up their children to slavery, they usually surrendered their daughters first.[112] The Mosaic law

---

106. Ibid. Premnath further notes: "Many factors drove the peasants into debt. First, the exactions in agricultural produce were heavy, sometimes more than half of the total produce. Prices tend to be the lowest at the time of the harvest. Illegal business practices on the part of the landowners further cut into the returns. Second, the common peasants bore the brunt of much of the taxation to support the program of the state. . . . Third, when the peasants were dependent primarily upon rain for agriculture, there were serious consequences if the rains failed. They were forced to borrow to feed the family. If the rains failed for subsequent seasons, the peasants went into deeper debt. Often, the peasants offered either the piece of land they owned or an article of value or a member of the family as collateral. Failure to repay mounting loans resulted in the foreclosure of land and/or being sold into slavery." Premnath, *Eighth Century Prophets*, 162.

107. Houston, *Contending for Justice*, 86–87.

108. Phyllis Bird, *Missing Persons and Mistaken Identities: Women and Gender in Ancient Israel* (Minneapolis: Fortress Press, 1997).

109. Houston, *Contending for Justice*, 63.

110. Bird, *Missing Persons*, 76.

111. Ibid., 77.

112. Ibid., 75.

specifically ensured the protection of women, particularly widows, and the fatherless and this was primarily through the family and kinship structure. So if the women were among the poor, it was because the male heads of the household had failed them. Houston states, "These are the people [referring to the widow and the fatherless] who have no rights, no fixed place in the structure of the family, particularly, one may surmise, after the dissolution of the extended family in urban conditions, which is why their position is precarious . . ."[113]

While Amos was concerned for the rights of those who were full citizens, Isaiah (5:8–10) and Micah (2:1–5) are specifically concerned with peasant families who were losing their lands. Many of the prophets (other than Amos) refer to the oppression of the fatherless and the widows. Jeremiah 7:6 and Ezra 22:7, 29 also refer to the oppression of the aliens in the land (the *ger*). Both male and female debt bondservants are mentioned in Jeremiah 34, many of whom would have been children (Neh 5:2–5), including girls (as referred to in Amos 2:7).[114]

The Mosaic law was clear that the status of Israelites who were slaves was temporary. Male salves (Exod 21:2–6) and female slaves (Deut 15:12–17) had to be set free after six years of service. At that point they had a choice of whether they left their master's house or remained. According to de Vaux, "These laws do not seem to have been strictly observed. According to Jer. 34:8–22 which is explicitly based on Deuteronomy, the people of Jerusalem had liberated their 'Hebrew' slaves, during the siege under Nebuchadnezzar; but when the siege was raised for a while, they seized them again. The prophet denounces this as a felony against their brethren and transgression of a law of God."[115] There was further provision for the liberation of slaves during the jubilee year (Lev 25:41–53). De Vaux adds, "There is no evidence that the law was ever applied, either before or after Nehemiah, who makes no reference to it when he orders a remission of debts, involving the liberation of persons held as security (Neh 5:1–13)."[116]

While God intended ancient Israel to reflect equity and justice in their society, what evolved was a stratified society with wealth and power concentrated within a small ruling elite living mainly in the cities. As a result

113. Houston, *Contending for Justice*, 63.

114. Ibid., 87.

115. de Vaux, *Ancient Israel*, 88.

116. Ibid., 88.

poverty increased because of the breakdown of the kinship structure and the most vulnerable in society were no longer taken care of. Poverty also increased because of oppression, brutality and injustices practiced by the wealthy elite. The oppression and injustice more often than not contributed to the breakdown of the kinship structure.

The Kingdom of God: The Ideal That Was Forgotten

The narrative of Scripture keeps the character of God central to how the history of Israel unfolds. Scripture provides a vision of the world based on the character of God. The Mosaic law reflected the kind of society that the creator King desired. In the midst of holiness, righteousness, and incredibly mighty power, the character of God is revealed along with the values that he desired for his kingdom. These included justice, compassion and care for the poor, the weak, the vulnerable and the outsider who did not belong. (Deut 10:19, Lev 19:10; 23:22; 25:35–43, Deut 24:19–21 Num 35:15, Exod 22:22–24, Deut 10:18; 24:17–21 all describe provisions in the law that ensured that the widows, the sojourners and "resident aliens," the non-Israelites under Israel's protection, the fatherless and the slaves – all who were poor and vulnerable, were protected and provided for.)

The kind of society that God had wanted for his chosen people in the Old Testament was to be a model of what his kingdom would be like when it is finally established in all its fullness. The prophets painted word pictures of the fleeting glimpses they had of this kingdom. One of the more descriptive pictures is in Isaiah 65:17–25. God's kingdom will comprise of new heavens and a new earth that he will restore. As God takes delight and pleasure in his people, there will no longer be any sorrow, weeping and crying. Children will no longer die in infancy (because of disease, malnutrition or abandonment) and adults will not die prematurely (because of chronic illnesses or sudden health crises). People will have secure shelters and homes that no one can take away from them (due to default on loans, soaring debt or wealthy land developers), neither will they become refugees, being driven from their homes. They will have food security and enough to eat as their own gardens and vineyards will yield rich harvests. They will be able to put in a hard day's work and be satisfied because what they earn and produce will be theirs to enjoy and not robbed from them by absentee landlords and exorbitant taxes. Their children will grow up secure in a family and not be sold into slavery because of debts that their parents cannot repay. The delight of God in them would be so great that before they can even express their thoughts and desires to him, he would have anticipated them and answered by providing their hearts' desires. Nature will be at peace and balance restored in the ecological system.

These glimpses of the kingdom of God were the very thing that the poor in ancient Israel and the refugees in exile yearned for, and by which they were sustained. Their hope was in God that he would one day bring this about and relieve them of their poverty and suffering. They yearned for a kingdom where they would not be oppressed but are able to live in security. Unlike later utopian visions of society, this was going to be ushered in by God himself rather than by social engineering.

As ancient Israel evolved as a political entity, a theocratic society based on worship of the living God who had revealed himself and governed by the Mosaic laws, it was gradually influenced by values and ethics of the surrounding nations. They forgot God's values. Jeremiah reminds the nation of what was important when he writes about the King (Jer 22:15–16), "he did what was right and just, so all went well with him. He defended the cause of the poor and needy, and so all went well. Is that not what it means to know me?" As pagan worship, idolatry, and social disintegration took hold in Israel, God sent prophets to warn them of impending judgment if they did not return to him. Finally he does judge them. His verdict is damning as they reject him as God worthy of worship and as King to be obeyed.

- They had betrayed him and his love for them. They were unfaithful to the covenant they had with God and they worshiped idols (Hos 2:1–3, 8–13; Amos 2:7b–8, 10–17; 5:25–27; Exod 32:1; Mic 2:1–2; Isa 5:8–24).

- They were unjust in their dealings and exploited the poor and the minorities in their midst (Amos 2: 6–7a; 5: 7–12; Mic 6:6–8).

In his judgment, God deported to Babylon the ruling elite, the wealthy of society, and the landowners – the very ones who had exploited the poor.[117] The warning of Exodus 22:21–24 had come true. "Do not mistreat or oppress a foreigner, for you were foreigners in Egypt. Do not take advantage of the widow or the fatherless. If you do and they cry out to me, I will certainly hear their cry. My anger will be aroused, and I will kill you with the sword;

---

117. The total population of Palestine at this point was probably about a million people with 800,000 in the Northern Kingdom and the remainder in Judah. According to evidence, Sargon II carried off 27,290 persons from Samaria. It is estimated that Nebuchadnezzar deported only about 10,000 from Judah in 597 BC, consisting mainly of people of rank and station, blacksmiths and locksmiths, mostly from the cities. De Vaux, *Ancient Israel*, 66–67. See also 2 Kgs 24:14–16.

your wives will become widows and your children fatherless." The ones who remained in the land were the poorest who previously had not owned any property. They were given vineyards and fields (even though this was short-lived) to prevent the fields from falling into disuse and provide subsistence for the Babylonian conquerors.[118] Though there is a return, a rebuilding and a partial restoration, the equitable, just and secure society that God has envisioned for his people seems to have died in the silence of biblical history.

The exile had a profound impact on how poverty was viewed. The exile experience allowed the entire population to feel that they were now part of the poor and oppressed. Pleins identifies four major changes that occurred that the postexilic compliers of the prophetic writings highlighted. First, the prophets now depicted poverty as evil. Second, the people must spare no effort to remove it from the community of God, and reforms and legislations must be enacted to ensure that. Third, God will ultimately eliminate all poverty in the future. And finally God has a special concern for the poor.[119] These perceptions would carry through to first-century Palestine.

It is important to note that God's judgment of his people for exploiting the poor was not just limited to Israel. God hates it when any nation abuses and exploits the poor. Ezekiel 16:49 gives the reason for God's judgment of Sodom. "Now this was the sin of your sister Sodom: She and her daughters were arrogant, overfed and unconcerned; they did not help the poor and needy." Professor of Old Testament at Gordon Conwell Theological Seminary, Timothy Laniak, explains that because human beings everywhere bear his image and likeness, God has a stake in how humans are treated.[120]

So What Does All This Mean?

A social-scientific and historical approach to the study of poverty in the Bible helps explain the history and the social, economical and political contexts that created and entrenched poverty in Old Testament society and which then are the reasons for the teaching on the issues of poverty, care of the poor and of justice.

---

118. Pleins, *The Social Visions*, 291, and Richard I. Bradshaw, "Exile," 1999, accessed 18 January 2013, http://www.biblestudies.org.uk/article_exile.html. cf. 2 Kgs 25:11–12 and Jer 39:10; 52:15–16.

119. Pleins, *The Social Visions*, 421.

120. Timothy S. Laniak, *Finding the Lost Images of God* (Grand Rapids: Zondervan, 2010), 48.

While there is acknowledgement that laziness and lifestyle choices are causes of poverty, in the Old and New Testaments, it is clear that greed caused the rich to usurp the land of the poor at every excuse. In addition the elite placed unbearable taxation systems on the poor peasants, which caused them to go into debt and ultimately end up in destitution.

God envisaged a just society, which would reflect his very nature and character. The laws he gave were to be the social contract of God's people, and they reflected the character of God. Since there is no duality in Hebrew thought, the physical realm was to reflect the reality of the spiritual realm. The unseen God is to be perceived not only through the laws that he gave and the narrative and teaching of the rest of the Bible, but *he is to be perceived through his creation, as well as the attitudes and practices of his people.*

This understanding of the causes of poverty is continued in the New Testament and is the context of much of Jesus' teaching.

4

The Biblical Basis to Understand the Poor and Poverty: The Gospels

Social-scientific and historic research has identified that the basic structure of society in Palestine during the period of the New Testament, especially the Gospels, was similar to the monarchic period, that of the time of the prophets, and the postexilic period.[1] However, the political landscape had changed with the Roman occupation.

This chapter will focus on the socioeconomic context of the Gospels rather than an analysis of the teachings on the poor and poverty. It will look at what did Jesus say about the poor and seek to understand the context within which he said it. How the early church responded to the poor in their midst and to poverty will be addressed in the next chapter.

In the New Testament there were two types of people who were poor. The first was a person who did manual labor. They worked in shops and fields and though they had no wealth or leisure time (like the wealthy did), they had sufficient resources to meet the very basic of needs. But they were poor. The second was someone who was a pauper and had been reduced to begging

---

1. Pleins notes that there are two contrasting views of what happened in the postexilic period. One view is that of domination and control, while the other view is that the harsh reality of the exile experience and the destruction of the elite created a kinship with the poor and that there was reconciliation between the various actor such as the rich and the poor and they tried to create a 'state' in the midst of the pressures of Babylonian and Assyrian assimilation. Pleins, *The Social Visions,* 389.

because they did not have enough to survive.[2] Professor of New Testament at Notre Dame University, Jerome Neyrey, in describing such a person quotes historian Gildas Hamel, "The *ptochos* was someone who had lost many or all of his family and social ties. He often was a wanderer, therefore a foreigner for others, unable to tax for any length of time the resources of a group to which he could contribute very little or nothing at all."[3]

Poverty, injustice and the poor were the focus of some of Jesus' teaching, most of which was within the context of the coming of the kingdom of God. In order to understand Jesus' teaching on poverty and to know who the poor Jesus was referring to were, it is important to understand the social and political contexts of the poor in first-century Palestine.[4]

First-Century Palestine

The Roman territory of Palestine was mainly an agrarian society with a few towns and cities. Richard Rohrbaugh, Professor of Religious Studies at Lewis and Clark College, writes that according to sociologist Robert Bellah at University of California, Berkeley, there were four classes in Palestinian society during this period. At the top were the urban elite who were the political-military elite and consisted of only about 1 to 2 percent of the total population. These consisted mainly of those involved in the administration of the Roman Empire and the Herod dynasty. While they were never a large number they were a very cohesive group. The second class, which was also primarily urban, was the cultural-religious elite. They had a stabilizing function in society as they provided the bureaucratic system necessary for governance. This was also a fairly small group.[5]

Rohrbaugh further states that another 13 percent of the population was composed of a lower middle class, which included those working in the trades: artisans and craftsmen who had shops in the market, merchants and traders. This group lived modestly and had the confidence that their resources would be able to meet their needs and any future emergencies. This group comprised

2. Jerome H. Neyrey, "Loss of Wealth, Loss of Family and Loss of Honour: The Cultural Context of the Original Makarisms in Q," in *Modelling Early Christianity: Social Scientific Studies of the New Testament in Its Context*, ed. Philip F. Esler (London: Routledge, 1995), 139.

3. Ibid., 140.

4. I am grateful to Gordon King for his insights.

5. Richard L. Rohrbaugh, "Ethnocentrism and Historical Questions about Jesus," in *The Social Setting of Jesus and the Gospels*, eds. Wolfgang Stegemann, Bruce J. Malina and Gerd Theissen (Minneapolis: Fortress, 2002), 27–35.

the bulk of a city's population.[6] The lowest class, the poor consisted of two kinds. About 75 percent of the population was peasants in rural areas with small landholdings or tenant farmers. They also included the day laborers (casual laborers), and slaves.[7] In today's classifications, they would be those in chronic poverty, which tends to be long term and intergenerational. The bottom 10 percent of the population was those living in extreme poverty.[8] These would include the beggars, the sick, the blind, the lame, the lepers, the destitute, orphans, widows, prostitutes, dung collectors and shepherds, among others.[9]

This breakdown is slightly different to what Bruce Longenecker suggests based on Steven Friesen and Walter Scheidel's models of the economic structure of the Greco-Roman world in the first century. Longenecker suggests the elites were about 3 percent, merchants, traders and artisans with moderate surplus about 17 percent, merchants, traders and artisans with minimum surplus about 25 percent, small farmer and traders at subsistence level around 30 percent, and all those below subsistence level about 25 percent. So between 80–85 percent of the population was either poor or lived at or slightly above the poverty line.[10]

According to historian Michael Rostovtzeff (1870–1952) at the University of St. Petersburg, there was a "general tendency throughout the empire towards the concentration of land in the hands of a few proprietors who lived in the cities... The land was owned by men who were not themselves experts in agriculture but were townsmen for whom land was a form of investment."[11] Wealth was generated through trade, through land ownership and from the produce of the land. While the wealthy mostly lived in urban areas, their wealth and affluence was based on them owning a disproportionate share of the farmland.[12]

---

6. Ibid., 37.

7. Ibid., 39.

8. These are those who barely have enough to get through each day and lived below subsistence level.

9. Longenecker, *Remember the Poor*, 46.

10. Philip A. Harland, "The Economy of First-Century Palestine: State of the Scholarly Discussion," in *Handbook of Early Christianity: Social Science Approaches*, eds. Anthony J. Blasi, Jean Duhaime and Philip-Andre Turcotte (Walnut Creek: Alta Mira Press, 2002), 515.

11. Michael Rostovtzeff, *The Social and Economic History of the Roman Empire*, ed. P. M. Fraser (Oxford: Clarendon Press, 1957 [1926]), 344.

12. Harland, "The Economy," 515.

While similar socioeconomic breakdowns exist in many countries in the world today, what was different in first-century Palestine was that the wealth and resources were limited. According to New Testament Scholar at Creighton University, Bruce Malina, and Rohrbaugh, the concept of "limited goods" is the key to understanding the dynamics of wealth and poverty and the attitudes towards the wealthy.[13] Modern economies operate on the basis of unlimited supplies of resources and commodities. If there is a shortage, more can be produced. So if one person receives more of anything, it does not automatically mean that another person receives less. Malina and Rohrbaugh explain the very different reality of first-century Palestine, which was based on "limited goods."

> But in ancient Palestine, the perception was the opposite: all goods existed in finite, limited supply and all goods were already distributed. This included not only material goods, but honor, friendship, love, power, security, and status as well – literally everything in life. Because the pie could not grow larger, a larger piece for anyone automatically meant a smaller piece for someone else[14] . . . Profit making and the acquisition of wealth were automatically assumed to be the result of extortion or fraud . . . To be labeled "rich" was therefore a social and moral statement as much as an economic one. It meant having the power or capacity to take from someone weaker what was rightfully his.[15]

Professor of ancient history at York University (Canada), Philip Harland, notes that most scholars acknowledge that the economic situation of the peasantry was precarious due to subsistence-level farming and the expenses for taxes, rents, and seed, as well as the threat of natural disasters and famine.[16] As taxation from the Romans and the demands from the temple authorities in Jerusalem increased, the poor were pushed further into destitution.[17]

---

13. See also Alicia Batten, "Brokerage: Jesus as Social Entrepreneur," in *Understanding the Social World of the New Testament*, eds. Dietmar Neufed and Richard E. DeMaris (London: Routledge, 2010), 168.

14. It is only when this is understood, is the concept of the Year of Jubilee (Lev 25:8–55) understood. All debts were to be cancelled, land that had been sold could be redeemed.

15. Bruce J. Malina and Richard L. Rohrbaugh, *Social Science Commentary on the Synoptic Gospels* (Minneapolis, MN: Fortress Press, 2003), 400.

16. Harland, "The Economy," 521, and Malina and Rohrbaugh, *Social Science*, 390.

17. Richard Horsley, *Jesus and the Powers: Conflict, Covenant and the Hope of the Poor* (Minneapolis: Fortress Press, 2011), 134.

Palestine, which was transitioning from a barter economy to a "money" based economy under the Romans, forced the poor to trade what little they had for survival and for their food needs to acquire money (coins) to pay their taxes and temple dues. Various scholars estimate that as much as 40 percent of what a peasant produced went towards taxes and religious dues.[18] Farmers were subjected to blackmail, bullying and over taxation (Luke 3:13–14). Besides this, as the cities grew, they required increasing amount of resources and food from the rural areas. The urban elite procured these on terms that they dictated to the poor, which were often grossly unfair. In addition, any emergencies such as accidents, ill health, and crop failure forced the poor into debt, with them having to borrow money at exorbitant rates.[19] If they failed to repay the loans, they would not only lose their land but also could also be enslaved or imprisoned (Matt 5:25–26). As a result, most of the peasants in the rural areas were poor and destitute.

Because of our supposedly egalitarian societies in the West, it is hard to understand the social impact of poverty in first-century Palestine (and in much of the Majority World today[20]). There was shame attached to being poor as it meant that with limited resources one could not fulfill one's social and religious obligations.[21] Jerome Neyrey writes, "Although most people had meager possessions and low status, there were families or kinship groups who could no longer maintain their inherited status in regard to marriage contracts, dowries, land tenure and the like. Loss of wealth translated into lower status, which meant loss of honor."[22]

The causes of poverty and oppression in the New Testament were very similar to those from the period of the monarchy in ancient Israel, though some of the oppressors had changed. Thomas D. Hanks, adjunct professor of Bible at Latin American Biblical University, San Jose, Costa Rica, makes an observation on the Hebrew vocabulary of poverty and oppression in the Hebrew Scriptures that further explains this relationship between the rich and the poor in Palestine. Hanks observes that the Hebrew words that described

---

18. Harland, "The Economy," 521. The estimates of various scholars range from 20–40 percent.

19. Ibid., 516, 520.

20. Also referred to as the Global South and the Developing World.

21. Malina and Rohrbaugh, *Social Science,* 390–391, 400.

22. Neyrey, "Loss," 140.

poverty "occurred overwhelmingly in connection with the vocabulary of oppression."[23] From that, Hanks makes four observations:

a) Oppression is a fundamental structural category of biblical theology

b) The theme is virtually absent in classical theology[24]

c) Oppression is viewed as the basic cause of poverty in biblical theology

d) Most English translations conceal the radical socioeconomic analysis of the Hebrew Scriptures.[25]

He notes that other than oppression, other causes of poverty are rarely mentioned. He follows this through into the New Testament. The Greek word *thlipsis* (especially in Jas 1:27) has been translated in the English translations of the New Testament as "difficulty," "suffering," "hardship," "distress," "oppression," "affliction" or "tribulation."[26] Hanks contends that the primary translation of *thlipsis* is "oppression." Arthur Glasser, writing about the message of the prophets, linked wealth with injustice, and concurs:

> When the prophets speak about poverty, however, they almost invariably relate it to the ways in which the rich people contribute to this acute problem. The two aspects of society are not independent phenomena. They are intimately interrelated. During the period of the monarchy the prophets constantly linked wealth with injustice; the oppressors of the poor were the rich. Furthermore, poverty was rarely portrayed as an accident. More often than not, it is determined by the structure of society. Poverty brings unnecessary misery to people, a misery that is heightened when it is realized that the poor are the victims of the injustice of others. (Isa 10:1–2; Jer 5:28; Ezek 16:49; 18:12–13; Amos 2:6–7)[27]

---

23. Hanks, *God So Loved*, 35.

24. A quick review of six major texts of systematic theology, only one had a chapter on the social dimensions of sin.

25. Hanks, *God So Loved*, 38–39.

26. Ibid., 50.

27. Glasser, *Announcing the Kingdom*, 118.

It is almost as if time had stood still and very little had changed during the hundreds of years between the period of the monarchy and first-century Palestine. In first-century Palestine, being rich was as much a social and moral statement as an economic one. Being rich meant that one had the power to take whatever one wanted from someone weaker because the poor were unable to defend themselves. It was synonymous with being greedy. It was assumed that acquiring wealth and making profit was only possible as a result of extortion or fraud[28] and at the expense of the poor.

Jesus – The Rich and the Poor

It is from this context that Jesus draws richly in his teaching using parables. First-century Palestine provided him the pictures of violence, oppression and poverty. Real life was the basis for his parables of the absentee landlord (the rich in Jerusalem who had their rural farm properties administered by others), tenant revolts, slavery, debt and debtors, day laborers waiting the whole day for employment, a widow pestering a corrupt judge to get justice, the rich farmer who hoards his grain, starving beggars, uncaring rich people, corruption and extortion.[29]

So when Jesus spoke about the poor, they were not a small section of society who had fallen on hard times and who deserved our compassion. He was referring to the majority (at least 80–85 percent of the total population) who were oppressed because of the greed and injustice of a small wealthy and powerful elite.[30] When he taught and preached, his listeners were the chronically poor and those in extreme poverty (who lived in the fringes of society), while some from the wealthy and elite sections of society listened in. He used parables about being exploited that they could relate to (Mark 12:40–44, Matt 18:21–35).[31] He spoke about a God who cared enough to feed the birds of the air and clothe the flowers of the field because they were worried about their next meal and did not have a spare set of clothes or enough warm clothing for the winter (Matt 6:25–34). He fed them as they listened to him teach, because they did not have enough food to bring with them (Matt

---

28. Malina and Rohrbaugh, *Social Science,* 400.

29. Luke 12:13–21; 16:1–15; 16:19–21, 18:1–14; Matt 18:21–35, 20:1–16.

30. Harland, "The Economy," 515.

31. Jesus' parables in Luke 14–20 provides insight in the daily social and economic challenges that poor peasants faced.

14:13–21). He healed them because they could not afford to go to the doctors (Matt 8:1–17, 9:1–8, 12:9–14, and so many more).

So whether in ancient Israel or in the New Testament world, the poor were those who were weak and marginalized because of the injustices of the social system.[32] They had few resources to survive and almost no social or legal protection.[33] They lived in shame because they could not meet their social obligations.[34] The Mosaic law was explicit in ensuring that they were to be provided for and protected. Yet the existing social system had abandoned them, and there was no social safety net when they were exploited by the wealthy and elite.[35] Jesus understood the vulnerability of the poor and the impact of an unjust society on them. He spoke out against greed and injustice (Matt 21:12–13; Mark 12:40–44) but he also showed them what the kingdom of God would be like – a just society where the weak and poor would no longer be vulnerable but valued (Matt 6:25–34).

Jesus, who came from the poorer sections of society (however, he was not destitute),[36] along with his disciples, shared the lot of the poor (Luke 9:58). Jesus did not seem to have a problem with the wealthy as long as they used their wealth for the common good, such as supporting parents (Mark 9:7–13), or lending to those in need without expecting a profit in return (Mark 5:42). The occasions when Jesus denounced the rich were when they oppressed the poor (Mark 12:40–44) and when riches became a dominating power in a person's life (Mark 10:17–22). However, Jesus was opposed to the

---

32. David Fiensy however clarifies this. He writes, "He [Jesus] criticized not the system so much as the dominant partners of the system: the aristocrats . . . When Jesus talked about the rich persons in such a critical way, he was referring to those 1,500 to 2,000 aristocrats living in Sepphoris and Tiberias. He said nothing that we know about the system as such. But he could be stingingly critical of the wealthy men and women who controlled it." David A. Fiensy, "Ancient Economy and The New Testament," in *Understanding the Social World of the New Testament*, eds. by Dietmar Neufeld and Richard E. DeMaris (London: Routledge, 2010), 205.

33. Ibid., 204.

34. Malina and Rohrbaugh, *Social Science,* 390–391, 400.

35. Fiensy refers to Hungarian economic historian, economic anthropologist and political economist Karl Polanyi. "Polanyi stated that in traditional ('primitive') societies starvation was not a threat unless the whole community starved at the same time since one could always count on help from relatives and neighbors (which must be reciprocated later)." Fiensy, "Ancient Economy," 203. Such communities that lived on the economic margins would be characterized by development practitioners as experiencing transitional poverty, which continues to keep them vulnerable and never allows them to get out of poverty (cf. chapter 7).

36. Richard L. Rohrbaugh, "Honor: Core Value in the Biblical world," in *Understanding the Social World of the New Testament*, eds. by Dietmar Neufeld and Richard E. DeMaris (London: Routledge, 2010), 120.

social, political and economic structure of society that allowed for the rich and powerful religious and political elite to abuse and oppress the poor.

Jesus not only ministered to the needs of the poor, but he also taught his disciples the value of giving. In Luke 6:30, Jesus said, "Give to everyone who asks you . . ." In Matthew 6:1–4 he said:

> Be careful not to practice your righteousness in front of others to be seen by them. If you do, you will have no reward from your Father in heaven. So when you give to the needy, do not announce it with trumpets, as the hypocrites do in the synagogues and on the streets, to be honored by others. Truly I tell you, they have received their reward in full. But when you give to the needy, do not let your left hand know what your right hand is doing, so that your giving may be in secret. Then your Father, who sees what is done in secret, will reward you.

Jesus was very clear that giving to the poor was not a choice or option that one had. It was a requirement as a follower of Christ, because he said, "When you give . . ." not "if you give . . ." He also taught that giving should be done in such a way so that it brings no attention to the giver. The giving and assistance was to be part of a person's life and not something exceptional.

In Matthew 25:31–46,[37] Jesus taught that he will judge his followers as to whether they met the needs of the poor or not. As seen from passages above, one of the signs of being his follower, a mark of being a disciple, was whether they were generous and compassionate.

---

37. "When the Son of Man comes in his glory, and all the angels with him, he will sit on his glorious throne. All the nations will be gathered before him, and he will separate the people one from another as a shepherd separates the sheep from the goats. He will put the sheep on his right and the goats on his left. Then the King will say to those on his right, 'Come, you who are blessed by my Father; take your inheritance, the kingdom prepared for you since the creation of the world. For I was hungry and you gave me something to eat, I was thirsty and you gave me something to drink, I was a stranger and you invited me in, I needed clothes and you clothed me, I was sick and you looked after me, I was in prison and you came to visit me.' Then the righteous will answer him, 'Lord, when did we see you hungry and feed you, or thirsty and give you something to drink? When did we see you a stranger and invite you in, or needing clothes and clothe you? When did we see you sick or in prison and go to visit you?' The King will reply, 'Truly I tell you, whatever you did for one of the least of these brothers and sisters of mine, you did for me' . . . Then they will go away to eternal punishment, but the righteous to eternal life."

Jesus – Injustice and Poverty

Was Jesus concerned only about meeting the needs of the poor or was he also concerned about the injustices that caused poverty? At the beginning of his ministry, Jesus stood in the synagogue in Galilee and read from the Old Testament. Luke 4:18–19 "The Spirit of the Lord is on me, because he has anointed me to proclaim good news to the poor. He has sent me to proclaim freedom for the prisoners and recovery of sight for the blind, to set the oppressed free, to proclaim the year of the Lord's favor."

The meaning of this passage is often debated between those who take it at supposed face value, that Jesus' mission was to bring social and economic justice,[38] and those who only perceive its spiritual dimensions. The pre-Lausanne 1974 evangelical understanding is reflected in English Presbyterian minister Matthew Henry's (1662–1714) commentary on Luke 4:18–19.

> By Christ, sinners may be loosed from the bonds of guilt, and by his Spirit and grace, from the bondage of corruption. He came by the word of his gospel, to bring light to those that sat in the dark, and by the power of his grace, to give sight to those that were blind. And he preached the acceptable year of the Lord. Let sinners attend to the Saviour's invitation when liberty is thus proclaimed. Christ's name was Wonderful; in nothing was he more so than in the word of his grace, and the power that went along with it. We may well wonder that he should speak such words of grace to such graceless wretches as mankind.[39]

Referred to by many as the "Nazareth Manifesto" and stated at the beginning of his ministry, it frames his mandate from God. But what did Jesus want to communicate by choosing these verses from the prophet Isaiah?

Scholar in Middle Eastern New Testament studies, Ken Bailey, provides a detailed analysis of this passage.[40] Using "Hebrew parallelism,"[41] a Jewish

---

38. Malina and Rohrbaugh, *Social Science,* 243. See also Gutierrez, *A Theology of Liberation,* 97, and Leonardo Boff and Clodovis Boff, *Introducing Liberation Theology* (Maryknoll: Orbis Books, 2008), 53.

39. Henry, *Concise Bible Commentary.*

40. Kenneth E. Bailey, *Jesus through Middle Eastern Eyes: Cultural Studies in the Gospel* (Downers Grove: IVP Academic, 2008), 147–162.

41. Ibid., 13. Bailey states (p. 149) that Jesus uses this Jewish rhetorical device for a Jewish audience that would appreciate the biblical artistry involved, where he weaves a number of Old Testament passages (Isa 61:1–2 and 58:6) together as he read the scroll.

rhetorical device, to analyze the structure of thought in the passage, he identifies the key actions in Luke 4:18–19 as:

The Spirit of the Lord is on me,
because he has anointed me
A. to *proclaim good news to the poor.*
   B. he has *sent me* to proclaim *freedom for the prisoners,*
      C. and *recovery of sight for the blind,*
   B. to *set the oppressed free,*
A. to proclaim the year of the Lord's favor.

Choosing the key action verbs, the structure reads as follows:

A. Preach
   B. Sent
      C. Sight
   B. Set [Send forth]
A. Proclaim

He uses the A-B-C-B-A format. The outer envelope of tasks (A) refers to proclamation. The second idea (B) in the parallelism refers to advocacy for justice. The climax of the message is at the center (C) and speaks of compassion (sight for the blind).

The question is, who are the poor being referred to in verse 18? There are two Hebrew words for poor used in Isaiah; one is ʿani (often translated "poor") and the other is ʿanaw (usually translated "meek"). They are used interchangeably. The text from which Jesus read, Isaiah 61:1, uses ʿanaw, which tends towards meaning "meek." Throughout Isaiah the two words appear fifteen times; three of them tend towards meaning those who don't have enough to eat; eleven of those times are oriented towards the humble and pious who seek God.[42] So while Jesus' audience were primarily those who were socially and economically poor, Jesus emphasizes the qualities of meekness, of "being humble and pious and sincerely seeking God."[43] Jesus knew that his audience would understand these qualities better than the rich,

---

42. Ibid., 158.
43. Ibid., 159.

because they had been abused and held in bondage because of injustice and robbed of their land and inheritance. They did not expect justice from their earthly political rulers but cried out to God for deliverance and justice. It is to these, those who had cried out to God, that the good news, the message of hope, is proclaimed that the kingdom of God is near.

The second idea (B) "to let the oppressed go free" (NLT) is from Isaiah 61:2 and 58:6. Isaiah was writing to the Jews in exile. The Persian Emperor, Cyrus the Great, had just conquered the Babylonian Empire and had allowed the various refugees living in Babylon to return home. So the phrase "letting the oppressed go free" is of refugees returning home. They would no longer be under bondage and be slaves. This is the imagery that Jesus evokes for those who are under the bondage of the wealthy. The promise of the kingdom of God is that they will be able to go back to their homes, which had been usurped by the wealthy. Justice will be done.

According to Bailey, the text in (C), "the opening of the eyes of the blind" in the Hebrew phrasing is ambiguous and literally reads, "The opening – to those who are bound." While most English translations use the standard wording, the Aramaic Targum of Isaiah nuances it, as it reads, "To those who are bound, be revealed to light."[44] The imagery is of those who have been living in the darkness of the dungeons are freed and come out into the light.

Bailey states that understanding Hebrew parallelism in the way Jesus uses the texts from Isaiah puts the Messiah's agenda of compassion at the core of Jesus' agenda and ministry. Bailey summarizes the message of Luke 4:18– 19 in saying that Messianic agenda was proclamation, advocacy for justice, and compassion. Relating it to the mandate and ministry of the church, he writes, "The *preacher* knows that those marching for justice are an important part of the team. Thoughtful *justice advocates* know that the justice of God must judge the justice for which they strive. Those who show compassion, in whatever form, realize that without a message that changes hearts and minds and without a just society, their work is incomplete."[45] He adds that each action is meaningful in and of itself, "but only together in their christological setting do they achieve their full healing power."[46]

So for Jesus, his work did not just comprise of proclaiming and training, nor was it only acts of compassion, or only of challenging the authorities

---

44. Ibid., 161.
45. Ibid., 162.
46. Ibid., 161.

and wealthy for their corrupt actions for social and economic justice. The "Nazareth Manifesto" clearly identified that compassion was at the core of his ministry and what he did. Out of that came the advocacy for justice and the proclamation of the good news that the kingdom of God had now come and will one day come in all its fullness.

Bruce Longenecker at St Andrews University (then) reflecting on Jesus' response to John the Baptist (Matt 11:4–6 and Luke 7:22[47]) writes, "Jesus' reply depicts a world in which healing blindness, curing diseases, restoring hearing and raising the dead were as exceptional as encouraging the poor. The astonishment that would have attended Jesus' miracles of power is, as we are led to think, comparable to the astonishment that would have attended Jesus' pronouncement of blessings for the poor."[48] The socioeconomic powers were so deeply entrenched that it would require a miracle for there to be justice in society.

So What Does All This Mean?

The structure of society and the causes of poverty in first-century Palestine were very similar to what it was in the period of the Divided Monarchy, that of the prophets, and the postexilic period. However, the political players had changed with the Roman conquests. The majority of the population (75 percent) lived in the rural areas and between 80–85 percent of the total population were poor – either they barely had enough to survive, or had to beg. The causes of poverty continued to be exploitation by the ruling business, political and religious elite.

It is within this context that Jesus ministered and taught. His audiences were predominantly the poor. He used their experiences of exploitation and surviving for his teaching and illustrations and he introduced them to the kingdom of God where there would be justice, and where God would provide all that they needed.

---

47. Matt 11–46, Jesus replied, "Go back and report to John what you hear and see: The blind receive sight, the lame walk, those who have leprosy are cleansed, the deaf hear, the dead are raised, and the good news is proclaimed to the poor. Blessed is anyone who does not stumble on account of me." And Luke 7:22, "So he replied to the messengers, 'Go back and report to John what you have seen and heard: The blind receive sight, the lame walk, those who have leprosy are cleansed, the deaf hear, the dead are raised, and the good news is proclaimed to the poor.'"

48. Longenecker, *Remember the Poor*, 120.

This provided the framework for Jesus' ministry. At the center was the demonstration of the compassion of God. This made God real to the people. Out of this flowed teaching and proclamation, and then advocacy for justice.

The review of the Old and New Testaments show that the cause of poverty was injustice. It is not the way God intended society to be, but with the introduction of the monarchy, society became stratified and wealth became increasingly concentrated in the hands of an elite resulting in the growth of large estates as the peasants slid deeper into poverty, with many loosing their land and even their freedom as they were sold into slavery. It is in this context that the prophets preach their message of justice, and where Jesus shows a preference for the poor.

5

Teachings and Practices of the Early Church: The New Testament and Church History

Did the early church continue in the teachings and traditions of the Old Testament and the Gospels with regard to compassion towards the poor and responding to poverty? There is the biblical evidence that needs to be examined. There is also church history, especially the teachings of the early church fathers, which are indicative of the values and attitudes of the early church. Besides that, what does research on the social history of the late Roman Empire show about the practice and impact of the Christians?

There were no specific studies done on poverty in ancient Rome till 1989 when Cambridge Classics scholar, C. R. Whittaker published a chapter entitled "The Poor" in a collection of studies published as *L'uomo Romano*.[1] Since then Princeton historian, Peter Brown's *Poverty and Leadership in the Later Roman Empire* published in 2002 has brought the discussion on the different attitudes towards poverty to the forefront. Much has been written since then, building on previous studies on antiquity (not necessarily focusing on poverty) done by German classical scholar, M. H. Bolkenstein and French historian and Byzantinist, Evelyne Patlagean.

This chapter will describe the context within which the early church lived so that its practice and teachings are better understood. It will then look at

---

1. Margaret Atkins and Robin Osborne, *Poverty in the Roman World* (Cambridge: Cambridge University Press, 2006), 1.

the practice of charity by the early church and its impact. And lastly it will explore the teachings of the early church fathers.

The Context of the Early Church

The ancient Roman Empire was a combination of agrarian rural communities and large urbanized areas with a city at its center. By the time Rome became an empire in the first century BC, it was the first western city to have a million inhabitants.[2] The Roman world was pre-industrial and its economy was mainly agricultural. The Roman economy was "underdeveloped" with life expectancy being low (between 20–30 years) and nutritional deficiencies widespread.[3] Wealth had been determined by access to land. But this began to change from 8 BC onwards with considerable urbanization in Greece and Italy. Significant numbers were employed as artisans and in service activities. They were reasonably fed. Many more were also employed as mercenary troops, infantry and rowers.[4]

In the rural areas able-bodied men could subsist by either growing their own food or gathering food from land beyond cultivation. But in times of scarcity, many sold themselves or their children into slavery.[5] Those who were not able-bodied or disabled, depended upon family and friends; and when this support was exhausted, they moved away to places where they had no social support, and poverty then became structural.[6]

Various models of analyzing the socioeconomic structure of society have been used. One model used extensively in New Testament studies is the binary model of the Greco-Roman economy, where an extremely small group of elite is contrasted with a large undifferentiated majority struggling at the subsistence level.[7] However, binary models are not true economic descriptors because there were significant variations within the grouping of the rich and the poor. Longenecker instead suggests a variation of University of Texas Professor Steven Friesen's non-binary economy of scale. Friesen's scale has seven levels, between those living at a subsistence level all the way

---

2. Ibid., 1.

3. Ibid., 4.

4. Ibid., 4–5.

5. Ambrose of Milan describes one such incident he witnessed, in his sermon, *On Naboth*.

6. Atkins and Osborne, *Poverty*, 5.

7. Longenecker, *Remember the Poor*, 40.

up to the imperial elites. Longenecker adjusts that to five levels and modifies the percentages at each level based on new research.[8]

- Elites (imperial, regional or provincial, municipal) 3%
- Those with a moderate surplus 15%
- Those who are near subsistence level but stable 27%
- Those at subsistence level and sometimes dipping below it 30%
- Those consistently below subsistence level 25%

What such a scale does not indicate is the quantity of wealth that the 3 percent elite controlled. Princeton University historian Peter Brown writes, "Wealth had to be seen to be believed. What was seen at the top – notably, but not exclusively at Rome – was expected to border on the incredible."[9] Among the many examples he gives, he mentions the young heiress Melania the Younger who is said to have enjoyed, around the year AD 405, an annual income of around 1,660 pounds of gold.[10]

In the Greco-Roman world political status was more important than the level of wealth. The distinction was between whether one was a citizen or not. A citizen could be wealthy or poor, but was rarely identified as such. That is why the poor were not thought of as a distinct social group. Citizens had economic benefits – such as landownership and political rights.[11] If some were occasionally spoken of as poor – they were citizens who were perceived to be in danger of impoverishment, of coming down in the world, not because they already lay at the bottom of society.

So any relief provided to the poor was based on political status. Those who were citizens received benefits from the emperor or the wealthy. For example, the great grain distribution of AD 58, because of a looming food scarcity, was restricted to only the citizens. Moreover, the wealthy focused on philanthropy that benefited the city, community and the temple rather than poor.[12]

Moses Finlay, a Classics scholar at Cambridge, observes that not even the state was concerned for the poor, excepting those in Rome, where the poor had become a political force as a result of the grain distribution which had

---

8. Ibid., 53.

9. Peter Brown, *Through the Eye of a Needle: Wealth, the Fall of Rome, and the Making of Christianity in the West, 350-550 AD* (Princeton, NJ: Princeton University Press, 2012), 16.

10. 753 kilograms of gold. Ibid., 17.

11. Atkins and Osborne, *Poverty*, 5.

12. Ibid., 6.

forced the elite to acknowledge the existence of large numbers of poor.[13] The huge needs of those who were not citizens, and were primarily poor, started changing the perception of people. There was finally a growing recognition of the presence of the poor.[14]

The Practices and Impact of the Early Church

The earliest communities that followed Christ did not have to be told to be compassionate to the poor and marginalized. They merely did what they had seen Christ do. They healed the sick and the crippled (Acts 3:1–10; 5:12–16). They made sure that no one among them was in need (Acts 4:32–36). They ensured that the most vulnerable in their communities were properly taken care of (Acts 6:1–7). They taught that the only sure sign of religion that God the Father accepted as pure and faultless (i.e. faith) was if the widows and orphans were taken care of (Jas 1:27). They said that one was saved by grace through faith and created in Christ Jesus to do good works (Eph 2:8–10). Ministering to the poor was just as important as having proper theology and missiology (Gal 2:1–10). Their preaching of justification by faith was to be complemented by their demonstrating the reality of the kingdom of God.[15]

As the church grew, they continued the practices and traditions that they had been taught. Brown refers to the Christians in the Roman Empire (AD 300–600) providing for the needs of the poor as a revolution that impacted the social imagination of the times.[16] The notion of *euergesia* (good works) in classical culture as something that the wealthy did was a civic virtue and contributed to the general well-being of society. They gave to institutions like the city or the temple, but not necessarily to the poor. Some poor did benefit through the services that were funded this way. But the poor were never the focus. It was the Christians, and particularly the bishops who were expected to be "lovers of the poor," a category that comprised those who were poor (deep poverty) and those who lived under the threat of poverty (shallow poverty).[17] In the fourth and fifth centuries as poverty increased in

---

13. Ibid., 12.

14. Ibid., 7.

15. See Longenecker's *Remember the Poor* for an extensive discussion of Gal 2:10.

16. Peter Brown, *Poverty and Leadership in the Latter Roman Empire* (Hanover: University Press of New England, 2002), 1.

17. Walter Brueggemann, "How the Early Church Practiced Charity," *The Christian Century* (14 June 2003): 30–31.

the eastern provinces of the Roman Empire, the cities were unable to absorb the poor who were not citizens. Brown writes, "The existing structures of the city and the civic model that had been associated with them collapsed under the sheer weight of a desolate human surplus, as the cities filled with persons who were palpably "poor." They could not be treated as citizens, neither could they be ignored. . . ."[18] It was the Christians who responded to the needs of the poor. Brown writes about these Christians, "They [lay and clerical alike] were themselves, agents of change. To put it bluntly: In a sense it was the Christian bishops who invented the poor. They rose to leadership in late Roman society by bringing the poor into ever-sharper focus."[19]

This ministry of compassion and charity as demonstrated by the lay people and the church leadership in the Roman Empire had a significant influence on the social value of the society. American Old Testament scholar and theologian, Walter Brueggemann, highlights the growing appreciation of the "legitimacy of the cry of the poor [that] created a social awareness that the powerful were obligated to provide justice and protection for the poor. Through the work of the bishops the poor were given a voice that created 'an advocacy revolution' . . ."[20] Brown refers to this change within the attitudes of the wealthy as being from patronage to *humnanitas*.[21]

It would be only appropriate to acknowledge that there was charity in Roman society, mainly in the form of alms giving. There were also examples of the extreme wealthy, such as the senator Petronius Probus, who used his enormous wealth to bestow gifts to "countless throngs of men" to ensure he held his followers.[22] However, Baylor theologian, Longenecker states that when Jesus described reality, "you will always have the poor among you," he implied that the elite had no intentions of changing the socioeconomic structures and the sub-elites certainly could not.[23]

M. H. Bolkenstein states that it was only in the early Roman Empire around the late first century AD that people saw the poor as being less morally corrupted and the giving of monetary relief to the poor as a virtue.[24] Bolkenstein states that this change was the result of what he called "eastern

---

18. Brown, *Poverty,* 8.

19. Ibid., 8–9.

20. Brueggemann, "How the Early Church," 30.

21. Brown, *Through the Eye,* 58.

22. Ibid., 59.

23. Longenecker, *Remember the Poor,* 107.

24. Atkins and Osborne, *Poverty,* 2–3.

influences," which caused priority to be given to the poor in the Greco-Roman world as it was in ancient Israel. He quotes Seneca in *Letters to Lucillius* (95.51) who says that the minimum moral demand on any man was to give a coin to the beggar and crust to the starving.[25] Others disagree; Brown places this change at around late antiquity with the conversion of Constantine in AD 312 and as a result of the charitable programs of the church leadership. Evelyne Patlagean states that it was due to the massive change in structure of society in late antiquity and the major demographic changes that were taking place.[26]

In contrast to the lack of concern in the ancient non-Judeo-Christian societies, the care for the poor was embedded within the theological traditions of early Judaism. Nicholas Wolterstroff, Professor of Philosophical Theology at Yale, writes, "Israel's religion was a religion of salvation, not of contemplation – that is what accounts for the mantra of the widows, the orphans, the aliens, and the poor. Not a religion of salvation *from this earthly existence* but a religion of salvation *from injustice* in this earthly existence."[27] Adolf von Harnack, in his monumental book *The Mission and the Expansion of Christianity,* stated that the "Gospel of Love and Charity" (*Evangelium der Liebe und Hilfleistung*), was the main factor in the rise of church.[28]

The concept of the love of the poor therefore did not naturally grow out of the Greek and Roman ideals of benefactors helping their city. Christian and Jewish charity was not just another form of charity and generosity being practiced among other forms – it was a completely new departure from existing values and practice. Brown writes, "It gained symbolic weight far out of proportion to its actual extent and efficacy."[29] However Brown clarifies, "Classical benefactors were not necessarily more hard-hearted. They simply looked out on society and saw, above all, cities and citizens, while Jews and Christians had come to see, rather, rich and poor"[30]

---

25. Ibid., 3.

26. Ibid.

27. Nicholas Wolterstorff, *Justice: Rights and Wrong* (Princeton: Princeton University Press, 2008), 115.

28. Adolf von Harnack, *The Mission and Expansion of Christianity in the First Three Centuries.* Trans. J. Moffat (New York: Harper & Brothers, 1961).

29. Ibid., 6.

30. Ibid., 9.

The Teachings of the Early Church

The impact of the charitable practices of the early church was significant and noticeable. The Roman Emperor, Julian the Apostate, in AD 362 while on his way to the Persian frontier, was appalled by the giving habits of his fellow pagans when compared with the charitable deeds he had seen among the Jews and Christians. Writing to Arsacius, the pagan high priest of Galatia, Julian states, "For it is disgraceful that, when no Jew ever has to beg, and the impious Galileans [Christians] support not only their own but ours as well, all men see that our people lack aid from us [that is from the pagan priesthood]."[31] It is apparent that by the fourth century AD, the charitable activities of the Christians were significant enough to come to the attention of the Roman Emperor.

Earlier in the second century, the Greek rhetorician and satirist, Lucian of Samosata (AD 125–180), who was not a follower of Christ, wrote what he saw in the Christians, (Peregrinus 13), "They despise all things indiscriminately and consider them common property . . ."[32]

The following review of the teachings of some of the early church fathers will only address the first four centuries (and a bit of the fifth century), the formative period when the theology and practice of the church was being established. It is also recognized that some of the writings of the early church fathers are actually transcribed sermons. Recognizing the genre of the particular text will help provide perspective on the content of the sermon as to whether hyperbole is involved in making a specific point.

Two documents are of significance during the first century. The first is the Didache (The Teaching of the Twelve Apostles), the oldest surviving written catechism from the late first century (probably between AD 70–90, though recent studies indicate that it could be as early as the 50s), variations of which were probably used widely in the Jesus groups and churches. It teaches generosity and charity.

> 1:5 Give to everyone who asks of you, and do not demand it back; for the Father wants something from his own free gifts to be given to all. Blessed is he who gives according to the commandment, for he is guiltless;

---

31. Quoted in Brown, *Poverty*, 2.

32. Lucian of Samosata, "The Passing of Peregrinus," (2001), accessed 15 June 2013, http://www.tertullian.org/rpearse/lucian/peregrinus.htm. Alternate translation, "Christians despise all possessions and share them mutually."

4:8 You shall not turn away from him who is actually in need, but share with your brother in all things and not say things are your own, for if you are partners in what is imperishable, how much more so in perishable things?

15:4 And your prayers and almsgiving and all your deeds, do as you find it in the gospel of our Lord.

In 1:5, the wording is almost identical to those of Jesus in Matthew 5:42 and Luke 6:30. The vertical and horizontal dimensions of spirituality are very clear in 4:8 and 15:4.

The second document of significance from the first century is attributed by some to **Clement of Rome**,[33] one of the earliest Apostolic Fathers of the church and the Bishop of Rome (either the third or fourth pope) from AD 92–99. His *First Epistle to the Corinthian Church* is one of the oldest extant Christian documents outside the New Testament and was read in churches along with other Epistles, some of which were later included in the New Testament canon. In chapter 33 he exhorts the Corinthians to not give up the practice of good works and love, as God himself is an example of good works.[34] Then writing specifically about the poor and charity (chapter 38), Clement states what should be the nature of the relationship between the rich and the poor:

Let the strong take care of the weak; let the weak respect the strong. Let the rich man minister to the poor man; let the poor man give thanks to God that he gave him one through whom his need might be satisfied.[35]

Polycarp (AD 69–155) was the Bishop of Smyrna and a friend of Ignatius. Both had been students together under the Apostle John. Polycarp writes: "When you can do good, defer it not, because 'alms delivers from death.' Be all of you subject one to another 'having your conduct blameless among the Gentiles,' that ye may both receive praise for your good works,

---

33. Modern scholarship has questioned the authorship of the *First Epistle to the Corinthian Church*. The letter is anonymous and does not include the name of Clement of Rome, but its style suggests that there was a single author. It was not accepted into the New Testament canon but is part of the Apostolic Fathers collection.

34. Philip Schaff, *The Apostolic Fathers with Justin Martyr and Irenaeus* (Grand Rapids: Classic Ethereal Library, 2001 [1885]), 23.

35. Ibid., 26.

and the Lord may not be blasphemed through you" (chapter 10).[36] Polycarp clearly identifies that the giving of alms and helping the poor was a powerful witness to the Gentiles, the assumption being that it was something that was so different than what the Gentiles were used to seeing.

The *Didache*, the writings of Clement of Rome, and Polycarp are significant because of their late first-century early second-century dates, and the fact that the writers had a direct connection with the first apostles. They, in effect, establish the connection and continuity between the teachings of Jesus and the apostles with the later church fathers.

Justin Martyr (AD 100–165) was an early Christian apologist. For Justin Martyr, the qualities of justice and philanthropy were critical because of the social structure of the Christian community in the middle of the second century. He describes the Christians at the bottom of the social ladder. These included the illiterate and those with simple and unrefined language (*First Apology* chapter 60), the needy, who included the orphans, the widows, the imprisoned Christians, and the strangers in the Christian community (*First Apology* chapters 13, 14, 15, 67). A fund had been set up for them (which was filled up every Sunday at the worship service) and food was provided for them (*First Apology* chapters 31, 67).[37] He writes further in chapter 15, "We, who valued above all things the acquisition of wealth and possessions, now bring what we have into a common stock, and communicate to every one in need."[38]

A few years after Justin Martyr's death, **Dionysius of Corinth**, around AD 170 attested to the generosity of the church in Rome, and wrote in his letter to the Roman Church about the practice of charity in Rome. **Eusebius**, Bishop of Caesarea quotes that letter in his writings: "From the beginning you had the custom of helping all of the brethren in many sorts of ways and sending support to many congregations in all cities. Through these gifts which you have been sending all along . . . you have eased the poverty of the needy."[39] Eusebius was then to add how the church in Rome had also helped churches in all Syria and Arabia. German theologian and Professor of New Testament, Peter Lampe, writes, "Eusebius can report no other Christian community

36. Ibid., 54–55.

37. Peter Lampe, *Paul to Valentinus: Christians in Rome in the First Two Centuries* (Minneapolis: Fortress Press, 2003), 100.

38. Schaff, "The Apostolic," 219.

39. Quoted in Lampe, *Paul to Valentinus,* 101, from the writings of Eusebius.

with a similar economic engagement not only for 'their own needy' but for many other Mediterranean cities as well."[40]

Earlier in the second century, **Aristides**, the Athenian philosopher who became a Christian writer, described the social consciousness of the Christians. In his *Apology*, which he addressed to Emperor Hadrian, Aristides writes about the moral quality of the lives of the Christians (apology 15):

> They have the commands of the Lord Jesus Christ himself graven upon their hearts . . . they despise not the widow, nor oppress the orphan; and he that has, gives ungrudgingly for the maintenance of him who has not. If they see a stranger, they take him under their roof, and rejoice over him as a brother; for they call themselves brethren not after the flesh but after the spirit. And they are ready to sacrifice their lives for the sake of Christ; for they observe his commands without swerving, and live holy and just lives, as the Lord God enjoined upon.[41]

The **Shepherd of Hermas** is a literary work dated either from the first or second centuries, with the consensus being that it is from around AD 160. Some early church fathers, including Irenaeus, considered it a canonical book. It was one of the most popular books among the churches in the second and third centuries and therefore was quite influential.[42]

It states that the widows and orphans were taken care of by the Christian community through subsistence provided by the deacons. The *Commandment Second* stated:

> Practice goodness; and from the rewards of your labors, which God gives you, give to all the needy in simplicity, not hesitating as to whom you are to give or not to give. Give to all, for God wishes his gifts to be shared among all . . . This service, then, if accomplished in simplicity, is glorious with God. He, therefore, who thus ministers in simplicity, will live to God.[43]

Clement of Alexandria (AD 150–215) was a theologian who taught in Alexandria. He writes extensively about wealth, poverty and charity in *Who*

---

40. Lampe, *Paul to Valentinus*, 101.

41. Aristides, "The Apology of Aristides," *Early Church Fathers – Additional Texts*, (2003), accessed 23 June 2013, http://www.tertullian.org/fathers/artistides_02_trans.htm.

42. Lampe, *Paul to Valentinus*, 98.

43. Ibid., 37.

Is the Rich Man That Will Be Saved? He does not condemn wealth but warns against loving riches and not being totally surrendered to God. He exhorts the rich to give to those in need.

> He bids Zacchaeus and Matthew, the rich tax-gathers, entertain him hospitably. And he does not bid them part with their property, but, applying the just and removing the unjust judgment, he subjoins, "To-day salvation has come to this house, forasmuch as he also is a son of Abraham." He so praises the use of property as to enjoin, along with this addition, the giving a share of it, to give drink to the thirsty, bread to the hungry, to take the houseless in, and clothe the naked. (XIII)[44]

Irenaeus (AD 130–202), the Bishop of Lyon in Gaul, was one of the great theologians of the early church. He had been a disciple of Polycarp. Writing around AD 180 in probably his most important work, *Against Heresies* (book 4, chapter 13):

> Instead of the tithes, which the law commanded, the Lord said to divide everything we have with the poor. And he said to love not only our neighbors but also our enemies, and to be givers and sharers not only with the good but also to be liberal givers toward those who take away our possessions.[45]

Tertullian (AD 160–220) was Christian author and theologian from Carthage in the Roman province of Africa. He writes (in *The Apology of Tertullian*, chapter 39) about the lifestyle of the Christian and how the church should collect money and provide for those in need:

> All here is a free-will offering, and all these collections are deposited in a common bank for charitable uses . . . for feeding the poor and burying the dead, and providing for girls and boys who have neither parents nor provisions left to support them, for relieving old people worn out in the service of the saints, or those who have suffered by shipwreck, or are condemned to the mines, or islands, or prisons, only for the faith of Christ . . . But we Christians look upon ourselves as one body, informed as it were by one soul; and being thus incorporated by love, we can never

---

44. Philip Schaff, *Ante-Nicene Fathers: Fathers of the Second Century*, Vol. II (Grand Rapids: Christian Classics Ethereal Library, 2001 [1885]), 861.
45. Schaff, "The Apostolic," 690.

dispute what we are to bestow upon our own members. Accordingly among us all things are in common.[46]

John Chrysostom[47] (AD 347–407), the Archbishop of Constantinople, was a prolific expositor of the Bible. He preached extensively on the issues of wealth and the social responsibility that the rich had towards the poor. He writes, "The rich are in possession of the goods of the poor, even if they have acquired them honestly or inherited them legally."[48] He adds, "Not to enable the poor to share in our goods is to steal from them and deprive them of life. The goods we possess are not ours but theirs."[49] In *I Corinthians: Homily 10:3* he says, "All the wealth of the world belongs to you and to the others in common, as the sun, air, earth, and all the rest . . . Do not say 'I am using what belongs to me.' You are using what belongs to others."[50]

One's intimacy with God can be affected by the lack of compassion and charity. Chrysostom writes, "When you are weary of praying and do not receive, consider how often you have heard a poor man calling, and have not listened to him."[51]

Basil of Caesarea (AD 330–379), sometimes also referred to as Basil the Great, was the Greek bishop of Caesarea Mazaca in Cappadocia, Asia Minor. As a priest he was known for his work among the poor and those who were underprivileged. In AD 368 when a severe drought hit Asia Minor, the result of which was exacerbated by the greed of some who held back some of the available grain in order to inflate prices, he preached a sermon entitled *To the Rich* (Homily VII) which was based on Matthew 19:16–22, where the rich young man asked of Jesus as to what he must do to inherit eternal life. In Homily VIII, where he addresses the issue of the drought and famine, and bases the text of his sermon on Amos 3:8, he states that the national disaster

---

46. Tertullian, *The Apology of Tertullian*, trans. William Reeves (London: Griffith, Farran, Okeden &Welsh, 1889), 110–111.

47. *Chrysostomos* meant "golden mouth," as he was known for his eloquence in preaching.

48. Quoted in Walsh and Langan, "Patristic Social Consciousness," in *The Faith That Does Justice,* ed. John Haughey (Mahwah: Paulist, 1977), 129.

49. Quoted in *Catechism of the Catholic Church,* 2nd ed., (Washington DC: United Sates Catholic Conference, 1994), # 2446.

50. Quoted in Walsh and Langan, *Patristic Social Consciousness*, 129.

51. Quoted in Donald Haggerty, *Contemplative Provocations* (San Francisco: Ignatius Press, 2013), chapter 11.

affecting the region can be traced to national sin, especially the neglect of the poor.[52]

Basil's ministry involved caring for the poor and the ill, and he organized soup kitchens during the famine that followed the drought. The gates of Caesarea were overcrowded because of the assistance that he provided. Basil gave away his own personal family inheritance so that the poor could be helped. He built a large complex outside Caesarea called the Basiliad, which included a hospice, a hospital and a poorhouse. Not only was he involved in acts of compassion, he was also concerned about justice. Some of his letters indicate that he worked to reform prostitutes and thieves, and he criticized public officials who failed in their duty to administer justice.

In his blistering *Sermon to the Rich,* Basil challenges the rich about their attitude towards wealth:

> Which things, tell me, are yours? Whence have you brought your goods into life? You are like one occupying a place in a theatre, who should prohibit others from entering, treating that as his own which was designed for the common use of all. Such are the rich . . . If each one would take that which is sufficient for his needs, leaving what is superfluous to those in distress, no one would be rich, no one poor . . . The rich man is a thief.[53]

He then bluntly states, "You have not shown mercy, you shall not receive mercy; you've not opened your home, you shall be evicted from the kingdom. You haven't given of your bread; neither shall you receive eternal life."[54]

So his exhortation to the wealthy in *Homily VI* based on Luke 12:18:

> Come then; dispose of thy wealth in various directions. Be generous and liberal in thy expenditure on the poor. Let it be said of thee, "He hath dispersed, he hath given to the poor; his righteousness endureth for ever." Do not press heavily on necessity and sell for great prices. Do not wait for a famine before thou openest thy barns. "He that withholdeth corn, the people

---

52. Philip Schaff, *Nicene and Post Nicene Fathers, Series II, Vol. 8* (Grand Rapids: William B. Eerdmans Publishing Company, 2001 [1885]), 110–111.

53. Peter Gilbert, ed., "St. Basil's Sermon to the Rich," *De Unione Ecclessiarum,* (2008), accessed 28 June 2013, http://bekkos.wordpress.com/st-basils-sermon-to-the-rich/.

54. Ibid.

shall curse him." Watch not for a time of want for gold's sake – for public scarcity to promote thy private profit.[55]

Ambrose (AD 339–397), Bishop of Milan, was one of the most influential persons of his time and was contemporary of Jerome and Augustine. His sermon, *On Naboth* is particularly striking, indicating a passionate commitment to alleviating the misery of the poor. Ambrose practiced what he preached: at the time of his ordination, he gave away all his property to the church and to the poor, after seeing to it that his sister Marcellina was provided for. Some years later, as we know from his own account in the treatise *On the Duties of Ministers* (2.28.136–43), he melted down the sacred vessels of the church at Milan in order to ransom captives. For this, the Arians, who were only too happy to find something to accuse him of, blamed him, but he defended himself by asserting that "the church has gold not for keeping but for disbursing and for aiding those in need."[56]

On Naboth is the clearest exposition of Ambrose's thinking on the wealthy and charity. In it, he compares the wealthy to King Ahab and the rich fool, and he rebukes their heartlessness towards the poor. He develops three key ideas: (1) The earth and its resources are the common property of all mankind. (2) Charity and almsgiving benefits both the rich and the poor. And (3) greed destroys not only those towards whom it is directed, but also those who harbor it. Boniface Ramsey, a biographer of Ambrose, writes, "These ideas were commonplaces in Christian antiquity, but rarely did other Western Fathers promote them as vigorously as did Ambrose in this writing."[57]

In *On Naboth* (1.2) he starts by challenging the rich about the fleeting nature of all wealth and possessions. "Nature, which begets everyone poor, knows no wealthy, for we are not born with clothing or begotten with gold and silver."[58]

In probably one of the best description in literature of the depths of misery that poverty inflicts on a person, Ambrose then tells of an incident, which he witnessed when a poor man was threatened with imprisonment because he had not been able to repay his debts. In order to delay his punishment so that he could find someone to help him, he had the option of selling one of his

55. Schaff, *Nicene and Post Nicene*, 99.

56. Boniface Ramsey, *Ambrose* (London: Routledge, 1997), 38.

57. Ibid., 117.

58. Ibid., 118.

sons. He then describes the torment. Ambrose wrote (5.21), "But the damage inflicted by poverty and the obligations of a father's love for his family were in conflict, with hunger demanding the sale and nature urging its duties." Finally, he ends his sermon by saying (12:53):

> It is not anything of yours that you are bestowing on the poor; rather, you are giving back something of his. For you alone are usurping what was given in common for the use of all . . . Hence Scripture says to you: Incline your soul to the poor, give back what is owed, and answer him with peaceable words in gentleness. (Sirach. 4:8)[59]

Gregory of Nazianzus (329–389 or 390) was the Archbishop of Constantinople and was a classically trained orator and philosopher. One of Gregory's most moving orations, *On the Love of the Poor,* is an appeal to a Christian congregation to notice the destitute (especially the homeless victims of an outbreak of leprosy) in their own city and to open their homes to them in compassion. It was probably delivered in Caesarea during the years 369–371. Like the two biblical homilies of Gregory of Nyssa dealing with the same theme, it seems to form part of a campaign to win public support for the efforts of Basil of Caesarea to organize relief for the poor and sick, a project that culminated in the opening of a new hostel for the homeless just outside Caesarea during the early years of Basil's work there as bishop (370–379).[60]

In Oration 14 *On the Love of the Poor,* Gregory identifies love and mercy as the basis for responding to the needs of the poor. In 14.5 he says, "And if, following the command of Paul and of Christ himself, we must suppose that love is the first and greatest of the commandments, the crowning point of the law and the prophets, I must conclude that love of the poor, and compassion and sympathy for our own flesh and blood, is its most excellent form."[61]

Gregory then appeals to their common humanity to offer kindness to those suffering. In 14.6 he says. "We must open our hearts, then, to all the poor, to those suffering evil for any reason at all, according to the Scripture that commands us to 'rejoice with those who rejoice and weep with those who weep.'"[62]

---

59. Ibid., 135.
60. Brian Daley, *Gregory of Nazianzus* (London: Routledge, 2006), 75–76.
61. Ibid., 78.
62. Ibid.

Gregory's message is a simple one; for the Christian, love for one's neighbor, especially those suffering and in need, is the most direct way of loving Christ.

So What Does This All Mean?

The context within which the early church lived its life had significant portions of its population marginalized and living in poverty. It was also a place where charity and concern for the poor was not common. The considerable philanthropy that existed was focused on the benefit of the city and the temple. It was the church and its leaders that brought the poor into focus.

The teachings of the church fathers in the first four centuries provide insight into the values, the prevalent thinking, and practice in the church during this period.[63] The church and the church fathers merely continued to teach what Jesus and the apostles had taught. This included compassion and charity for the poor, the vulnerable and the marginalized. However, there is very little, if any at all, on justice for the poor and marginalized, which was so much part of the teaching of the Old and New Testaments. Maybe, this was an acknowledgement by the church leaders that the structure of society could not be changed. They also believed that wealth was from God, but it was to be used for the benefit of all, especially those in need. However, they repeatedly acknowledged that much of the wealth was gotten unjustly, often at the expense of the poor.

Second, during the first two centuries, when the church comprised mainly the middle and lower classes of society, with a few who were wealthy, the focus of the teaching was on ensuring that resources were shared, and that those in extreme poverty were taken care of. By the third century, as more of the wealthy joined the church, the teaching challenged their values and often shamed them to be generous and address the needs of the poor.

The first six hundred years was a period when much theology was being formulated and theological debates tore the Christian community apart. While they believed that correct theology was important, compassion for the poor and those suffering was equally central to the Christian faith. The central truth throughout all the teaching was that the only way one could

---

63. The review in this chapter has not covered all the relevant church fathers such as Cyprian, Augustine and St. Bede, among others.

demonstrate that they were true followers of Christ, was if they showed mercy and compassion towards the poor.

The next chapter will trace the theological and missiological discussion that have framed the issue of whether the church should be responsive to issues like poverty and injustice.

6

Theological Challenges

Our theology has an impact upon our compassion and how we relate to the poor. While Jesus spoke about the poor and met their needs on occasion, many contend that this was not at the core of his message of salvation, but was only a secondary issue. The issue as to whether the community of faith should relate to social problems, has deeply divided the church during the past two centuries. Much of this divide is based on three theological premises.

The first of these is in understanding what the gospel is, as many contend that Jesus and Paul had different understandings of the gospel. The second theological issue is in understanding what is meant by "righteousness." Lastly, the difference in understanding when Christ will return and when the thousand-year reign of Christ will occur by postmillennialist and dispensationalist theories has influenced how the church should relate to society and whether it should address social issues. These three issues are interlinked and each has contributed to a historical split within Protestant Christianity.

What Is the Gospel? – The Teachings of Jesus versus Paul

Oxford University New Testament theologian, David Wenham, articulates the first of these theological issues by wondering what the relationship is between the teachings of Jesus and those of Paul. How important was the historical Jesus and his teachings to Paul? Wenham writes, "The accusation sometimes made is that Paul was not trying to be faithful to Jesus – hence his apparent lack of interest in Jesus – and that his is a different religion from that of Jesus, not a legitimate development of it."[1]

---

1. David Wenham, *Paul: Follower of Jesus or Founder of Christianity* (Grand Rapids: William B. Eerdmans Publishing Company, 1995), 9.

This difference is brought into sharp focus when trying to understand what the gospel is. Is the good news that the "the kingdom of God has come"? After all Jesus proclaimed, "The time is fulfilled, and the kingdom of God has come near; repent, and believe in the good news" (Mark 1:15). And then later, "And this good news of the kingdom will be proclaimed throughout the world, as a testimony to all the nations" (Matt 24:14). Or is the gospel "justification by faith," as Paul proclaimed (Rom 3:27–28; Rom 4:2, 5–6; 5:11; 9:30–32; 10:4–6; 1 Cor 4:7; 2 Cor 12:9)? It would seem that for Paul the gospel was all about Jesus Christ, his death and resurrection. He writes in Romans 1:1–4, "the gospel of God, which he promised beforehand through his prophets in the Holy Scriptures, the gospel concerning his Son, who was descended from David according to the flesh and was declared to be the Son of God with power according to the spirit of holiness by resurrection from the dead, Jesus Christ our Lord."

The understanding of what is the good news – the gospel – is critical in determining whether the church should be involved in addressing social issues. If the gospel is only about believing that God has forgiven my sins through the death and resurrection of his Son Jesus Christ, then the focus of any ministry is to ensure as many people as possible know and understand this and have the opportunity to accept the forgiveness that God offers. Everything else in this world is secondary or unnecessary. However, if the gospel is the good news that the kingdom of God has finally come, then the focus of ministry is not only on how people can enter the kingdom through the forgiveness that God offers through his Son (John 3:3), but also to ensure that the reign of God and his powerful presence impact all spheres of life. The understanding is that God not only redeems human beings, but also his entire created universe.

There have been different understandings about what constitutes this kingdom. The Jews yearned for liberation from debt, from economic and political oppression, particularly Roman oppression. They were not interested in, as N. T. Wright states, a "*post-mortem* disembodied bliss, but for a national liberation . . . Hope focused on the coming of the kingdom of Israel's God."[2] Their understanding of kingdom was of a king, of a people and of a law that governed the people. It was of a physical and political entity in time and a specific geographical space.

---

2. N. T. Wright, *The New Testament and the People of God, Vol. I* (Minneapolis: Fortress Press, 1992), 170.

For Jesus, the kingdom of God (*basileia tou Theou*) was not a geographic or political realm but the "dynamic reign of God."[3] In trying to explain how different this reign of God was from the traditional Jewish understanding of an earthly kingdom, Wenham explains, "Some scholars believe that the expression 'kingdom of God' refers in a rather loose way to God's kingship: Jesus called people to reckon with God as King and with his powerful presence in the world. Most, however agree that the expression suggests more specifically the coming of the day of divine liberation and of the new society."[4] He states that the kingdom of God proclaimed by Jesus is the "eschatological kingdom" – the one that is to come in the last days. It would usher in the divine rule and the new world order the Jews were looking for.

However, this was not just a future event. Jesus' announcement of the appearance of the kingdom (Mark 1:15; Matt 12:28) was an eschatological in-breaking or *inaugurated eschatology* – meaning that the future was now present. Professor of New Testament Exegesis and Theology at Fuller Theological Seminary, George Eldon Ladd's (1911–1982) book title describes it well: *The Presence of the Future*. South African biblical scholar Derek Morphew describes it as, ". . . there is both 'kingdom now' and kingdom 'not yet.'"[5] The reign of God, which will one day come in all its fullness, has already started with the coming of Christ. It was evident in the healings and deliverances from bondage that Christ performed. Righteousness in relationships and forgiveness for sins were signs that the kingdom was already here.

With the future breaking in now, Jesus through his teaching and actions showed what the reign of God is like. It meant good news for the poor because one day there would be justice and freedom from exploitation by the rich. Those living on the edges of society, the lepers, prostitutes and tax collectors, would be treated with the dignity of God created human beings. Justice would reign and there would be peace from the violence that had torn the land. The process had begun with Christ's first coming, giving us glimpses of what it would be like when Christ returns and the reign of God is evident in all its fullness, which will be the fulfillment of Revelation 11:15 – "The kingdom of the world has become the kingdom of our Lord and of his Messiah, and he will reign for ever and ever."

---

3. Scott McKnight, "Jesus vs. Paul," *ChristianityToday.com* (2010), accessed 5 December 2010, http://www.christianitytoday.com/ct/2010/december/9.25.html, and Wenham, *Paul,* 35.

4. Wenham, *Paul,* 35–36.

5. Derek Morphew, *Breakthrough: Discovering the Kingdom* (Cape Town: Vineyard International Publishing, 1991), 202.

South African theologian and Professor of Missiology at the University of South Africa in Pretoria, David Bosch (1929–1992) has described the reign of God through the incarnated Christ as an assault on evil. He says it is interesting to note the "religious" words (as we now understand them) used by the gospel writers to describe Jesus' response when confronted with demon possession, sickness and exploitation. For example, the word "to save" (*sozein* in Greek) is used by the gospel writers in at least eighteen cases in reference to Jesus healing the sick. Similarly, the word "forgiveness" (*aphesis* in Greek) has a wide range of meanings, which include freeing of bonded slaves, cancellation of monetary debts, eschatological liberation and the forgiveness of sins.[6] These imply that the reign of God in his kingdom was not just something spiritual and in the future, but was a present reality that could be experienced in the midst of evil, suffering and injustice. Bosch concludes, "In Jesus' ministry, then, God's reign is interpreted as the expression of God's caring authority over the whole of life."[7]

Paul made only thirteen references to the kingdom[8] because his focus was on matters related to the church, eschatology (to a certain extent), and foremost on matters related to salvation (especially justification). It seems he rarely talked about the poor, and when he did his concern was mainly for the poor in Jerusalem. This has been strongly countered by Bruce Longenecker in his book *Remember the Poor*.[9] Longenecker contends that Paul's concern for the poor was not just Jerusalem centric but was for the poor everywhere. Jesus, in contrast to the prevalent thinking about Paul, inaugurates his ministry in the synagogue at Nazareth with passages from Isaiah by focusing on the poor, the oppressed and those suffering: "The Spirit of the Lord is on me, because he has anointed me to preach good news to the poor. He has sent me to proclaim freedom for the prisoners and recovery of sight for the blind, to release the oppressed, to proclaim the year of the Lord's favor" (Luke 4:18–19).

However, upon closer examination, this disconnect is less obvious. Paul was very familiar with the concept of the kingdom of God and understood it just as Jesus did. For him, as people believed, they were called to the kingdom (1 Thess 2:12), the kingdom of light (Col 1:12). The kingdom was not

---

6. Bosch, *Transforming Mission*, 33.

7. Ibid., 34.

8. Rom 14:7; 1 Cor 4:20; 6:9–10; 15:24; 15:50; Gal 5:21; Eph 5:5; Col 1:13; 4:11; 1 Thess 2:12; 2 Thess 1:4–5; 2 Tim 4:1; 4:18.

9. Longenecker, *Remember the Poor*.

associated with outward rituals like food and drink but with manifestations of the Spirit of God in the individual and the community of faith (Rom 14:17). The kingdom was both present now (Rom 14:17) and yet something in the future – yet to come (1 Cor 6:9–10; 15:24).

Wenham mentions two reasons why Paul may not have used kingdom language and motifs much.[10] First, the "kingdom of God" language, which Jesus used so often, would have been very familiar and easily understood by the Jews of first-century Palestine, but would have meant nothing to Paul's Greek-speaking Gentile readers.[11] Second, the "kingdom and king" language, was sensitive enough in Jesus' rural and Jerusalem contexts. When Herod the Great heard from the Magi who had come looking for Jesus at the time of his birth, he was disturbed to hear the newborn referred to as the "King of the Jews" (Matt 2:1–3). It would have been even more sensitive in the context of the Roman Empire and some of the people Paul related to. It was an act of treason to pledge allegiance to a king other than Caesar.[12] So while Paul clearly understood the reality of the kingdom of God that Jesus spoke of, his writing and language were adapted to influence a very different audience with a different worldview but with similar social problems.

However, the understanding of the kingdom of God was central in Paul's thinking. Though Paul may not have used the term "the kingdom of God" frequently in his writings, it was something that he preached about consistently. At Ephesus he told the elders, "Now I know that none of you among whom I have gone about preaching the kingdom will ever see me again" (Acts 20:25). When Paul was imprisoned in Rome before his execution, Luke writes, "For two whole years Paul stayed there in his own rented house and welcomed all who came to see him. He proclaimed the kingdom of God and taught about the Lord Jesus Christ – with all boldness and without hindrance!" (Acts 28: 30–31).

In preaching on the theme of the kingdom of God, Paul knew he was providing an alternative to Caesar's empire and all the values it stood for. This kingdom had now established itself within the Roman Empire, bringing

---

10. Wenham, *Paul,* 78–79.

11. Wenham quotes F. W. Beare. Paul's use of different language was "the transposing of the gospel into the language and thought forms of another people, the kind of adjustment that was needed if the gospel of Jesus was to be brought effectually into the Greek world." Wenham also suggests that there is a possible parallel in the Gospel of John where John prefers "eternal life" to "kingdom" terminology. Wenham, *Paul,* 78.

12. Ibid., 79.

different values. Herein lay the danger that the Christians and their message posed to the Roman Empire. N. T. Wright states, "If Paul's answer to Caesar's empire is the empire of Jesus, what does this say about this new empire, living under the rule of its new Lord . . . This counter empire can never be merely critical, never merely subversive. It claims to be the reality of which Caesar's empire is the parody. It claims to be modeling the genuine humanness, not least the justice and peace, and the unity across traditional racial and cultural barriers, of which Caesar's empire boasted."[13] The modeling of genuine humanness included caring for the poor, a value that was rare in the Roman Empire and the kingdoms that preceded it.

Why is having a proper understanding of what the gospel is so important? The narrative throughout the Bible is not just about God wanting to reconcile individuals to himself, but it is of a God wanting to dwell with his creation and to establish his kingdom, his reign and authority, here on earth. It is only in this context that 1 Peter 2:9 can be understood, "But you are a chosen people, a royal priesthood, a holy nation, God's special possession, that you may declare the praises of him who called you out of darkness into his wonderful light." Because God has chosen us and is establishing his kingdom among us (a holy nation), we serve as priests. As priests of God, God has shown us what he wants and how he wants us to live. "And what does the Lord require of you? To act justly and to love mercy and to walk humbly with your God" (Mic 6:8).

Skye Jethani, the senior editor of *Leadership Journal*, uses the phrase "making the invisible kingdom visible,"[14] which is probably one of the best descriptions of the church addressing physical and social needs. Bosch describes the motivation for making this kingdom visible:

> Those who know that God will one day wipe away all tears will not accept with resignation the tears of those who suffer and are oppressed *now*. Anyone who knows that one day there will be no more disease can and must actively anticipate the conquest of disease in individuals and society *now*. And anyone who believes the enemy of God and humans will be vanquished will already

13. N. T. Wright, "Paul's Gospel and Caesar's Empire," in *Paul and Politics*, ed. R. A. Hosley (Harrisburg: Trinity, 2000), 182–183.

14. Skye Jethani, "Making the Invisble Kingdom Visible," (6 May 2013), accessed 13 May 2013, http://www.outofur.com/archives/2013/05/making_the_invi. html?utm_source=parse&utm_medium=Newsletter&utm_term=12502841&utm_ content=174724452&utm_campaign=2013.

oppose him *now* in his machinations in family and society. For all of this has to do with *salvation*.[15]

Proclaiming salvation is about making the invisible kingdom visible.

Because of this *perceived* difference in the teachings of Paul versus the teaching of Jesus, there is a deep divide on whether addressing the needs of the poor and injustice are part of the mandate and mission of the church.

Righteousness

The second theological issue that has a significant impact on whether the church has a social responsibility is how the concept of righteousness is understood.

The root of the Hebrew word for righteousness (*sedeq, sedaqa, saddiq*) connotes conformity to an ethical or moral standard.[16] The meanings of the word include rightness, lawful, and justice.[17] The word describes three aspects of personal relationships: ethical, forensic and theocratic. The ethical aspect involves how people relate to each other. "The man who is righteous tries to preserve the peace and prosperity of the community by fulfilling the commands of God in regard to others."[18] In the post-exilic period, the word developed to mean benevolence, almsgiving, etc. as the acts of a godly man.[19]

However, British New Testament scholar, James D. G. Dunn (formerly at Durham University) explains that there are significant differences between the Greek and Hebrew understandings of righteousness. Dunn states that according to the Greek worldview, "righteousness" is an idea or ideal "against which the individual and individual action can be measured."[20] It is a state of moral perfection. In Hebrew thought "righteousness" is understood more as a relational concept – "as the meeting of obligations laid upon the individual by the relationship of which he or she is part."[21]

---

15. Bosch, *Transforming Mission*, 400.

16. R. Laird Harris, Gleason L. Archer, Jr., and Bruce K. Waltke, *Theological Workbook of the Old Testament* (Chicago: Moody Publishers, 1980), 752. For a detailed analysis of the word, see pages 752–755.

17. Strong's Concordance 6664 *tzedek* – righteous, integrity, equity, justice, straightness.

18. Harris, Archer, and Waltke, *Theological Workbook*, 753.

19. Ibid., 754.

20. James D. G. Dunn, *The Theology of Paul the Apostle* (Grand Rapids: William B. Eerdmans Publishing Company, 1998), 341.

21. Ibid.

The understanding of "the righteousness of God" is more in line with Hebrew thought, where God's righteousness can be understood as God's faithfulness to his people. German theologian G. Schrenk states that *sedaqa* implies a relationship. He writes, "This linking of right and salvation is most deeply grounded in the covenant concept. *Sedaqa* is the execution of covenant faithfulness and the covenant promises. God's righteousness as his judicial reign means that in covenant faithfulness to his people he vindicates and saves them."[22] Simply put, Dunn summarizes that God's righteousness was the "fulfillment of his covenant obligation as Israel's God in delivering, saving, and vindicating Israel, despite Israel's own failure."[23] So, just as God was righteous in his relationship with Israel, he is righteous with the rest of his creation also (Rom 1:16–17).

So "righteousness" is also understood as God's faithfulness to fulfill his obligations to human beings and his creation, because as creator he has a relationship with them. Even though they are fallen and marred by sin, God has an obligation to redeem them and he is faithful to do that through Christ. Understanding God's righteousness as obligation in the context of a relationship, explains why God is concerned about the poor. The poor are not just marred by sin, but also by social and economic oppression and injustice. The Psalmist identifies God as "A father to the fatherless, a defender of widows, is God in his holy dwelling. God sets the lonely in families, he leads out the prisoners with singing: but the rebellious live in a sun-scorched land" (Ps 68:5–6). God's redemption is not just spiritual, but addresses the totality of human beings in every sphere of their lives. Therefore because of his righteousness God restores human beings (and his creation) to the condition he intended for them.

This understanding of righteousness explains what is meant when it states in Matthew 1:19 that Joseph was a righteous man. He was a person who would fulfill his obligation to Mary to not only do what is right but also care for her in the context of his relationship to her. Similarly, Cornelius is referred to as being righteous (Acts 10:22) and says that he gave generously to those in need and prayed to God regularly (Acts 10:2). He fulfilled his obligation to those in need and to God.

As human beings receive the righteousness of God through Christ, they are then able to fulfill their obligation not only to God, but also within the

---

22. Quoted in Harris, Archer, and Waltke, *Theological Workbook*, 755.
23. Dunn, *The Theology of Paul*, 342.

social context they live in. Proverbs 29:7 says, "The righteous care about justice for the poor;" and Ephesians 2:10, "For we are God's handiwork, created in Jesus Christ to do good works."

This understanding of righteousness as obligation is central to the discussion in this book. It is also a concept that is fundamental in the major religions of the Near East. University of California historian Gildas Hamel states that the Hebrew word in the Old Testament and the Arabic word in Islam for charity are the same, *tzedakah* or *sedaquah* and *sadaqa*. While in Islam *sadaqa* is a term for charitable and voluntary gifts, Hamel writes that in Judaism "the most frequent word used by the rabbis to express charity, *sedaquah*, meaning 'righteousness' or justice, reveals a basic attitude, namely that of the donor's obligation and the poor's right."[24] Jewish religious writer and translator Philip Birnbaum in commenting on Book VII of Maimonides' *Mishneh Torah* says that the charity to the poor was an act of justice and moral behavior. He adds that Judaism considers as a legal claim that has to be honored, the right of the poor to food, clothing and shelter. "*Tsedekah* is not an act of philanthropic sentiment but an act of justice."[25]

One's understanding of righteousness will influence whether an individual and community of faith will be involved in addressing the issues of social injustice. If the understanding of righteousness is only that of moral perfection, the focus is primarily on attaining that moral perfection through Christ and maintaining it.[26] If righteousness is also understood as an obligation in the context of the social relationships one has, then the focus will also be on addressing the needs of the poor, the marginalized and others suffering in society.

Understanding the Millennium and the Attitude towards the Poor

Over the past three centuries there has been a growing concern to improve the world we live in. Much of the focus has been on dealing with social problems and improving the quality of life. Terms like "human rights" and the "rights of the individual" are now part of most discussions on social change. This desire has now permeated the church and has influenced theology.

---

24. Gildas Hamel, *Poverty and Charity in Roman Palestine: First Three Centuries CE* (Berkeley: University of California Press, 1990), 216.

25. Philip Birnbaum, *Mishneh Torah: Maimonides' Code of Law and Ethics* (New York: Hebrew Publishing Company, 1974), 156–157.

26. This is seen mostly clearly in movements such as the Holiness Movement among others.

Veteran missionary and theologian, Bishop Lesslie Newbigin (1909–1998) has written, "The inner relationship between this expectation of a new world and the Christian gospel of the reign of God is one of the issues that must be discussed in any contemporary theology of mission."[27]

The word *millennium* has moved from theology (particularly eschatology) to everyday usage.[28] The millennium in Scripture refers to the thousand-year period of Christ's rule (Rev 20:6). There is much confusion and controversy as to when this period is and as to how it will be inaugurated. How this is understood impacts how the church relates to society, and whether the church should be involved with the poor and issues of injustice.

One perspective, known as *premillennialism*,[29] is that the millennium will happen *after* Christ's second coming. A variation of premillennialism is dispensationalism. This perspective believes that the church will be secretly "raptured" by Christ seven years before the second coming of Christ.[30] This will then be followed by seven years of great tribulation, which will then be followed by the millennium. The church will not be on earth during the great tribulation and the millennium.

Another perspective is *amillennialism*, which defines the present church age starting with the book of Acts as the millennium. American Presbyterian theologian Oswald T. Allis (1880–1973) writes:

> The view, which has been most widely held by opponents of Millenarianism, is associated historically with the name of Augustine. He taught that the millennium is to be interpreted spiritually as fulfilled in the Christian church. He held that the binding of Satan took place during the earthly ministry of our Lord (Luke 10:18), that the first resurrection is the new birth of the

---

27. Lesslie Newbigin, *The Open Secret: Sketches for a Missionary Theology* (Grand Rapids: Eerdmans, 1995), 7.

28. We talk of the new millennium, of Millennium Development Goals and the giant millennium Ferris wheel in London.

29. The movements and groups that believe in premillennialism were and still are, conservative evangelicalism, fundamentalism, Pentecostalism, the holiness movement and Adventism, among others.

30. There are some who believe that the rapture will take place three and a half years into the seven-year period. They are referred to as believing in the mid-tribulation rapture. There are others who believe that the rapture will take place at the end of the tribulation. Others believe in the pre-tribulation rapture.

believer (John 5:25), and that the millennium must correspond, therefore, to the interadventual period or church age.[31]

The millennial is thus symbolic rather than a literal thousand years and it is Christ's rule through the church. Some take *amillennialism* further and say that the church age will culminate in a period of glory for a thousand years, when the church will triumph in the world before Christ's second coming. This is known as *postmillennialism* (described below).

The following discussion of postmillennialism and dispensationalism is not an in-depth analysis or critique of either theology. The aspect that will be discussed is how each theology's understanding of when Christ will return and when his thousand-year reign will take place, influenced how they relate to society, its social problems and the poor.

Postmillennialism

Postmillennialism has its roots in the Enlightenment and its reaction to what was referred to as the "dark ages" and the teachings of the medieval church. The idea was that through scientific progress human beings now had an optimistic vision that they could create a better world. A number of key Christian leaders provided the theological framework for postmillennialism. Joseph Mead (1586–1639), Anglican biblical scholar, believed that "the discoveries of the Enlightenment meant that history did not have to be reversed in a cataclysmic manner. The dark ages could merge gradually into the new world order of the millennium through historical progress."[32] The great evangelist and revivalist Jonathan Edwards (1703–1758) ascribed to this. Edwards "saw great significance in the settlement of the New World (America) and believed that it would usher in the millennium in about the twentieth century."[33]

Postmillennialists differ among themselves on how the gospel through the church will impact society. The Puritans believed in a *Revivalist postmillennialism* doctrine that society could only be transformed through changing the hearts and minds of people. There was an optimism, very much part of postmillennial thinking, that they were well into Calvin's third and

---

31. Oswald T. Allis, *Prophecy and the Church* (Phillipsburg: P & R Publishing, 1945), 2–3.
32. Morphew, *Breakthrough*, 260.
33. Ibid., 261.

final stage of history[34] and on the verge of extending Christ's kingdom to the ends of the earth.[35] In contrast, *Reconstructionist* postmillennialism believed that along with the "grass roots, bottom up approach" of preaching the gospel to change the hearts and minds of people, that Christians and the church should be involved in changing political and legal institutions in society. This "top down" approach would primarily be done through Christian education.

This optimistic vision of the future and of the role of the church to bring it about had a significant influence in the evolution of the Social Gospel. Christian theologian and Baptist pastor, Walter Rauschenbausch (1861–1918) writes:

> Theology has often received its most fruitful impulses when secular life and movements have set it new problems."[36] By applying Christian ethics, which were based on the message of the gospel, social problems could be tackled. These problems included injustice and discrimination, racial tensions, poverty and slums, child labor, education (both poor quality and the lack of education), crime, access to health care and clean water and most other social problems. Bishop Lesslie Newbigin states that in the period following World War I, one of the most popular biblical texts among missionaries was John 10:10 "I came that they may have life, and have it abundantly."

---

34. Charles L. Chaney, *The Birth of Missions in America* (Pasadena: William Carey Library, 1976), 32–33; "Calvin postulated a tri-epochal program of time between the coming of the Holy Sprit and the second advent of Christ. The first period was that of the Apostles, during which the gospel was offered to the whole world. The second epoch was the period of the manifestation of the Antichrist. Calvin understood his own age to be that of the most effective work of Antichrist. This explains why all of Calvin's theology was written to people in the throes of persecution. His theology was to the church under-the-cross. The final period was that of the great expansion of the church. During this epoch the fullness of the Gentiles would come in, the ends of the earth would come to Christ, and the Antichrist would be defeated."

35. Bosch, *Transforming Mission,* 313.

36. Walter Rauschenbusch, *A Theology for the Social Gospel* (New York: The Macmillan Company, 1917), i. He writes further, "If theology stops growing or unable to adjust itself to its modern environment and meet its present tasks, it will die. Many now regard it as dead. The social gospel needs a theology to make it effective; but theology needs the social gospel to vitalize it." (p. 1).

Newbigin writes, "'abundant life' was interpreted as the abundance of the good things that modern education, healing, and agriculture would provide for the deprived peoples of the world."[37]

Christian missions changed as a result. Director Emeritus of the Overseas Ministries Study Center in New Haven, Connecticut, Gerald Anderson, identifies four major shifts in thinking and strategy that occurred by the early 1900s. The first was that other religions were no longer thought to be entirely false. The second was that the work in missions was less focused on preaching and more on a broader range of transformational activities. The third was that the focus was now on salvation for life in the present world. And finally that the focus of missions had shifted from the individual to society.[38]

The American Presbyterian, James Dennis (1842–1914) the author of the three-volume *Christian Missions and Social Progress,* wrote in 1906 about "the contribution of Christian mission to social progress."[39] Its impact cannot be underestimated. Missiologist Eugene Smith describes the result:

> The missionary movement made a prime contribution to the abolition of slavery; spread better methods of agriculture; established and maintained unnumbered schools; gave medical care to millions; elevated the status of women; created bonds between people of different countries, which war could not sever; trained a significant segment of the leadership of nations now newly independent.[40]

Most of the Social Gospel leaders tended to be theologically liberal[41] and the gospel message of "salvation through Christ alone" was often lost in the midst of all the work that was being done. Though the movement peaked in the early twentieth century, strands of it resurfaced in the civil rights movement in the US in the 1960s and more recently in movements like Christians against Poverty. Strong influences of the Social Gospel still exist in

---

37. Newbigin, *The Open Secret*,103.

38. Gerald H. Anderson, "The American Protestants in Pursuit of Missions 1886–1986," *International Bulletin of Missionary Research* 12 (1988): 104.

39. Quoted in Bosch, *Transforming Mission,* 294.

40. Eugene L. Smith, *Mandate for Missions* (New York: Friendship Press, 1968), 71.

41. There were exceptions – such as Robert Wilder, John R. Mott, Robert E. Speer and J. H. Oldham who acknowledged "a profound spiritual experience," which put them at odds with others within the Social Gospel movement. However, they chose to stay within the mainline churches that had become increasingly theologically liberal. Bosch, *Transforming Mission,* 324.

many of the historical Protestant churches and in their missions departments, as well as in some Christian relief and development NGOs.

Dispensationalism

One of the strongest influences on evangelical theology over the past 150 years has been dispensationalism. From its beginning with John N. Darby (1800–1882) and the Plymouth Brethren movement, till recently, it has influenced much of mainstream Evangelical and Pentecostal theology. Because of their strong belief that the kingdom of God is yet to come and that social conditions and personal morality will decline as the "end times" approach, dispensationalists feel that nothing can or should be done to change society in the meantime. This thinking was reinforced by 2 Peter 3:10, "The heavens will disappear with a roar; the elements will be destroyed by fire, and the earth and everything in it will be laid bare." Since the present earth will be destroyed when Christ returns, there was no need to try and seek any improvement. Michael Pocock, Department Chair and Senior Professor of World Missions and Intercultural Studies at Dallas Theological Seminary, affirms this idea when he writes that, "things on earth will get progressively worse and will culminate in a unique time of terrible tribulation."[42] Darby himself wrote, "I believe from Scripture that ruin is without remedy," and that Christians should expect "a progress of evil."[43]

Because of dispensationalism's origins as a separatist movement that sought separation from church structures, the attitude of separatism influenced their relationship with broader society and the issues it faced as well.[44] Their identity is that they are a heavenly people of God and part of the invisible church. In sharp contrast to postmillennialism, dispensationalists are pessimistic about social progress in society, as they believe that genuine change in society can only come about through the conversion of individuals. Bosch identifies the difference in approach between the two eschatological frameworks as one being "a service to the body" and on a gradual improvement of society towards the millennium versus "a service to the soul" as the world

---

42. Michael Pocock, "Destiny of the World and the Work of World Missions," *Bibliotheca Sacra Vol. 145,* (1988): 438.

43. Quoted in G. Carter, *Anglican Evangelicals: Protestant Secessions from the Via Media, c. 1800–1850 (Oxford Theological Monographs),* (Oxford: Oxford University Press, 2001), 220, 226.

44. Bosch, *Transforming Mission,* 318.

gradually deteriorates before the coming of Christ and the millennium.[45] The basic thinking within dispensationalism is to focus on individual sin rather than structural sin in society. However, there was recognition that conversion did have a social impact. The language used was that individual conversion was the "root" and the social impact was the "fruit."[46]

The impact of believing that they should separate themselves from a progressively evil society and that they will one day be taken out of this world has had a significant influence on how they relate to this world. Professor of New Testament at Wesley Theological Seminary, Craig Hill, states the sense of pessimism, fatalism and the abandonment of social responsibility that such a belief fosters.

> The hope of impending departure can lead believers to abandon interest in the world and its problems. The expectation of deteriorating conditions prior to the soon-approaching rapture is morally corrosive, encouraging pessimism, fatalism, and the forsaking of political responsibility. Disengagement from the problems of the world is ethically indefensible, but it is all too common among today's prophecy elite. Their books tell us that nuclear war is inevitable, that the pursuit of peace is pointless, that the planet's environmental woes are unstoppable, and so on.[47]

In their battle against Liberal Theology (and the Social Gospel), the focus of the dispensationalists was on defending the inspiration and authority of the Bible, the deity of Christ, the resurrection and the uniqueness of Christ. They narrowed their focus on what they considered were the most important doctrines in the Bible. Addressing social needs were seen as secondary. Dispensationalists saw the influence of humanism in the Social Gospel as if it were a denial of faith.[48] This attitude is summarized by dispensational Bible teacher David L. Burggraff: "Reform was no substitute for regeneration, and

---

45. Ibid., 315.

46. Ibid., 318.

47. Craig C. Hill, *In God's Time: The Bible and the Future* (Grand Rapids: Eerdmans, 2002), 208.

48. Al Tizon writes, "The preoccupation with defending orthodoxy against the liberal modernist tide produced what became known by the 1920s as fundamentalism, a movement that eventually came to represent the "militantly conservative wing" of evangelicalism." Tizon, *Transformation after Lausanne*, 23.

even successful reform may be nothing more than a satanic device to lure people away from saving faith in Christ."[49]

Having said that, there were dispensationalists who were involved with social reforms between the 1870s and the 1920s. These included A. J. Gordon, Arthur T. Pierson, William Bell Riley, and John Roach Straton, among others. Timothy Webber at Denver Seminary in his survey of American premillennialism summarizes the range of attitudes towards social change. "Some premillennialists condemned all reform efforts as unsuitable for those who expected Christ momentarily; but others believed that until Christ does appear, Christians should engage in certain kinds of reform activity and do whatever possible to slow down the inevitable decline and breakdown of the social order."[50]

The Great Reversal

In the early 1800s there was a spirit of cooperation across the denominations and there was no clear dividing line between pre- and post-millennialists. However by the 1830s a fierce spirit of competition arose among the denominations.[51] This culminated in the theological split by the 1920s between the Liberals (postmillennialist) and Fundamentals (who were predominantly dispensationalists), which polarized the issues with little middle ground. Burggraff writes, "Fundamentalists came to oppose social reform in the 1920s not primarily because they were theologically predisposed to reject the concept, but because the modernists had endorsed it so completely."[52] The tragedy was that in an effort to save the key evangelical doctrines regarding salvation along with the need for personal morality and the urgency of evangelism, they abandoned the balance of Scripture and a strong tradition of social responsibility.

Theologian Carl F. H. Henry, who helped define modern evangelical theology, wrote about what came to be called "the great reversal." "Whereas once the redemptive gospel was a world-changing message, now it was

---

49. David L. Burggraff, "Determining Our Place in Our World or Social Responsibility versus Irresponsibility," *A Dispensationalist Fundamentalist Ponders the Difficult Charge of Social Irresponsibility,* accessed 8 December 2010, http://bobbixby.wordpress.com/2010/09/01/a-dispensationalist-fundamentalist-ponders-the-difficult-charge-of-social-irresponsibility/.

50. Timothy P. Weber, *Living in the Shadow of the Second Coming,* 2nd ed. (Grand Rapids: Zondervan, 1983), 83.

51. Bosch, *Transforming Mission,* 315.

52. Burggraff, "Determining Our Place."

narrowed to a world-resisting message . . . Fundamentalism in revolting against the Social Gospel seemed also to revolt against the Christian social imperative . . . It does not challenge the injustices of totalitarianisms, the secularisms of modern education, the evils of racial hatred, the wrongs of current labor-management relations, and the inadequate bases of international dealing."[53]

Bosch commenting on the split between the "service to the body" and the "service to the soul" writes that both perspectives on their own were the church's inadequate responses to the problems of society and the solutions that the Enlightenment proposed.[54] This separation of evangelism and disciple making from programs that focus on justice and compassion are reflected in church structures. Mission that focuses on conversion and discipling is expressed mainly in the local church, in its congregational life.[55] While programs and initiatives that focus on God's justice and compassion are mainly carried out by non-local (para) church agencies, or committees and boards that are either ecumenical or at a denominational level. Bishop Newbigin felt that evangelism, as well as compassion and justice for the poor, should be expressions of the reality of Christ in the life of a local congregation. He writes:

> Christian programs for justice and compassion are severed from their proper root in the liturgical and sacramental life of the congregation, and so loose their character as signs of the presence of Christ and risk becoming crusades fueled by moralism that can become self-righteous. And the life of the worshipping congregation, severed from its proper expression in compassionate service to the secular world around it, risks becoming a self-centered existence serving only the needs and desires of its members.[56]

The "great reversal" not only split the Protestant church but also robbed local congregations from being able to experience and express the reality of God's salvation more fully.

---

53. Quoted in Rodger C. Bassham, *Mission Theology 1948–1975: Years of Worldwide Creative Tension, Ecumenical, Evangelical, and Roman Catholic* (Pasadena: William Carey Library, 1979), 176.

54. Bosch, *Transforming Mission*, 315.

55. There are exceptions to that as ministries such as Campus Crusade, the Navigators, InterVarsity Christian Fellowship, Every Home Crusade and others were non-church based ministries that focused on evangelism and disciple making.

56. Newbigin, *The Open Secret*, 10–11.

7

Healing the Divide

Modern Missions

It is often stated that modern missions, starting around the late 1700s, understood the teachings and examples of Christ, of the apostles and of the early church fathers, and that right from the beginning the focus of missions was both the verbal proclamation of the gospel, and addressing social and physical needs. While William Carey's only colleague when he sailed for India in 1793 was a medical man, John Thomas, and the team that the London Missionary Society sent to the Pacific in 1796 included a surgeon,[1] in the early years of the missionary movement there wasn't a clear theological understanding of whether social issues should be addressed.

Regardless of this lack of clarity, in 1865, William Booth (1829–1912), a former Methodist minister in England, started working with the "undesirables" of society. These included drug and morphine addicts, prostitutes and alcoholics. Industrialization in Britain had created significant social problems and a large portion of the population was either unemployed or living in very poor and unhealthy conditions. Booth felt that the church had a responsibility to show the love of Christ to those who were unemployed or living in very poor and unhealthy conditions.

There was much discussion within the mission agencies and sending churches as to the role of education in missions. The question was whether there was value in education besides making a population literate so that they could read the Bible. Education was seen by some as a tool to develop societies and for the poor to find a way out of poverty. Thomas Smith, a Church of Scotland missionary to India, at the 1860 Liverpool Conference on Missions

---

1. Walls, *The Missionary Movement*, 211.

discussed whether a missionary should teach anything else other than the gospel. His conclusion was that education was "a legitimate method of fulfilling the great obligation of Christian missionaries" because heathenism (as stated by Smith) was embedded in the educational system and what was taught was that there was no distinction between moral good and evil.[2]

In the Middle East, the first American Protestant missionaries arrived in Lebanon in the early 1820s. They soon discovered that the conversion of a Muslim within the Ottoman Empire was extremely difficult because of a possible death penalty for the convert.[3] Over time, since the majority of the converts were from the historical churches in the region and almost none from the Muslim community, questions were raised about the focus of the mission. Rufus Anderson, who was the senior secretary of the Prudential Committee of the ABCFM[4] in Boston, after a number of trips to the region, referring to the historical churches in the Near East, wrote, "They need to be reminded of things, which, amid ages of political revolution and degradation, they have forgotten. They need to see – as Muslims also need to see – 'living exemplification of the gospel' with all its benevolent influences on society, culture and the nation."[5] Anderson was very involved in the debate around mission strategy, the question being "civilization or Christianization." He was against the "civilizing mission" of overseas missions, which often resulted in the imposition of western cultural and religious patterns, and favored an approach that focused on the message of the gospel alone.[6] Yet Protestant and Catholic missions established schools and colleges as part of their mandate.

There was a similar discussion around medical missions, though the humanitarian imperative made the argument for medical missions much easier. Andrew Walls, the British missiologist, writes about a small book entitled *Murdered Millions* published in 1894, whose author George Dowknott argued that western Christians would be guilty of murder on a massive scale if they failed to reduce the mortality rates by means of medical missions. Walls summarizes Dowknott's argument, "There is little point . . .

2. Ibid., 203.

3. Habib Badr, "American Protestant Missionary Beginnings in Beirut and Istanbul: Politics, Practice and Response," in *New Faiths in Ancient Lands*, ed. Heleen Murre-van den Berg (Leiden: Brill, 2006), 213.

4. American Board of Commissioners for Foreign Missions (ABCFM).

5. Quoted in Badr, "American Protestant Missionary," 224.

6. Ellen Fleischmann, "Evangelization or Education: American Protestant Missionaries, the American Board, and the Girls and Women of Syria (1830–1910)," in *New Faiths in Ancient Lands*, ed. Heleen Mutre-van den Berg (Leiden: Brill, 2006), 271.

in speculating on the eternal future of the heathen when their present state is so pitiable."[7]

But medical missions were not just about healing sick bodies, but also about providing an opening for the gospel. This was given prominence at the 1860 Liverpool Conference, when the London Missionary Society appointed William Lockhart as the first genuine medical missionary.[8] He was also the first Protestant missionary in China. His work was the beginning of full-fledged medical missions, which was more than previous missionaries dispensing medicines as they preached the gospel.[9]

As these issues were addressed, mission strategy began to include evangelism, church planting, Bible translation, providing health care and education, setting up orphanages, and doing advocacy. Their advocacy addressed justice issues like *sati* (widow burning) and young girls forced into temple prostitution in India, foot binding of children in China, and slavery in Africa, the UK, and the US, among others.

The Impact of Liberation Theology

This book has focused primarily on the discussion over the past two hundred years within modern Protestant missions on the place and primacy of evangelism versus addressing social and economic needs. The issues were not the same within the Catholic Church. Yet by the 1960s, with the evolution of Liberation Theology, the issues of poverty, political power and justice were to question the role of the Catholic Church in society. While evangelicals are critical of Liberation Theology, it has succeeded in highlighting specific issues that the church had forgotten. It was to have a profound impact not only on how community development was to be done, but also in influencing some aspects of evangelical theology and practice. So it is an important milepost in this discussion.

Liberation theology started as a movement in Latin America in the 1950s and the 1960s. Gustavo Gutiérrez, a Peruvian theologian and Dominican priest, who had spent much of his life living and working among the poor and oppressed in Lima, Peru, coined the term in 1971 when he wrote *A Theology of Liberation: History, Politics and Salvation.* It was intended to be a Christian

---

7. Walls, *The Missionary Movement*, 213.

8. Though there had been a surgeon on the team that was sent by the LMS to the Pacific, he was not considered a medical missionary.

9. Walls, *The Missionary Movement*, 213.

response to the reality of poverty and the conditions in which the majority of Latin Americans lived. In an interview he said, "I am firmly convinced that poverty – this sub-human condition in which the majority of humanity lives today – is more than a social issue. Poverty poses a major challenge to every Christian conscience and therefore to theology as well."[10]

Gutiérrez's starting point was not eschatology or the kingdom of God, but in understanding the realities of his society, especially poverty and oppression, through the framework of his Christian faith. Gutiérrez states:

> People today often talk about contextual theologies but, in point of fact, theology has always been contextual . . . When Augustine wrote "The City of God," he was reflecting on what it meant for him and for his contemporaries to live the gospel within a specific context of serious historical transformations. Our context today is characterized by a glaring disparity between the rich and the poor. No serious Christian can quietly ignore this situation . . . Theology does not pretend to have all the technical solutions to poverty, but it reminds us never to forget the poor and also that God is at stake in our response to poverty.[11]

The core of his premise was that poverty and injustice are sins manifested in an unjust social structure. He identified two kinds of poverty – hunger for God (spiritual poverty) and hunger for bread (material poverty). God values the former and hates the latter.[12]

Liberation theology has been criticized particularly because of its supposedly Marxist analysis of society. In the 1950s and 1960s, Marxism had found deep resonance with the poor and marginalized in Latin America. The Catholic Church, because of its dominance in society and its political influence, felt particularly vulnerable. The most severe criticism against it however came from within the Catholic Church itself. Cardinal Ratzinger (who later became Pope Benedict XVI), in 1983, published ten observations critically examining Liberation Theology.[13] He remained opposed to its

---

10. Daniel Hartnett, "Remembering the Poor: An Interview with Gustavo Gutierrez," *America, The National Catholic Weekly*, 2003, 3 February, accessed 14 December 2010, http://www.americamagazine.org/content/article.cfm?article_id=2755.

11. Ibid.

12. Gutiérrez, *A Theology of Liberation*, 171.

13. Cardinal Joseph Ratzinger, "Liberation Theology: Preliminary Notes," in *The Ratzinger Report*. Reprinted in *The Essential Pope Benedict XVI*, eds. J. F. Thornton and S. B. Varenne (New York: Harper, 2007).

teaching and took disciplinary action against many of the key leaders – including the Brazilian Catholic theologian, Leonardo Boff.

Gutiérrez explains what he sees as the impact of a theology of liberation. "We will have an authentic theology of liberation only when the oppressed themselves can freely raise their voice and express themselves directly and creatively in society and in the heart of the people of God . . . when they are the protagonists of their own liberation."[14] So in effect, while Liberation Theology saw the poor as victims of oppression, it also saw that they had the ability to create the kind of society that pleases God and work towards it.

Gutiérrez believed that the church was an institution in the community and bore responsibility to be a prophetic voice, reminding people of God's standards. He states, "Now we know that poverty is not simply a misfortune; it is an injustice . . . Christians cannot forgo their responsibility to say a prophetic word about unjust economic conditions."[15]

Evangelicals have also struggled with Gutiérrez's concept of God's "preferential option for the poor." They are concerned about what this means in reference to salvation. Are the poor saved (blessed) just because they are poor? It is important to hear Gutiérrez explain what the term "the preferential option for the poor" means.

- The term poverty refers to the real poor. This is not a preferential option for the spiritually poor . . . The spiritually poor are the saints! The poverty to which the option refers is material poverty. Material poverty means premature and unjust death. The poor person is someone who is treated as a non-person, someone who is considered insignificant from an economic, political and cultural point of view . . . But even though the poor remain insignificant within society, they are never insignificant before God.

- God's love has two dimensions, the universal and the particular . . . God's love excludes no one. Nevertheless, God demonstrates a special predilection towards those who have been excluded from the banquet of life.

- In English, the word "option" merely connotes a choice between two things. In Spanish, however, it evokes the sense of commitment. The option for the poor is not optional, but is incumbent upon every Christian. It is not something that a Christian can either take

---

14. Gutiérrez, *A Theology of Liberation,* 174.
15. Hartnett, "Remembering the Poor," 2003.

or leave . . . it involves standing in solidarity with the poor, but it also entails a stance against inhumane poverty.[16]

Evangelicals, especially in Latin America, were forced to evaluate their understanding of how to relate to society because of the impact and influence of Liberation Theology.

The World Council of Churches

Other streams within the church built on the thinking of Liberation Theology and its starting point of the need for relevance of the Christian faith to society and its problems. Jürgen Moltmann, reflecting on his involvement in the 1973 Bangkok Assembly of the World Council of Churches themed "Salvation Today," writes in his autobiography, "We tried to find a comprehensive understanding of salvation and withstood western emphasis on the salvation of the individual."[17] Section II of the *Minutes and Report of the Bangkok Assembly 1973*, often referred to as the theology of the Bangkok Assembly, states that salvation was total liberation involving economic justice, political freedom and cultural renewal.[18] Section II states:

> As evil works both in personal life and in exploitative social structures which humiliate mankind, so God's justice manifests itself both in the justification of the sinner and in social and political justice . . . we see the struggles for economic justice, political freedom and cultural renewal as elements in the total liberation of the world through the mission of God. This liberation is finally achieved when "death is swallowed up in victory" (1 Cor 15:55). This comprehensive notion of salvation demands of the whole of the people of God a matching comprehensive approach to their participation in salvation. . .
>
> Within the comprehensive notion of salvation, we see the saving work in four social dimensions:
>
> a) Salvation works in the struggle for economic justice against the exploitation of people by people.

---

16. Ibid.
17. Jürgen Moltmann, *A Broad Place: An Autobiography* (London: SCM Press, 2007), 171.
18. Quoted in Moltmann, *A Broad Place,* 173–174.

b) Salvation works in the struggle for human dignity against political oppression of human beings.

c) Salvation works in the struggle for solidarity against the alienation of person from person.

d) Salvation works in the struggle of hope against despair in personal life.

In the process of salvation, we must relate these four dimensions to each other. There is no economic justice without political freedom, no political freedom without economic justice. There is no social justice without solidarity, no solidarity without social justice. There is no justice, no human dignity, no solidarity without hope, no hope without justice, dignity and solidarity.

The World Council of Churches believed that the social, political and economic transformation of the world based on the justice of God was the mission and mandate of the church. A 1967 World Council of Churches report states, "We have lifted up humanization as the goal of mission because we believe that more than others, it communicates in our period of history the meaning of the Messianic goal."[19]

The Fundamentalist Evangelical Reaction

The more fundamentalist evangelical churches during this period remained very focused on evangelism. In preparation for the World Council of Churches Assembly in Uppsala, Sweden in 1968, Donald McGavran, a veteran missionary and one of the founders of the Church Growth Movement, in a special issue of the Church Growth Bulletin reacted against the emphasis on social and physical need. He argued for the primacy of the spiritual dimension of salvation over social issues.

By "the two billion" I mean that great number of at least two billion, who either have never heard of Jesus Christ or have no real chance to believe on him as "Lord and Savior." These inconceivable multitudes live and die in a famine of the Word

---

19. World Council of Churches, *The Church for Others and The Church for the World* (Geneva: World Council of Churches, 1967), 78.

of God, more terrible by far than the sporadic physical famines, which occur in unfortunate lands….

By "betray" I mean any course of action, which substitutes ashes for bread, fixes the attention of God's children with the flesh when they long for the spirit. By "betray" I mean planning courses of action whose sure outcome will be that the two billion will remain in their sins and in their darkness, chained by false and inadequate ideas of God and humanity.[20]

For McGavran, the confusion lay in understanding the mission and mandate of the church. He writes, "In some circles, everything is called mission – feeding the hungry, educating the ignorant, healing the sick, building bridges of friendship between nations."[21] For him, "A chief aim of Christian mission is to proclaim Jesus Christ as divine and only Savior and persuade men to become his disciples and responsible members of his church."[22]

This perspective is still very prevalent among many evangelicals today. Wolfgang Simon, the author of the *Starfish Manifesto* and church growth consultant, asks:

Does Jesus expect that the world will be transformed before or after his return? After. Does he indicate that the character of this world, its soul, its nature, its ethos, can ever be transformed? No. Did he authorize his disciples to transform the world? No. Did he advise his disciples what methods they should use to transform the world? No.[23]

His conclusion is that any attempt at social transformation is a waste of time. He writes, "Let's face it: developed pagans are, yes better pagan – but they are still pagan."[24]

It is important to understand the theological basis of what McGavran, Simon and some of the evangelicals are saying. McGavran wrote, "Salvation

---

20. Donald McGavran, "Will Uppsala Betray the Two Billion," *Church Growth Bulletin: Special Uppsala Issue* IV, no. 5 (May 1968).

21. Donald McGavran, ed., *Eye of the Storm: The Great Debate in Mission* (Waco: Word Books, 1972), 65.

22. Ibid., 56.

23. Wolfgang Simon, *The Starfish Manifesto* (Antioch: Asteroidea Books, 2009), 6875–6878, Kindle ed.

24. Ibid., 6954–6956, Kindle ed.

is a vertical relationship. . . . The vertical cannot be displaced by the horizontal. Desirable as social ameliorations are, working for them must never be substituted for the biblical requirements of 'salvation.'"[25] Their understanding of mission is based on the aspect of human beings they consider most important, namely the spiritual. Professor Matthew John of Serampore College in India reacts against this when he writes, "The concern for man's immortal soul, which is made in the image of God hides the fact that according to the Bible it is man, the whole man – not merely his soul – that is said to be created in the image of God."[26]

The discussion still remains very polarized as to whether the mandate and priority of the church is evangelism or whether it also include addressing social and political issues like poverty, injustice and oppression.

Lausanne 1974 and Beyond

David Bosch, reflecting on this polarization, provides a balance when he writes: "We have to affirm that redemption is never salvation *out of* this world but always salvation *of* this world. Salvation in Christ is salvation in the context of human society en route to a whole and healed world."[27] Bosch goes on to say that any interpretation of salvation has to operate within a comprehensive christological framework, which includes his incarnation, earthly life, death, resurrection, and the second coming of Christ. These taken together constitute the work of Christ as he inaugurated salvation, and is the model for us to emulate in our ministry. This was the balance that many evangelicals were trying to achieve. The process culminated with the International Conference on World Evangelism in Lausanne in 1974.

In preparing for the 1974 Lausanne Conference, and then during the conference, a number of evangelical leaders led by John Stott struggled to find the balance between evangelism and addressing social needs. They tried to avoid "schizophrenic positions" and extremes as they sought to understand what salvation and ministry means for the individual and society, body and soul, present and future.[28] Aware of the questions being asked by Liberation Theology and the discussions at the World Council of Churches,

---

25. Donald McGavran, "Salvation Today," in *The Evangelical Response to Bangkok*, ed. Ralph Winter (Pasadena: William Carey Library, 1973), 31.

26. McGavran, *Eye of the Storm*, 117.

27. Bosch, *Transforming Mission*, 399.

28. Ibid.

the main streams of the evangelical community was forced to re-examine their theology. One of the questions they explored was "the relationship of evangelism and social concern, raised by the rapid growth in awareness of poverty and injustice in the world and the effects of (natural and human-made) disasters."[29]

The resulting Lausanne Covenant emphasized evangelism, but placed it within a Christian presence in the world and discipleship. Affirmation 4 "The Nature Of Evangelism" states ". . . evangelism itself is the proclamation of the historical, biblical Christ as Savior and Lord, with a view to persuading people to come to him personally and so be reconciled to God. In issuing the gospel invitation we have no liberty to conceal the cost of discipleship . . . The results of evangelism include obedience to Christ, incorporation into his church and responsible service in the world."[30]

There was also recognition of the social responsibility of Christians among many of the evangelicals. Affirmation 5 "Christian Social Responsibility" states:

> We therefore should share his [God's] concern for justice and reconciliation throughout human society and for the liberation of men and women from every kind of oppression . . . Although reconciliation with other people is not reconciliation with God, nor is social action evangelism, nor is political liberation salvation, nevertheless we affirm that evangelism and sociopolitical involvement are both part of our Christian duty. For both are necessary expressions of our doctrines of God and man, our love for our neighbor and our obedience to Jesus Christ . . . The salvation we claim should be transforming us in the totality of our personal and social responsibilities. Faith without works is dead.[31]

However, in trying to connect evangelism and social responsibility within the mission of the church, the Lausanne Covenant stated *the primacy of evangelism*. In affirmation 6 "The Church and Evangelism" it states, "In

---

29. Tom Houston, "The Story of the Lausanne Covenant: Case Study in Cooperation," 2013, accessed 23 July 2013, http://www.lausanne.org/en/gatherings/global-congress/lausanne-1974/story-of-the-covenant.html

30. The Lausanne Movement, *The Lausanne Covenant,* 2013, accessed 23 July 2013, http://www.lausanne.org/en/documents/lausanne-covenant.html.

31. Ibid.

the church's mission of sacrificial service evangelism is primary. World evangelization requires the whole church to take the whole gospel to the whole world."[32]

While the Covenant explicitly affirmed evangelism as primary, the major breakthrough of 1974 Lausanne Conference was the rediscovery by the wider evangelical community that addressing the social needs of the community is a mandate for the church, as is evangelism. However, Bosch explains the danger of not understanding the relationship between the two. "The moment that one regards mission as consisting of two separate components one has, in principle, conceded that each of the two has a life of its own. One is then by implication saying that it is possible to have evangelism without a social dimension and Christian social involvement without an evangelistic dimension. What is more, if one suggests that one component is primary and the other secondary, one implies that one is essential, the other optional."[33]

Nine years later, the 1983 Wheaton Consultation developed a more holistic understanding of mission by developing a biblical, theological and practical understanding of the term "transformation." Track III in the Wheaton 1983 Statement reads, "Transformation is the change from a condition of human existence contrary to God's purposes to one in which people are able to enjoy fullness of life in harmony with God."[34]

The Micah Declaration 2001 and Integral Mission

The 2001 consultation in Oxford sought to explain the relationship between the Great Commission (Matt 28:19–20) and the Great Commandment (Matt 22:37–40). This consultation produced the "Micah Declaration" which states:

> Integral mission or holistic transformation is the proclamation and demonstration of the gospel. It is not simply that evangelism and social involvement are to be done alongside each other. Rather, in integral mission our proclamation has social consequences as we call people to love and repentance in all areas of life. And

---

32. Ibid.

33. Bosch, *Transforming Mission*, 405.

34. Tizon, *Transformation after Lausanne*, 8–9.

our social involvement has evangelistic consequences as we bear witness to the transforming grace of Jesus Christ.[35]

The Micah Declaration finally provided the right balance between the verbal proclamation of the gospel and the demonstration of its reality. Neither operates independently and each has significant implications for the other. It finally laid to rest theologically the great divide of the past hundred and fifty years, resulting in a deeper and clearer understanding of what is the mandate of the church.

---

35. Micah Network, *Micah Network Declaration on Integral Mission* (Oxford: Micah Network, 2001), 1.

8

Transformation or Witness:
The Challenge
of Transformation

Any study of compassion and of a Christian response to poverty will invariably at some point ask the question of whether there is a biblical basis for community development and social transformation. Does the compassion of God focus on only meeting immediate needs through charity or is God concerned with the underlying issues that cause poverty and in the transformation of the world?

The word transformation is now part of the vocabulary of most Christian development NGOs and is even used by government agencies such as USAID. Part of the question is whether the only accepted strategies to address social issues such as poverty are those that are explicitly mentioned in the Bible (such as charity), or whether the church can borrow concepts from economics and the social sciences (such as community and economic development and other poverty alleviation strategies) to accomplish its mission. But more importantly, are the values, the goals and objectives of economists and development professionals compatible with goals of the mission of God (*missio Dei*) and are they within the biblical mandate of the church? Is the mission of God only about improving the quality of life of the poor and ensuring that they have secure livelihoods or is it something more?

There is a certain simplicity in the various campaign slogans – "Make Poverty History"; "Jubilee 2000, a debt free start for a billion people"; "Stop Hunger Now"; "No Child for Sale" – which give a vision of what the world could be and the certainty that dramatic social and political change for the better is possible. They mirror the enthusiasm and confidence of a younger generation who want to change the world. While their objective is to advocate for specific social issues, the impression among the public is that by being part of a campaign and by lobbying those in power for the right legislation, the world can be changed.

Understanding Development and Transformation

To understand what is meant by development and transformation, it is important to have clarity as to what is meant by poverty. The United Nations describes poverty:

> It means lack of basic capacity to participate effectively in society. It means not having enough to feed and clothe a family, not having a school or clinic to go to, not having the land on which to grow one's food or a job to earn one's living, not having access to credit. It means insecurity, powerlessness and exclusion of individuals, households and communities. It means susceptibility to violence, and it often implies living in marginal or fragile environments, without access to clean water or sanitation.[1]

Robert Chambers highlights the dimensions of powerlessness, isolation and voicelessness to the understanding of poverty – that these dimensions of marginalization are both causes of poverty and the result of poverty.

As a result, the process needed for social, political and economic change, and transformation is far more complex and often times messy. Change involves dealing with competing interests, different visions of what the world could be, and the egos and personal agendas of leaders. While there have been individuals who have changed the course of history using peaceful means, in each case they were able to do so because of strategic historical opportunities which provided access to resources and a network of supporting actors.

On the other hand, development (understood by economists and development practitioners to be a systematic process of improving the quality of life of individuals and communities[2]) is a complex process. It

---

1. United Nations Educational, Scientific and Cultural Organization (UNESCO). "Statement of Commitment for Action to Eradicate Poverty Adopted by the Administrative Committee on Coordination," 20 May 1998, accessed 2 February 2012, http://www.unesco.org/most/acc4pov.htm.

2. There is no one agreed upon definition of development. However, the concept involves an economic, political, social and cultural process of planning to improve the quality of life and wellbeing of individuals and ensuring the common good of communities in a defined area. It encompasses the human rights of individuals and ensures the protection and sustainability of the environment. It ensures inclusiveness and social justice. The socioeconomic indicators of

involves many different individuals, groups and institutions, policies all the way from the community level to the international, and a wide range of resources. It requires intangibles such as the willingness and commitment to change, as well as tangibles such as political allies, bureaucratic mechanisms, and institutions that enable change to actually happen. Development and social change involve the empowerment of communities who have been marginalized from the mainstreams of society and ensuring the availability of services for them.

However, social change, resulting in improved quality of life, is not necessarily always planned. It can also happen through the informal process of *non-movements*, which sociologist Asef Bayat describes as the process of large numbers of ordinary people whose "fragmented but similar activities trigger much social change."[3] Examples of non-movements are large numbers of migrants from rural areas who move into urban settings; urban slum dwellers who encroach upon government land to extend their meager dwelling; inhabitants of poor section of cities who illegally tap into electricity and water connections. Each of these has a huge impact on communities and society and in some way marginally improve the quality of life of individuals and families but not necessarily the community at large.

Yet "development" remains a complex and ambiguous term fraught with political and social meaning. David Lewis, professor of Social Policy and Development at the London School of Economics (LSE), explains that in different contexts the term can be used as a verb, adjective, or concept. He writes:

> As a verb, "development" refers to activities required to bring about change or progress, and is often linked strongly to economic growth. As an adjective, "development" implies a standard against which different rates of progress may be compared, and it therefore takes on a subjective, judgmental element in which societies or communities are sometimes compared and then positioned at different "stages" of an evolutionary development schema. Indeed, development is often understood in Darwinian

---

development include access to education and health services, reduction of child and maternal mortality rates, development of civil society organization (CSOs) and civic participation, improvement in employment, employment security and income, the existence of a social security net, and reduction in crime.

3. Asef Bayat, *Life as Politics: How Ordinary People Change the Middle East* (Stanford: Stanford University Press, 2010).

terms as a biological metaphor for organic growth and evolution, while in a Durkheimian[4] sense it can be associated with ideas about the increasing social, economic and political complexity in transitions from "traditional" to "modern" societies. At the same time, "development" has also come to be associated with "planned social change" and the idea of an external intervention by one group in the affairs of another. Often this is in the form of a project, as part of conscious efforts by outsiders to intervene in a "less-developed" community or country in order to produce positive change. Finally, within radical critiques, development is viewed in terms of an organized system of power and practice, which has formed part of the colonial and neo-colonial domination of poorer countries, by the West.[5]

The ambiguity is not limited to terms such as "development," but also with "transformation." *Change, development, poverty alleviation,* and *transformation* are words and concepts that permeate the conversations not only of development practitioners and academics, but also of politicians and diplomats. It has now also become very much part of the discussion as to what is the mission of the church, as the concept of development has been increasingly embraced as a fundamental mission of the church. It is no longer good enough to be compassionate and charitable by setting up food banks, digging wells, building schools, or assisting individuals in need. The causes of hunger, unemployment, homelessness and disease have to be addressed. Poverty has to be eradicated. As a matter of fact, acts of charity that address the immediate needs are often looked down on as being inadequate responses to poverty. The assumption is that the only acceptable response is a process of empowerment and social change, which lead to transformation of communities.

But is transformation of communities and of this world a biblical concept? Is it a mandate for the people of God? Is transformation without addressing the spiritual dimensions of life, which influence values and ethics, sustainable? Is transformation possible on this side of eternity?

These seem strange questions to ask. After all isn't a better world everyone's desire? Don't people everywhere dream of life being a little less

---

4. Emile Durkheim was a French philosopher and sociologist.

5. David Lewis, "Anthropology and Development: The Uneasy Relationship," in *A Handbook of Economic Anthropology,* ed. James D. Carrier (Cheltenham: Edward Elgar, 2005), 474.

burdensome? Aren't visions of utopia (however defined) the rhetoric of the political and religious elite, and the dreams of the poor and oppressed? Why would Christianity and Christians even question these desires? What remains unclear is what does the concept of transformation actually mean; what are visions of transformation? The irony of the dreams of utopia is found in the word that Sir Thomas More chose to describe a fictional island in the Atlantic Ocean, which was the ideal society. Writing in 1516, he was probably intentional in naming his book *Utopia*,[6] which in Greek means "no place" (οὐ "not" and τόπος "place"), implying that it doesn't exist.

While utopia may remain a dream, Bishop Lesslie Newbigin, who had been a veteran missionary in India, wonders if there is a step beyond simply addressing needs – namely that of justice. The poor are not satisfied by only having some of their needs met. They demand that the injustices that are at the root of poverty also be addressed. Bishop Newbigin, reflecting on his experience and the changing nature of missions, writes:

> The discussion about the role of "services" in the missionary work of the church is now thus replaced by a new discussion. We are no longer thinking about "services" such as have been traditionally offered by the (Christian) rich to the (pagan) poor in the form of schools, hospitals, and agricultural programs. We have now to listen to the missiology formulated within the consciousness of the Christian who is part of the poor world, a missiology centered in the demand for liberation in the name of God's justice. It is in these terms that we must face in our day the question of the relation between preaching of the gospel and action for God's justice as part of the church's mission.[7]

What Bishop Newbigin is referring to is Micah 6:8 which identifies part of what is central to the heart of God and therefore is part of the mission of the church. "He has shown you, O mortal, what is good. And what does the Lord require of you? and therefore is part of the mission of the church with your God." From our study so far it is clear that the verbal proclamation of the gospel cannot be separated from addressing physical and social needs. But is seeking justice for the poor and the oppressed the same as transformation as development practitioners and economists understand the concept to be?

---

6. In English, "eutopia" derives from the Greek, meaning "good place." The identical pronunciation of the two words gives the concept double meaning.

7. Newbigin, *The Open Secret*, 5.

The Impact of Missions

Robert Woodberry in his ground breaking research, *The Missionary Roots of Liberal Democracy*,[8] has shown definitively the impact of historical Protestant missions in the nineteenth and twentieth centuries in improving the quality of life of local populations and laying the groundwork for representative democracy to take root, where the individual was empowered to be part of the mainstream of the political discourse in their country. He identifies specifically the investments that mission agencies and missionaries made into mass education, mass printing, newspapers, voluntary organizations, and the codification of legal protections for non-whites in the nineteenth and early twentieth centuries. They were also involved in major colonial reforms and were the crucial catalyst for the initiation and spread of religious liberty as a formal legal right (as opposed to an informal practice of toleration). As Woodberry states, these "fostered conditions made stable representative democracy more likely – regardless of whether many people converted to Protestantism."[9]

Woodberry's research confirms what many had known anecdotally and intuitively about the impact of missionary schools, colleges and hospitals. Missionaries worked to ensure mass literacy so that the Bible was accessible to everyone and that they were able to interpret it with a certain level of competence. The result was that it reduced the barriers between the elites in society and others. Their efforts to address social evils such as *sati* (burning of widows along with their deceased husbands) in India, slavery, and foot binding of girls in China (to name just a few) are well documented. It was missionaries during this period who introduced major advances in agriculture, tackled diseases such as leprosy, and helped improve the status of women.

Yet somehow in the post-colonial era through the assertions of Post-Colonial Theology, the efforts and the impact of the missionary initiatives, particularly in education and medical services, were reinterpreted and dismissed as being the tools of the colonial powers to control local populations.[10] However, Sri Lankan theologian D. Preman Niles provides a

---

8. Robert D. Woodberry, "The Missionary Roots of Liberal Democracy," *American Political Science Review* 106, no. 2 (May 2012).

9. Ibid., 245.

10. Insight into this thinking can be gained from K. C. Abraham, ed., *Third World Theologies: Commonalities and Divergence* (Maryknoll, NY: Orbis, 1990), in particular the documents

corrective when he writes that the early missionaries were craftsmen, small traders, shoemakers, printers, ship builders and schoolteachers.[11] He writes about William Carey, the father of the modern missionary movement, ". . . it was his social background and his identification with people of his class in countries to which he went that influenced his attitude and shaped his theology."[12] Niles contends that they were never part of the colonial enterprise at home and rarely aligned with people in power. "A missionary movement arose with the desire not to exploit nations but to take to them a divine treasure."[13] Accordingly they did not see people in their countries of service as a "lower order of creation" to be exploited. Therefore many of the early missionaries could critique and resist the slave trade and the sugar industry. "At a time when state churches either overtly or covertly colluded with national political and military powers, the dissenters trod a different path both at home and abroad. Non-conformism was at one and the same time a political position and theological conviction. These missionaries were not mere evangelists. They were also social reformers who challenged what they deemed to be wrong in society, theirs as well as those to which they went."[14] Niles concludes, "Understood as an intrinsic part of evangelical and pietistic commitment, this social and critical dimension, which affirmed the worth and dignity of every person, gave the early missionary movement its distinctive character."[15]

The impact of the church on society through missions was not just limited to the global south, in the missionary receiving countries. In the Europe (especially in Britain), during this period, Christians endowed with a social conscience shaped by the teachings of the Bible and what they understood the gospel to be, led in some of the major reform movements. Slavery in the British Empire was abolished because of the efforts of William Wilberforce and others who were part of the Clapham group.[16] The Earl of Shaftesbury Anthony Ashley Cooper pioneered labor reform through child labor laws and

from the 7th International Conference of the Ecumenical Association of Third World Theologians (EATWOT) 1986.

11. Niles, *From East and West*, 74.

12. Ibid., 74.

13. Ibid.

14. Ibid., 77.

15. Ibid.

16. Also known as the Clapham sect or the Clapham saints, the group consisted of social minded reformers who were members of the Church of England active between 1790–1830 and was based in Clapham, London.

prohibiting women to work in the mines. Theodor Fliedner in Germany and Elizabeth Fry and John Howard in England were pioneers in prison reform.

By the late 1800s through to the mid-1900s many of these missionary efforts were driven primarily by a Postmillennial Theology that had deep roots in the Enlightenment, with its focus on scientific progress transforming society. Postmillennialism with its optimistic vision that human beings could now create a better world, gave birth to the Social Gospel, the understanding of which fueled the Protestant missionary and social reform movements at its height in the late nineteenth century. The schools, colleges, and hospitals, as well as efforts to address social ills, were intended to break the hold of evil in society and progressively usher in the reign of God, culminating in the return of Christ. Education, for example, was more than just a tool for literacy to enable people to read the Bible. It was believed that society could be transformed through education, and that poverty could be alleviated. Thus the 1860 Liverpool Conference on Missions affirmed education was "a legitimate method of fulfilling the great obligation of Christian missionaries."[17] The debate around mission strategy was the question whether the mission of the church was "education or evangelism" or more broadly whether it was "civilization or Christianization."[18]

The impact of the church on society was not just a phenomenon of Protestant and Catholic missions during the nineteenth and twentieth centuries. The early church, believing that compassion for the poor was central in what it meant to be a people of God (Gal 2:10), responded to the growing poverty within the eastern provinces of the Roman Empire, especially around the fourth and fifth centuries. As the cities were unable to absorb the poor, it was the Christians who responded to their needs. Earlier, in AD 252 it was the Christians in Corinth who responded to the plague in the city by ministering to those who had been left on the streets to die. These early Christians also opposed slavery, infanticide, gladiatorial combat, and the degradation of women. As both Peter Brown and Walter Brueggemann have pointed out, it was this ministry of compassion that influenced the shift in attitudes within Roman society from one of patronage for the benefit of the city to one of compassion for the poor.[19] The hospices and orphanages

---

17. Walls, *The Missionary Movement*, 203.

18. Fleischmann, "Evangelization or Education," 271.

19. Brown, *Through the Eye*, 58, and Brueggemann, "How the Early Church," 30.

established during this period became the models for social institutions that would benefit society.

Vincent Donovan, writing in *Christianity Rediscovered* after seventeen years as a missionary in Africa, adds a note of caution in the midst of the euphoria of the social impact of Christian missions. "The gospel is not progress or development. It is not nation building. It is not adult education. It is not a school system. It is not a health campaign. It is not a five-year plan. It is not an economic program. It is not a ranching scheme or water development. It is not an independence movement . . . It is not violent revolution."[20] Donovan does not deny the impact of Christian missions on society but rather applauds it. He continues, "To see the gospel as adaptable and applicable to real life in all its dimensions is good. No one would deny the connection between the gospel and development."[21] Instead he asks the question that is central to the mission of God – what is the gospel?

The Challenge of Transformation

The word "transformation" is used very loosely today. It is used synonymously with the word "change." However, the word "transform" is defined as "to change something *completely* and usually in a good way."[22] In the New Testament the Greek word is *metamorphoo* meaning to change into another form, altered, and is used in the passive voice to refer to Christ's transfiguration.[23] The implication is that the change is not incremental, but is radical and holistic in nature. Most community development projects address incremental change and are not truly transformative in nature.

Mark Dever, senior pastor at Capital Hill Baptist Church and a trustee of the Southern Baptist Theological Seminary, in a debate with Jim Wallis of *Sojourners* on whether the church should be involved in issues of justice and social transformation, stated: "I certainly see the local church caring for the poor among its own number. We're worse than infidels if we don't do that. We have a special responsibility to make sure our brothers and sisters in Christ don't starve and are cared for. Beyond that it is appropriate to care for the

---

20. Vincent J. Donovan, *Christianity Rediscovered* (New York: Orbis Books, 2003) 123.

21. Ibid., 123.

22. "Transform," Merriam-Webster.com, accessed 25 October 2014, http://www.merriam-webster.com/dictionary/transform, 2014.

23. Vines Expository Dictionary of New Testament Words, accessed 26 October 2014, http://www.menfak.no/bibelprog/vines?word=%AFt0003059.

poor outside the church, but that is something for all humans made in the image of God to do, and Christians can certainly help. But the church isn't called to solve societal ills."[24] Devers wonders if addressing social issues is really the mandate of the church, when he feels it should really be a concern for everyone in society. While he is correct in that, the question hinges on what is meant by "church."

The Desire for Transformation

The issue is **not** whether transformation of society is a good thing. Everyone desires that. The challenge theologically is whether transformation is possible on this side of eternity. Throughout the Bible there are images of transformed communities such as in Isaiah 2:4 and Micah 4:3 where swords will be turned into plowshares and where there would be no more wars and violence; Isaiah 65:17–25, where there would be no child mortality nor child labor, where there would be no premature death and starvation, and people would not be driven from their home. Are these meant to be a reality that is possible, or is it an ideal to strive for, but one which will only be fulfilled when the kingdom of God is manifested in all its fullness here on earth at the end of time?

The desire for a world where there would be no pain or sorrow, and where there is justice, peace and equality, is deeply rooted in the cultural unconscious and consciousness of society. This is not just a recent phenomenon of modern civil society and NGOs seeking to improve the lives of the poor and of ensuring that the human rights of all are safeguarded. Literature, which is often a window into the soul of a culture, is replete with visions of an ideal society where there would be no injustice or poverty. Besides Sir Thomas More's *Utopia*, Plato, writing in *The Republic* around 380 BC, discussed the concept of justice and what a just state would look like. In 1627, English statesman, philosopher and scientist, Sir Francis Bacon wrote the *New Atlantis* about a fictional utopian community in the Pacific Ocean that embodied all the ideals of the human race. Karl Marx along with Friedrich Engels in 1848 envisaged a radical vision for society in the *Communist Manifesto*, advocating for political, social and economic equality. Edward Bellamy in 1888 published *Looking Backwards*, describing a socialist paradise. This deep longing for justice and equality is reflected in the fact

---

24. "Personal but Never Private," *ChristianityToday.com, 13 September 2010*, accessed 14 September 2010, http://www.christianitytoday.com/le/2010/summer/personalneverprivate.html.

that *Looking Backwards* was the third largest bestseller of its time. In 1905 H. G. Wells' *A Modern Utopia* described a postmodern world, where social, economic and racial barriers would not exist. James Hilton writing *Lost Horizon* in 1933 described the mythical kingdom of Shangri-La hidden in the inaccessible mountainous regions of Tibet as a paradise on earth. The American architect, designer and futurist Buckminster Fuller (1895–1983) presented a vision for a technological utopia.

This desire for utopia is not just a western tradition. Most of the great religions of the world have concepts and visions of a religiously defined utopia or paradise, whether it was a place, a state of mind or a mystical experience. The Chinese concept of the Great Unity (*datong*) described in *Liji* (Record of Rites), one of the classics of Confucianism, provides a vision where there is peace, with everyone and everything is in its rightful place. *The Peach Blossom Spring* written by the Chinese poet Tao Chien (AD 365–427, sometimes also referred to as Tao Yuanming) about a peaceful rural society – the perfect utopian community.

While revolutionaries tried to transform societies and writers painted word pictures and created visions of what society could be, many were frustrated with the inability to transform society at large and withdrew to create communities such as communes, ashrams, and eco-villages, each with a vision of what a perfect world would look like. The Christian world has not been immune from utopian communities. They yearned for what they saw modeled in Acts 2:42-44. "They devoted themselves to the apostles' teaching and to fellowship, to the breaking of bread and to prayer. Everyone was filled with awe at the many wonders and signs performed by the apostles. All the believers were together and had everything in common. They sold property and possessions to give to anyone who had need." The earliest known formal Christian monastic community meant to reflect these ideals was organized by St Pachomius in AD 318 when he gathered his followers into a communal living arrangement. Others followed, the more famous among them being St Catherine's Monastery in the Sinai, established between AD 527–565.

The settling of the New World provided opportunities for various religious groups to start anew and try and create the ideal community. The largest groups were the Amish, the Mennonites, the Moravians, and the Anabaptist Hutterites, who created their own communities, which were characterized by simple living and pacifism. While many of these Christian communities withdrew from the mainstreams of society because of persecution or a perceived threat to their beliefs and lifestyle, most were also motivated to create communities that honored God and reflected his values, as they understood them.

There is no disputing the fact that because of science and technology, the quality of life of vast numbers of people across the planet has improved. Harvard University professor Steven Pinker writes in *The Better Angels of Our Nature: Why Violence Has Declined*[25] that since 1945 there has been a decline in inter-state wars, military coups, and deadly ethnic riots, and that the average number of deaths per conflict have been significantly reduced. Along with other statistics, Pinker's contention is that the world is becoming a better and less violent place. There is hard evidence that deadly diseases such as polio have been eradicated, global hunger and the percentage of people living in poverty have declined, and that child and maternal mortality rates have decreased. These are the result of stable governments, progress in human rights, new instruments of international humanitarian law, and the use of science and technology. As commendable, and in some cases dramatic, as the changes have been, no one can honestly claim transformation.

Reality Check

The dreams of utopia were countered by warnings of perfectly organized or engineered societies that go wrong. The disturbing and terrifying images of dystopia ("a society characterized by human misery, as squalor, oppression, disease, and overcrowding"[26]) are portrayed in George Orwell's *Nineteen Eight-Four* and its vision of a totalitarian state, Anthony Burgess' *A Clockwork Orange*, where the question is at what cost can society be reformed, Aldous Huxley's *A Brave New World* and *Brave New World Revisited*, where science and technology create a new world, and psychologist B. F. Skinner's *Walden Two*, where humans have no free will or soul but are the product of variables in their environment.

The yearning to return to a long lost paradise or striving for a better future where technology and scientific progress will provide answers for all that ails society, are deeply embedded in the human psyche. These yearnings for a better life are also a fundamental part of Christian consciousness. The biblical narrative starts with the existence of a paradise created by God, a

---

25. Steven Pinker, *The Better Angels of Our Nature: Why Violence Has Declined* (New York: Allen Lane, 2011).

26. "Dystopia," Dictionary.com, 2014, 19 accessed June 2014, http://dictionary.reference.com/browse/dystopia.

paradise long lost. The Bible also looks forward to a transformed society when the kingdom of God becomes a reality in all its fullness here on earth. "They will be his people, and God himself will be with them and be their God. He will wipe away every tear from their eyes. There will be no more death or mourning or crying or pain, for the old order of things has passed away" (Rev 21:4).

The challenge to social transformation is the darkness and evil that is enmeshed with human nature and lurks within the human soul. As Orwell, Burgess, Huxley and Skinner have tried to paint with word pictures, efforts to intentionally and forcibly create a new society will not only fail but can also have terrifying consequences. Paulo Freire, the Brazilian educator and philosopher in his groundbreaking book *The Pedagogy of the Oppressed*, described how liberation and transformation improperly led and implemented could lead to further oppression. For Freire, because poverty and oppression are so self-destructive, the process by which the poor are liberated from their bondages of poverty is critical. He writes, "Attempting to liberate the oppressed without their reflective participation in the act of liberation is to treat them as objects that must be saved from a burning building."[27] If the process is not managed properly, "the oppressed, instead of striving for liberation, tend themselves to become oppressors."[28]

The history of colonization in the nineteenth and twentieth centuries highlighted the fact that the issue is not whether development is good, but *what are the agendas motivating development* and *who benefits from development*. Any discussion on transformation has to answer these two questions. This is the debate from which Post-Colonial Theology draws it critique of the modern missionary movement. These issues are just as relevant today as they were during the period of colonization. There are numerous examples, that in spite of efforts at providing education and healthcare, the policies of development often had severe negative long-term consequences because the underlying motive was to increase the wealth of the colonizing powers and the elite and not necessarily to benefit the local communities. One of the earliest anthropological studies on this was by Godfrey Wilson, the first director of the Rhodes-Livingstone Institute, who in 1942 documented how colonial policies in Zambia (formerly Northern Rhodesia) in an effort at economic development, structured industrialization and urbanization in

---

27. Freire, *Pedagogy of the Oppressed*, 52.
28. Ibid., 29–30.

order to discourage permanent settlement of migrant workers. This resulted in social instability with massive levels of male migrants moving back and forth between rural and urban communities.[29] His conclusion was that development policies as they were being implemented at the time were having huge negative social impact on families and communities. While the economy of the country grew and developed, the social impact of the economic development policies was devastating.

More recently, the World Bank's Structural Adjustment Programs (SAPs) aimed to bring fiscal discipline to certain countries so that they could pay back the massive debts they had incurred from international banks. The objective of good governance by reducing debt was that governments would be able to invest in the well-being of the citizens of the country. Economist Edwin M. Truman at the Peterson Institute for International Economics, responding to William Easterly's defense of structural adjustment in *IMF and World Bank Structural Adjustment Programs and Poverty*, highlighted the negative social and economic impacts.[30] The results of the SAPs showed a negative impact on the poor, as reduced spending on health, education and social welfare programs severely affected the middle class and the poor. While the borrowing countries were held accountable for the repayment of loans regardless of the negative consequences on the local population, the lending banks were never challenged and held responsible for their poor risk analysis before making the loans. The injustice of this is that the consequences of bad decisions and mismanagement by those in power (the leaders of the borrowing countries and the heads of the banking institutions) were borne entirely by the poor with no accountability or repercussions for those in positions of power.

The Bible identifies this darkness in the human soul that undermines attempts at transformation. "The heart is deceitful above all things, and desperately sick; who can understand it?" (Jer 17:9). "To the defiled and unbelieving, nothing is pure; but both their minds and their consciences are defiled" (Tit 1:15–16). "Also, the hearts of the children of man are full of evil, and madness is in their hearts while they live, and after that they go to the dead" (Eccl 9:3). "For from within, out of the heart of man, come evil

---

29. Godfrey Wilson, *An Essay on the Economics of Detribalization in Northern Rhodesia, Part II*, Rhodes-Livingstone Papers, no. 6 (Livingstone, Rhodesia: Rhodes-Livingstone Institute, 1942).

30. William Easterly, "IMF and World Bank Structural Adjustment Programs and Poverty," in *Managing Currency Crises in Emerging Markets*, ed. Michael P. Dooley and Jeffrey A. Frankel (Chicago: Chicago University Press, 2003), 383–390.

thoughts, sexual immorality, theft, murder, adultery, coveting, wickedness, deceit, sensuality, envy, slander, pride, foolishness. All these evil things come from within, and they defile a person" (Mark 7:21–23). In a postmodern age of pluralism where it is politically incorrect to disparage anyone, the reality of the sinfulness of human beings is a hard reality to accept. While this does not negate the image of God with all the abilities and potential inherent in each person he created, the influence and impact of sin on God's creation cannot be dismissed. This is a fundamental understanding of the Christian faith and is a reality in most human endeavors and relationships.

However, evil is not just a reality within the individual human soul. Baptist pastor William Rauschenbusch distinguishes between individual sinfulness and the sinfulness of the social order. Writing in 1917, he states:

> The individualistic gospel has taught us to see the sinfulness of every human heart and has inspired us with faith in the willingness and power of God to save every soul that comes to him. But it has not given us an adequate understanding of the sinfulness of the social order and its share in the sins of all individuals within it. It has not evoked faith in the will and power of God to redeem the permanent institutions of human society from their inherited guilt of oppression and extortion. Both our sense of sin and our faith in salvation have fallen short of the realities under its teaching.[31]

American theologian, Reinhold Niebuhr distinguishes between individuals and institutions such as banks, churches, governments, corporations and the military. He states that evil is often thought of as an individual trait, whereas institutions may in effect represent a far more insidious evil that is more likely to abuse power and is usually more resistant to change.[32] There are social, legal and economic structures in society that are unjust and inherently evil. These may be in the form of deeply imbedded social attitudes, legal and economic systems, or religious and social practices that discriminate against specific people, groups and individuals. Racism, apartheid, communalism, sexual exploitation, female genital mutilation, political oppression, hyper patriotism, human trafficking, and ethnic cleansing are just some examples of how these socially imbedded attitudes

---

31. Rauschenbausch, *A Theology,* 5.

32. Reinhold Niebuhr, *Moral Man and Immoral Society: A Study of Ethics and Politics* (New York: Scribner's, 1932), *passim.*

surface in everyday life. Often these attitudes are institutionalized through laws, economic policies or institutions that discriminate against particular groups or favor the wealthy, the elite and specific social groups.

Walter Wink, Professor Emeritus at Auburn Theological Seminary, explains that God creates civil, socioeconomic and legal institutions and systems, which Colossians 1:16–17 describes as "thrones or powers or rulers or authorities," for his purposes. These institutions and systems are given by God in order to bless human beings with peace and security and to enable them to prosper, what Wink refers to as the humanizing purposes of God. But Wink points out that "an institution becomes demonic when it abandons its divine vocation – that of a ministry of justice or a ministry of social welfare – for the pursuit of its own idolatrous goals."[33] What God had created for his purposes is warped and corrupted by misuse of power and by greed. German theologian Karl Heim (1874–1958) describes what this "demonization," the perversion of what is good, looks like.

> Nothing that God has created is protected from this demonization. Everything can be seized by it. Therefore there is demonic self-adulation of the ego, the image of God; a demonic sexuality of which man is no longer the master; the demonism of technology; the demonism of power, the demonic degeneration of nationalism. There is demonism of piety, and prayer itself can get lost in demonic convulsion . . . Even the gift of the Holy Spirit can be demonized. The satanic element in the matter lies in this: the demonic power depends entirely on God and what he has created. It possesses nothing that does not come from God. Whatever is demonized and turned against God is always but a distorted image of the glory of God.[34]

Wink then states that any attempt to transform social systems without also addressing the spiritual nature of these institutions and systems is doomed to failure. In any attempt at social transformation, not only the practices and policies of the institutions that are not aligned with the values of God would need to be changed, but the institutions themselves will also need to be redeemed, the underlying values and attitudes prevalent in the institution and system would need to be addressed.

33. Walter Wink, *Engaging the Powers: Discernment and Resistance in a World of Domination* (Minneapolis: Fortress Press, 1992), 72.

34. Quoted in Georg E. Vicedom, *The Mission of God* (St Louis: Concordia, 1965) 19.

The dreams of a better world and of transformation, justice and prosperity are deeply imbedded in human consciousness and are not uniquely Christian. However, it is only the biblical narrative that identifies the cause of injustice and human suffering as rebellion against God. As human beings became separated from the creator God in their desire to be independent, "their thinking became futile and their foolish hearts were darkened" (Rom 1:21). Being cut off from God who is their source of life, their values and attitudes darken and are transformed by greed, power and a self-centered pursuit of what only benefits them and their community.

Therefore the challenge of transformation here on earth before the end of created time is how does one sustain change when individuals and social institutions are warped by sin. The issue is not whether change is possible. The question revolves around the concept of transformation. *Efforts* put into social, economic and political transformation have tremendous value and do benefit many over the short to medium term, but at some point the reality of sin changes relationships and the objectives of transformation. There is tremendous value in ensuring that services like health care, education, water and sanitation are available, that justice issues and social inequality are addressed, and that new laws are enacted to ensure continuity of the changes. The lessons from the history of early Israel is that while they were given the laws and guidelines to ensure social justice and care for the poor, because they did not guard against the temptations of power and greed by the elite, Israel's social contract that was based on justice and equity, and the values that reflected the nature and character of God, was derailed. The 1983 Wheaton Consultation defined transformation as "the change from a condition of human existence contrary to God's purposes to one in which people are able to enjoy fullness of life in harmony with God."[35] While this may be the goal, is it realistic to expect all human beings in a community on this side of eternity to be able to maintain a depth of harmony with God that results in sustainable transformation?

Every NGO and social service organization involved in improving the quality of life of the poor and marginalized has examples of challenges when attempting transformation. A water project that is meant to provide clean water to a community, is undermined by a municipal official, who only agrees to ensure the supply of water if he is bribed. Access to a newly dug well in a village is denied to lower caste members of a community by the upper

---

35. Tizon, *Transformation after Lausanne*, 8–9.

castes. A food security farming project is undermined by a multinational that provides terminator seeds and encourages greater use of pesticides and fertilizers in order to ensure larger sales, none of which the farmers can afford over time. An education project is rendered ineffective because the teachers do not teach properly but encourage the students to come to them for private tuition after school (and having to pay an extra fee) if they want to pass. Funds for a community development project are misappropriated by the project manager and his friends. Large-scale development projects are not immune. A cooperative that is meant to empower a group of farmers is somehow hijacked by specific individuals for personal gain and power. The construction of a road into a remote and isolated area in order to enable access of teachers and doctors into the area, and also enable villagers access to markets in the larger towns, is not only delayed because bribes were not paid to the appropriate officials, but there were also compromises in the quality and quantity of the material used for construction. As a result the road deteriorated very quickly, making access into the area challenging again.

While the desire to "change the world" is worthy of pursuing, the reality is that transformation is complex and often not properly understood. Transformation is not achieved only by a set of activities. Projects and initiatives that do not address underlying values and attitudes have a high probability of failing. Transformation cannot happen just by addressing the physical realities of the world and focusing only on the improvement in the quality of life. For transformation to be sustainable, attitudes, values and ethics that often have their foundations in the spiritual dimensions of life, have to also be addressed. In social change initiatives and project planning, rarely if ever, is the reality and influence of sin factored in – the sin within individual human hearts and the sinfulness inherent in many social, legal and economic structures.

The Theological Basis for Transformation

So does this mean that transformation is not biblical and something that the church and Christians should not be involved in? It is abundantly clear from our study so far that showing charity towards the poor and those on the margins of society is a responsibility that is integral to the faith of individual Christians and of the church community. This is summed up in the exhortation to "do good" (Gal 6:9–10).

It is then wise, whenever possible, that acts of charity are not only an immediate response to a need but are properly planned. This planning involves two dimensions. Where it is possible to identify the root causes of the need, these then should also be addressed so that people do not continue to be dependent on others. In order to do this, the question that needs to be asked is *why* an individual or a community is poor or lacks specific services? A proper analysis needs to be done as to *why* children may be suffering from poor health or are unable to access schooling, *why* farmers are unable to produce more abundant crops, or *why* marginalized families in the urban areas are unable to earn enough to meet their daily needs. Addressing the root causes of poverty makes the acts of charity far more effective and has a long-term impact on the families and communities.

The second dimension deals with ensuring that the changes that are planned to help families and communities are sustainable. It is easy to build a school building, but who pays for the ongoing expenses of teachers, the teaching material, and the maintenance of the building and facilities? It is one thing to introduce a new farming technique that will improve crop yield, but is it financially viable for the farmers over the long term? In establishing microcredit programs, is it possible to ensure that the lending institution is sustainable so that it can pay salaries, do the training of the beneficiaries, and pay the rent and other expenses, while continuing to make fresh loans? There is value in a food bank providing access to food for desperate individuals and families. But are there ways for the families to have sustained food security after their initial needs are met?

This type of planning to move beyond acts of charity is part of development. It ensures that in assisting the poor, the results are sustainable and that the communities do not become dependent on continuing acts of charity and then revert to poverty when the assistance stops. So, sustainable change is an issue of being wise and of good stewardship.

However, it is important to move beyond issues of improving the quality of life of the poor and ensuring justice for the marginalized, and position the discussion of transformation within a larger biblical and theological paradigm. The desire among Christians for transformation is rooted in an understanding that the world is not the way God intended it to be. While all would agree with this, there are significant differences on what should be done, if anything.

God and the Created World

The starting point to understand this theologically is to see how God views the material world that he created and the social systems and cultures he allowed human beings to develop in order that he might bless them. When God created the material world, he pronounced it as "good," meaning that it was pleasing to him.[36] The word "good" also refers to having a practical and economic benefit,[37] implying that what God had created is of value. God not only delights in his creation, which is an esthetic and scientific masterpiece,[38] his creation was meant to be a blessing and of value to all who are part of it. He then gives stewardship of his created world to human beings (Gen 1:28). Psalm 115:16 states, "The earth he has given to humankind." Unfortunately, rebellion and separation from the creator God affects all of creation. Genesis 3:17–18 and Romans 8: 19–21 describe the impact upon the physical world, as death and decay become part of everyday reality. Romans 1:28–31 describes the impact of the rebellion on families and communities as it frays the social fabric of society.

The biblical narrative is one of redemption and restoration. At the end of time, all the nations of the earth will acknowledge Christ as King and live in obedience to his laws (Rev 21:23–26). "On each side of the river stood the Tree of Life . . . and the leaves of the tree are for the healing of the nations. No longer will there be any curse" (Rev 22:2–3). The curse that warped and defaced the physical world starting in Genesis 3:17 will finally be broken. While there will be judgment of those who have perpetuated evil (Rev 20:11–15, 21:8), God will bring comfort, healing and renewal to those who have suffered tragedy, injustice and abuse (Rev 21:3–4).

The world God created, delights him. When, because of rebellion it became dysfunctional, destructive and decaying, he set in motion a plan to redeem the world and restore it to his original purpose. Within this narrative, the challenge is understanding 2 Peter 3:10, "The heavens will disappear with a roar; the elements will be destroyed by fire, and the earth and everything in it will be laid bare." Depending on one's theological perspective there are different understandings of what it means. One perspective is that the physical

---

36. The Hebrew root word is *tub* which means pleasing or good.

37. Harris, Archer, and Waltke, *Theological Workbook*, 345.

38. Victor Alexander (*Genesis*, 2008) translates the word "good" in Genesis 1 as beautiful. This would be in line with Harris, Archer and Waltke, *Theological Workbook*, 345, where beauty is one of the five general areas of meaning of the word.

and material world will be destroyed and those who have been redeemed by Christ will be taken away to a disembodied bliss in another dimension beyond space and time.

However, juxtaposed with 2 Peter 3:10, Revelation 21:1–2 indicates some kind of continuity in the midst of discontinuity. "Then I saw 'a new[39] heaven and a earth' for the first heaven and the first earth had passed away."[40] Some dimensions and aspects of present reality ends and something new starts. However, there is also continuity. Later in Revelation 21:24 and 26 it states that the nations[41] are present in this new earth, as well as some sociopolitical structure because in verse 24 it refers to the leaders of the nations. Revelation 22:2 states that the nations will be healed. The key to understanding this discontinuity and continuity is in understanding what happens when God does destroy the earth as part of his judgment. The only other time he had done that was during the great flood. Earlier in 2 Peter 3:6–7, Peter draws a parallel between Noah's flood and the impending destruction by fire. By doing so Peter is drawing attention to fact that the physical world continued to exist after the flood along with a remnant of humanity and a very basic social

---

39. Ellicott's Commentary states that there are two Greek words that are translated as "new" in English translations of the New Testament. "One of these (*neos*) relates to time; the other (*kainos*) relates to quality. The one would be applied to what had recently come into existence; the other to what showed fresh features. The tomb, for example, in which our Lord's body was laid was new, not in the sense that it had been recently hewn out of the rock, but in the sense that it had never been used before; it may have been long made, but it was one wherein never man was yet laid. To describe it the second word (*kainos*) is used (Matt 27:60 and John 19:41). In the same way, the wine-skins (called "bottles" in our English version) required for the new wine were not necessarily wine-skins only just prepared for service, but they were skins which had not grown withered, but retained their freshness and elasticity. Here, again, the second word (*kainos*) is employed to describe them. Now, it is this latter word which is used throughout this chapter, and, indeed, throughout the book of Revelation. The newness which is pictured is the newness of freshness: the old, decaying, enfeebling, and corrupting elements are swept away." Revelation 21:1, Ellicott's Commentary for English Readers, 2004–2014, accessed 13 September 2014, http://biblehub.com/commentaries/revelation/21-1.htm.

40. "The theological question as to whether the old world will pass away in such a manner, that from it, as a seed, the new will arise, or whether an absolutely new creation, after the entire annihilation of the old world, be referred to, is indeed to be decided least of all from the Apocalyptic description; yet this description is not opposed to the former view, which, according to Scripture, is more probable than the latter." "Revelation 21:1," Meyers New Testament Commentary, 2004–2014, accessed 13 September 2014, http://biblehub.com/commentaries/revelation/21-1.htm.

41. The concept of nation that is used in the New Testament derives from the Greek word *ethnos*, which has been variously translated as tribe, people group, political nations of the world, and even refers to the Gentiles and pagans. Paul even uses the term to refer to Gentile Christians. "Ethnos," The NAS New Testament Greek Lexicon, accessed 31 August 2014, http://www.biblestudytools.com/lexicons/greek/nas/ethnos.html.

order – the family. The purpose of the judgment of God is not destruction but purification and restoration. The Prophet Malachi (3:2–3) refers to God's judgment at the end of time as a refiner's fire. Jesus himself referred to "the renewal of all things, when the Son of Man sits on his glorious throne" (Matt 19:28).

In trying to understand the roots of why many Christian see the material world as being evil and therefore to be despised, N. T. Wright points to the influence in many streams of theology of Plato's dualistic understanding of reality, which separates the physical from the spiritual. "The dualist supposes that, to escape evil, one must escape the physical, created universe."[42]

In contrast, Romans 8:19–21 states that God's creation is not condemned for destruction but will be liberated. "For the creation waits in eager expectation for the children of God to be revealed. For the creation was subjected to frustration, not by its own choice, but by the will of the one who subjected it, in hope that the creation itself will be liberated from its bondage to decay and brought into the freedom and glory of the children of God." Wright concludes, "Matter is to be redeemed."[43] British theologian, theoretical physicist and Anglican priest, John Polkinghorne provides perspective when he writes: "Where will this new 'matter' of this new world come from? I suppose that it will come from the transformed matter of this present world, for God cares for all of his creation, and he must have a destiny for the universe beyond its death, just as he has a destiny for us beyond ours."[44]

God's ultimate affirmation of the physical world is the incarnation. He identifies himself as Immanuel (God who is with us) not in some vague spiritual sense, but by physically becoming part of his creation. His identification with his creation is total. John 3:16 states, "For God so loved the world that he gave his one and only Son, that whoever believes in him shall not perish but have eternal life." The Greek word for world in this passage is *kosmos*, which literally means an ordered system like creation.[45] German

---

42. N. T Wright and M. Borg, *The Meaning of Jesus* (London: SPCK, 1999), 199.

43. N. T. Wright, *Surprised by Hope* (London: SPCK, 2007), 222.

44. J. Polkinghorne, *Serious Talk, Science and Religion in Dialogue* (Valley Forge: Trinity Press International, 1995), 108.

45. According to the Holman Bible Dictionary, in the New Testament three words are translated as "world": *oikoumene* (15 times, "the inhabited earth"), *aion* (over 30 times, similar to the Hebrew *olam* meaning "long duration," "age," or "world"), and *kosmos* (188 times). However, the word "world" has a number of nuances in the way it is used. "1) The whole created order. Paul before the Areopagus in Athens spoke of 'the God who made the world and everything in it' (Acts 17:24 NIV). 2) The earth and its inhabitants. John 1:9 refers

theologian Wolfhart Pannenberg stated, "God didn't have to create the world. But after he decided to create the world, he was bound to that decision. Given the fact that the created world exists, God's divine nature is bound up with his kingdom over this world."[46] God's delight is not just human beings, who are the pinnacle of creation, but all that he has created. Jesus places his love for human beings and their salvation and restoration to him within the context of his love for all that he has created.

God then reaffirms his commitment to his creation through the cross at Golgotha. Douglas John Hall writes:

> It will not – cannot – opt for a doctrine of redemption, however theologically or spiritually appealing, that in effect bypasses or contradicts the biblical affirmation of creation. What God loves and is determined to save is not an abstraction and not a "savable" *part* of the whole, but the real world in all its inseparableness and interrelatedness. God is as firmly committed to the life of this world as that cross was planted in the ground at Golgotha, that is, (symbolically) at the very center of death's apparent sovereignty.[47]

The biblical narrative has never been one of complete total destruction. Even when God judges, because he is the Creator and giver of life, he redeems and restores. In Genesis 3 he judged Adam and Eve and cursed the earth, yet they become the very material with which he started the process of redemption and restoration of his original creation. *This then is the mission of God, not only the redemption and salvation of human beings, but of all that he has created. Thus will the kingdom of God have come as he reaffirms his authority over all of creation.* Hall highlights how God sees his creation. "[It] is not that God thinks humankind so wretched that it deserves death and hell, but that God thinks humankind and the whole creation so good, so beautiful, so precious in its intention and its potentiality, that its actualization, its fulfillment, its redemption is worth dying for."[48]

---

to 'the true light which enlightens everyone was coming into the world' (NRSV). 3) The arena of human activity. This especially pertains to wealth and material goods. 'The cares of this world' can choke out the word (Mark 4:19)." "World, The," Holman Bible Dictionary, 1991. http://www.studylight.org/dictionaries/hbd/view.cgi?n=6478. Accessed 7 September 2014.

46. Thomas Jay Oord, "Pannenberg Dies; An Interview," posted on 8 September 2014, accessed 13 September 2014, http://thomasjayoord.com/index.php/blog/archives/pannenberg_dies_an_interview/

47. Hall, *The Cross, 36.*

48. Ibid., 24.

The world – the physical, social and cultural – is the context within which God chose to bless human beings. It is his intention to redeem all three as he redeems human beings. His plan never changed. As human beings partner with God in his mission, he asks them to be stewards of what he has created. Community development and social responsibility are simply outworkings of that stewardship.

The Continuity of Creation

If the incarnation is God's affirmation of the world he created, the resurrection is God's guarantee of the continuity of his creation after created time ends. Having seen that God values the created world and not only human beings, the second theological issue to consider, is the relationship between the world as we know it and reality beyond time. Is the way we live here on earth and what we do reflected in any way in the kingdom when it is revealed in all its fullness beyond time, or is there a total disconnect between the two?

There can only be speculation as to what happens when created time ends and this material world transitions into eternity. Various theological streams have different explanations about what happens on this side of created time and its relationship with eternity. However, the only definitive instance the world has of this transition is the resurrection of Christ. Polkinghorne explains that it is only the resurrection of Jesus Christ that explains the relationship between the world in created time and the new world beyond time. He writes, "That is why the empty tomb is so important. Jesus' risen body is the transmuted and glorified form of his dead body. This tells us that in Christ there is destiny for matter as well as for humanity. In fact, our destinies belong together, precisely because humans are embodied beings."[49]

Neo-Orthodox theologians, while acknowledging the centrality of Christ in the redemption narrative, do not believe in the bodily (physical) resurrection of Christ. Swiss theologian Emil Brunner wrote:

> Emphasis upon the empty tomb led to the medieval conception
> of the "resurrection of the body," with its drama of the Last Day,
> and the opening of the graves . . . Resurrection of the body, yes:
> Resurrection of the *flesh*, no! The "Resurrection of the body" does
> not mean the identity of the resurrection body with the material
> (although transformed) body of the flesh; but the resurrection of

---

49. Polkinghorne, *Serious Talk*, 108.

the body means the continuity of the individual personality on this side, and on that, of death.[50]

So according to Brunner there is a disconnect between the material reality in created time and the reality of eternity. The material world that God created ceases to exist. It is this understanding that undergirds some of Neo-Orthodoxy thinking that there is no need for the resurrection to complete redemption. Brunner states that Jesus' victory "is connected not so much with the fact of Easter as with the fact of Good Friday . . . for there the Incarnation of the Son of God – paradoxically – reached its climax."[51]

Robert Duncan Culver in his "Big Book," *Systematic Theology: Biblical and Historical* summarizes the historical theological perspective of the resurrection since the early church. He writes:

> Jesus came forth from the grave in the same body laid in the grave. The incarnation . . . of the Son of God that began at the conception of Jesus is permanent. An incarnation without flesh is a contradiction of terms. That is why the grave is empty. That body was and is a permanent part of the Lord's human nature, in which he ascended to heaven and shall return . . . The ancient creeds made a special point (perhaps in response to Gnostic and Manichean heresies already prevalent) that his was a resurrection of "the flesh" or "in the same body" (in parallel with "suffered in the flesh; and rose again").[52]

The physical resurrection of Christ then is a preview of what God intends to do with all of his creation. 1 Corinthians 15:53–54 states, "For the perishable must clothe itself with the imperishable, and the mortal with immortality. When the perishable has been clothed with the imperishable, and the mortal with immortality, then the saying that is written will come true: 'Death has been swallowed up in victory.'" This is the transformation that God intends to do – to take what is mortal and perishable and clothe them with immortality so that they would be imperishable and free from death and decay. While the passage in Corinthians refers specifically to human beings, it is his model for all that he has created. The apostle Paul writing to the Colossian Christians,

---

50. Emil Brunner, *The Christian Doctrine of Creation and Redemption, Dogmatics II* (Philadelphia: Westminster Press, 1952), 372.

51. Ibid., 372.

52. Robert Duncan Culver, *Systematic Theology: Biblical and Historical* (Fearn, Scotland: Christian Focus Publications, 2005), 608.

parts the curtain of time and provides a glimpse of the magnificence of God's plan to reconcile to himself through the sacrifice of Christ everything that has been fragmented and separated from him, so that one day Christ will reign over all of creation for eternity.

> The Son is the image of the invisible God, the firstborn over all creation. For in him all things were created: things in heaven and on earth, visible and invisible, whether thrones or powers or rulers or authorities; all things have been created through him and for him. He is before all things, and in him all things hold together. And he is the head of the body, the church; he is the beginning and the firstborn from among the dead, so that in everything he might have the supremacy. For God was pleased to have all his fullness dwell in him, and through him to reconcile to himself all things, whether things on earth or things in heaven, by making peace through his blood, shed on the cross. (Col 1:15–21)

God's objective is to restore and bring wholeness to the world he had created and not to destroy it and start all over again and create something new from scratch. So there is continuity between this world limited by time and space, and eternity. What we do and how we live in created time has eternal consequences. Our efforts don't just end with death. It is not just about moral living, but is also about stewardship of what God created physically, of what he decreed about social relationships, and of what he enabled human beings to develop culturally. Ron Sider describes the resurrection as the key to understanding why striving for transformation and justice on this side of eternity is not a futile effort that will end when created time and space and the world as we know it ends.

> There is continuity and discontinuity between our work now and the coming kingdom, just as there was between Jesus of Nazareth and the risen Christ. Jesus of Nazareth was raised from the dead. There is discontinuity between the social justice we create now and the final kingdom. But there is continuity. This groaning creation will be restored. The Tree of Life is for the healing of the nations, purged from sin and evil. Working for peace and justice is not based on naïve thinking that there will be transformation – but with an understanding of where history is going. The word transformation is still valid for changes in the here and now.

There will be times when sin and evil will reign while at other times there will be season of peace and justice.[53]

It is because of the challenges of sin and evil, Scriptures exhorts us to "not become weary in doing good, for at the proper time we will reap a harvest if we do not give up." (Gal 6:9) and in 1 Peter 4:19, "So then, those who suffer according to God's will should commit themselves to their faithful Creator and continue to do good." N. T. Wright states that "to do good" was a phrase that was in regular use in Paul's world referring to financial contributions in civic and community life.[54] The acts of goodness that Paul encouraged were focused on the poor and social problems.

Transformation Is a Biblical Concept

So transformation is a valid biblical concept. *But it is God who transforms and he invites us to partner with him.* God is already in the process of redeeming human beings and creation, and will transform all when created time melds into eternity. On this side of eternity, Christians are urged to "do good to all people" (Gal 6:10) and be faithful stewards of the world that God has created (Gen 1:28). However, among Christian development professionals, the power of God is often functionally not part of their consciousness in planning social change. The reality is that development and efforts at transformation are anthropocentric, where human beings see themselves central and the main actors of social change. The focus is on mobilizing the community, on getting the community assessment and project designs right, and on implementing properly, while ensuring participation, local ownership and sustainability. The assumption is that if this is done effectively, transformation will occur. If it does not, then the planning or the process was flawed. What is ignored is that God is the author of history and is involved not only in the rise and fall of nations, but is present in local communities seeking ways to accomplish his will and establish his kingdom. Our prayers, rather than being "Lord bless the work of our hands," should be, "Lord, where and how are you already working, and how do you want us to be involved."

The principle of the centrality of God in any kind of ministry is stated in 1 Corinthians 3:6, "I planted, Apollos watered, but God was causing the

53. Ron Sider, Lecture, Acadia Divinity College, Acadia University, Wolfville, NS, 27 May 2013.

54. N. T. Wright, *Paul for Everyone: Galatians and Thessalonians* (London: SPCK, 2002) 79.

growth." It is not that human effort is of no value, as Paul and Apollos were both involved using their gifts within their calling. God requires us to be agents of change, but it is God who transforms. As co-laborers with God in his mission, Christians work for change and social justice so that human beings can enjoy the blessings of God in this life. Yet this needs to be done with a deep and constant awareness that evil is real, that human beings are sinful and that sin permeates and warps social, economic and political structures.

While change is possible, evil pushed back, and the quality of the life improved, *complete, lasting* and *sustainable* social transformation on this side of eternity will never be a reality, because we live in the in-between times where evil and the kingdom of God coexist in this world. Jesus described it as the wheat and tares growing side by side till the end of time (Matt 13:2–30). The two World Wars, the ongoing brutality of conflicts using the latest advances in technology, the genocides and ethnic cleansings, the perverseness of human trafficking, and the continuing reality of gross injustice have destroyed any illusions of the continual improvement of the world in spite of the advances in the quality of life for many. Even in the Scandinavian countries that enjoy the highest quality of life and peace, there are dark under currents of racism and discrimination. It is disconcerting to see a new generation of Christians naively believe that this world can be transformed on this side of eternity, as it shows a lack of understanding of the concept of sin and how insidious, corrosive and destructive evil is. They are unaware of the frustrations and disillusionment that are involved, nor do they know how to address the issues of sin imbedded in society or how to confront evil without it destroying them in turn.

There is a major difference between believing that one can transform the world, and being a partner with God in the transformation that he is bringing about. Ron Sider provides perspective and identifies what the true motivation should be when he stated (as quoted above), "Working for peace and justice is not based on naïve thinking that there will be transformation – but with an understanding of where history is going."

There are some who equate the biblical concept *shalom* from the Old Testament with idea of transformation; that transformation of the world is the *shalom* that God promised, and is therefore what we as the people of God should strive for. John Stott cautions against this. While the Old Testament described the concept to include political and material well-being, this was limited to ancient Israel. In the New Testament the peace that is promised is reconciliation and fellowship with God through Jesus Christ and reconciliation with each other (Eph 2: 13–22). There are material blessings to being a child of God, but the New Testament is also full of verses referring to the people of God suffering in this life. Stott writes about *shalom*:

> Moreover, he does not bestow it on all men but on those who belong to him, to his redeemed community. So *shalom* is the blessing the Messiah brings to his people. The new creation and the new humanity are to be seen in those who are in Christ (2 Cor 5:17) . . . In many ways we see the righteousness of the kingdom, as it were, "spilling over" into segments of the world and thus to some extent blurring the frontiers between the two.[55]

In the midst of the discussion on social transformation, there is a lesson from the early missionaries that should not be forgotten. As D. Preman Niles pointed out, they were also social reformers. But what was central in what they did, was that they "affirmed the worth and dignity of every person."[56] The individual is important. Whether transformation takes place or not, affirming the worth and dignity of each individual is at the core of any act of charity, any ministry that is done, or any project that is implemented. By affirming the worth and dignity of the poor, the broken and the marginalized, they get a glimpse of the character of God. They begin to understand how God sees them – that they are people of tremendous value. This then is the starting point of bearing witness to who God is.

---

55. John Stott, *Christian Mission in the Modern World* (Downers Grove: IVP Books, 2008), 31.
56. Niles, *From East and West*, 77.

9

Transformation or Witness: Being a Witness

The miracles and good works of Jesus are often referred to as signs that the kingdom of God had come. When John the Baptist, sitting in jail awaiting his execution, wondered if Jesus was really the long awaited Messiah, Jesus sent word back saying in Luke 7:22, "Go back and report to John what you have seen and heard: The blind receive sight, the lame walk, those who have leprosy are cleansed, the deaf hear, the dead are raised, and the good news is proclaimed to the poor." Earlier, at the start of his ministry, Jesus had proclaimed in Luke 4:18, "he has anointed me to proclaim good news to the poor. He has sent me to proclaim freedom for the prisoners and recovery of sight for the blind, to set the oppressed free." These were the signs that he was the deliverer sent from God.

Jesus demonstrated that he is King and had authority over disease, illnesses and over all of creation. He had the power to forgive sin and break the bondages that warp human beings. Wherever he was allowed to exert his authority, there was life, healing and justice. Jesus himself explained this in John 10:10, "The thief comes only to steal and kill and destroy; I have come that they may have life, and have it to the full." The two messengers from John the Baptist were witnesses of what Jesus had done and they were sent back to John to tell him about it.

The critics of Christians involved in community development, social justice issues, and ministries of healing, education and empowerment of the poor, state that the miracles, healings and the good works of Jesus were signs that he was the Messiah and not examples for us to emulate. Somehow they miss the point. Jesus was demonstrating what the kingdom of God is like, what the world would be when God reigns and exerts his authority in all areas of life. Jesus through his actions was a prophetic witness, pointing to the day when, "'he will wipe every tear from their eyes. There will be no more death' or mourning or crying or pain, for the old order of things has passed away." (Rev 21:4). *This* is the ministry that the people of God, the church, are called to. Karl Barth describes the mission of the church. "To set up in the world a new sign which is radically dissimilar to [the world's] own manner and which contradicts it in a way which is full of promise."[1] As children no longer die from polluted water, as families are able to enjoy food security, as there is social and economic justice, as human beings are not trafficked but live secure in their own homes, and as peace and reconciliation take place, the reality of the authority and the reign of God is demonstrated in each and every one of those situations, because only he is the source of all life. It is through these experiences that they can then be introduced to the giver of life.

Sometimes the distinction is made between the *miraculous* works of Christ and the more mundane work of community development and ensuring social justice – that the two are not the same. The method and the means are often confused with the result. The result that God always intends is that he wants to give life and ensure justice. He uses a variety of means to do that. Sometimes he may choose the dramatic to demonstrate his power very visibly and miraculously and bring healing or change. At other times he chooses to work through the wisdom, skills, technology and abilities that he has given human beings to bring good to others and bless people. Romans 5:20 states, "But where sin increased, grace increased all the more." As human beings' ability to wreck destruction and exploit evil has increased, God in his grace has given humans the ability to cope with the consequences of their action. For example, the discovery of morphine in the early 1800s enabled soldiers to cope with their horrific injuries during the American Civil War and then in World War I. The discovery of penicillin by accident in 1928, along with morphine and sulfa drugs enabled doctors to provide some comfort during the murderous killings of World War II. Proverbs 2:6 (CEV) states, "All wisdom comes from the Lord, and so do common sense and understanding." It is this wisdom from God that enables human beings to find solutions to world hunger, grinding poverty, diseases that kill and maim, and social problems. They are as much part of the continuing work of Christ in this world as were his miraculous deeds.

---

1. Karl Barth and Thomas Forsyth Torrance, *Church Dogmatics: The Doctrine of Reconciliation, Volume 4, Part 3.2: Jesus Christ, the True Witness* (New York: T&T Clark International, 2004), 779.

Being a Witness

Being involved in addressing social issues is not only an act of compassion or about transformation, but is also about being a prophetic witness to the kingdom of God. For Jesus, the good news was that the kingdom had finally come (Mark 1:14), even if it was not manifested in all its fullness yet. The image he uses is of a seed being planted which then grows into a fully mature tree and becoming a blessing (Matt13:31). He then states, "And this good news of the kingdom will be proclaimed throughout the world, as a testimony to all the nations" (Matt 24:14). The proclamation of the gospel is not just an individualized message about the forgiveness of personal sins, but is much larger and more profound, reflecting the magnificence, greatness and wisdom of God. It is that the kingdom of God has come and that God is bringing all of creation back under his authority and one day it will be revealed, "The kingdom of the world has become the kingdom of our Lord and of his Messiah, and he will reign for ever and ever" (Rev 11:15). The great mysteries of God's will and his intentions have now been revealed. "With all wisdom and understanding, he made known to us the mystery of his will according to his good pleasure, which he purposed in Christ, to be put into effect when the times reach their fulfillment – to bring unity to all things in heaven and on earth under Christ" (Eph 1:8–10). God is reaffirming his authority over all creation and restoring his kingdom.

The forgiveness of personal sin is only the first step that enables individuals to enter the kingdom of God. The repentance that is required to enter the kingdom of God is not only confession of sin, but also understanding the depth and extent of our rebellion. Repentance then, is about turning back and acknowledging that Christ is King and learning to live under his authority. The good news is about the kingdom of God and a King who welcomes us back. German missiologist Paul Loffler wrote, "The beginning of the kingdom through Christ's entry into the human history is the main context of conversion in the New Testament."[2] Therefore talking about conversion without reference to God's kingdom, robs the full meaning of what conversion is all about.

Various dictionaries define a "witness" as someone who having been present, and therefore having seen, heard or experienced, can give a first hand

---

2. Paul Loffler, "Conversion in an Ecumenical Context," *The Ecumenical Review* 19, no. 3 (1967): 257.

account.[3] The Apostle John gives various accounts of this. In John 1:35–42, Andrew is invited by Jesus to come and spend a day with him. His encounter with the living Christ must have been so profound that he goes to find his brother Simon (Peter) to tell him who Christ is. Later in chapter 4 the Apostle John writes about the Samaritan woman at the well and her transforming encounter with Christ. In verse 39, John records, "Many of the Samaritans from the town believed in him because of the woman's testimony." In chapter 5 when Jesus heals the crippled man at the pool of Bethesda, in verse 15 John writes, "The man went away and told the Jewish leaders that it was Jesus who had made him well," even though he could not explain anything else beyond that. John then in his old age writes, "That which was from the beginning, which we have heard, which we have seen with our eyes, which we have looked at and our hands have touched – this we proclaim concerning the Word of life . . . We proclaim what we have seen and heard" (1 John 1:1, 3).

This understanding permeates the Old Testament also. The Psalms connect the personal experience of God and the proclamation of what they have experienced. "The Lord lives! Praise be to my Rock! Exalted be God my Savior! He is the God who avenges me, who subdues nations under my feet, who saves me from my enemies. You exalted me above my foes; from violent people you rescued me. Therefore I will praise you, Lord among the nations; I will sing the praises of your name" (Ps 18:46–49). Having experienced God's power, deliverance, mercy and compassion, David is a witness of who God is and what he is able to do. This then is the model of being a witness.

Being a witness is *not just* about proclaiming a biblical and theological truth about what God has done, but is *also* about sharing the experience of the reality of the living God who has revealed himself through Christ. During the Syrian crisis, as many Arab pastors and their teams were helping those who had lost their homes and were barely surviving, they would ask the families, most of whom were Muslim, whether they could pray for them. One pastor recounts that the reaction of most of the families was one of astonishment. Would God actually hear them if they prayed? These were devout Muslim families who prayed regularly. Yet they were never sure that God actually heard them. The pastor said that he would assure them that God

---

3. The Greek word is *martus*, meaning a witness in both a historical and legal sense. In the New Testament the word has referred to the original (eye) witnesses, the disciples, and to the post resurrection witnesses of Christ. The word as a noun has been used to refer to martyrs. Finally it is used to refer to those who have experienced redemption through Christ and then bear witness to others of their experience.

would hear them if they approached him and prayed in the Name of Jesus. With their permission, as he prayed for them, the families would invariably be overwhelmed, unable to believe that God actually cared what happened to them and would hear their prayers and the horrors of their pain.

What they were experiencing was what Martin Buber, the Jewish philosopher, referred to as the "I and Thou encounter." In such an encounter with the Eternal Thou (not an object or a philosophical system but a Person), what they entered into was a relationship where God became real and gave meaning to their existence.[4] The pastor's witnessing was very simple. Rather than providing statements about who God is and what he has done in Christ, which many Muslims have a hard time accepting, he simply asked them to come and see who God is and what he is able to do. As they encountered God, they were then much more open to hearing about Christ.

Unfortunately, witnessing has been reduced to a verbal proclamation of truth, and believing required only giving mental assent to the truth. The loss of understanding of what *Immanuel* – God with us – means, is reducing the Christian faith to merely an mental acknowledgement of the truth about God as summarized in the creeds and to a set of ethical teachings. Ron Sider emphasizes, "The ethical teachings of Jesus are not the core of the Christian faith. At the center of the Christian faith is an I-Thou encounter with the living God and experiencing forgiveness of sins and the empowering to live a transformed life."[5] The ethical teachings flow out of the transforming I-Thou encounter with God revealed in Christ. It is only then can they be lived out as they were intended.

The church's responsibility, as part of the mission of God, is the proclamation of the King and his kingdom, that his reign will one day be established here on earth. The seemingly invisible kingdom is revealed in Christ and is made real to people through "doing good" – the works of compassion, striving for justice, planning for change and community development, providing relief in disasters. The danger of focusing only on the kingdom of God is that Christianity is reduced to a set of ethical teachings and actions, which is no different than any other religion or philosophy. It is like focusing on the laws and values of the kingdom without every acknowledging that there is a king. Proclaiming the King is about introducing them to Christ and explaining our relationship with him. Focusing only on the King without

---

4. Martin Buber, *I and Thou* (New York: Scribner, 1958).
5. Sider, Lecture, 2013.

recognizing his kingdom deprives human beings from experiencing the richness of life and blessings that God has provided through all of his creation.

Bearing Witness

The followers of Christ are witnesses of God's work in their midst. As they submit to the authority of Christ by following the lead of the Holy Spirit and learning obedience to the Word of God, they see relationships reconciled, answers to prayer, addictions broken, experience protection, and have wisdom in perplexing circumstances. They get to know the God of all comfort and experience the comfort of God in the midst of tragedies and unexplainable evil. They know the reality of David's experience in Psalm 23:4, "Even though I walk through the darkest valley, I will fear no evil, for you are with me; your rod and your staff, they comfort me." As their bodies grow old or as disease ravages who they are, rather than growing bitter and angry, they experience the presence and strength of God in ways that cannot be explained. Even in the midst of the pain and confusion of unanswered prayer, there is a presence that assures them of the future. Being a witness means proclaiming this God that they experience in their midst – the God who now dwells with them.

Large segments of the church today are afraid to speak of the experience of the reality of God revealed in Christ. There is a very deep fear that supposedly subjective experiences will detract from what the truth of God's salvation is and thus lead to wrong theology. *There are enough examples to justify the fears.* However, the Christian faith is not just about believing propositional truths and having correct theology, but is also about transformed lives. This includes our feelings and emotions, which are as much part of who we are as created by God, and are not secondary to our intellect.[6] The purpose then of faith and theology is to help us understand and make sense of what we experience. Douglas John Hall writes. "Yet the whole purpose of faith is to

---

6. The word "mind" is often thought to refer only to thoughts and intellect. There is a common perception within Christian circles that a transformation of one's thoughts will transform the total being. This is Rational Emotive Therapy rather than a biblical concept. The Greek word for "mind" (as in Rom 12:1–2) is *nous*. The word is defined as "the mind, comprising alike the faculties of perceiving and understanding and those of feeling, judging, determining, the intellectual faculty, the understanding reason in the narrower sense, as the capacity for spiritual truth, the higher powers of the soul, the faculty of perceiving divine things, of recognizing goodness and of hating evil, the power of considering and judging soberly, calmly and impartially, a particular mode of thinking and judging, i.e. thoughts, feelings, purposes, desires." "Nous," The NAS New Testament Greek Lexicon, 1999, accessed 15 September 2014, http://www.biblestudytools.com/lexicons/greek/nas/nous.html.

free us for life – for full and actual living – and to illumine the meaning of what occurs to us, *not* to insulate us from all the confusing and negating dimensions of our finitude, but to give us the courage to enter more deeply into the unknown that is around us and within us."[7]

There is another dimension of being a witness. The experience of the reality of God is not just at the personal level. A local community of faith is a demonstration and a visible example of what the kingdom of God looks like – of what a community could be if Christ were allowed to reign. It is about "making the invisible kingdom visible."[8] As Karl Barth mentioned, it is a sign that provides an alternative example of what the world could be. The Old Testament provides glimpses and paints word pictures of a world where God reigns and his values permeate every aspect of society. The Laws of Israel highlighted his character. God values justice, compassion and care for the poor, the weak, the vulnerable and the outsider who did not belong. His laws made provision for the widows, the fatherless, the slaves, the sojourners and "resident aliens," the non-Israelites under Israel's protection – all who were poor and vulnerable.[9] In the New Testament, Jesus' healings, providing for the hungry, affirming those who lived on the margins of society, and condemning injustice were all prophetic acts pointing to what his kingdom is like. In his last discourse to the disciples, Jesus identifies love for each other as *the defining mark* of being his followers. "By this everyone will know that you are my disciples, if you love one another" (John 13:35). Jesus is not referring to having good feelings towards other Christians, but rather the practical demonstrations of love by caring for one another, being reconciled in relationships, and having compassion for those within the community who are broken and living on the margins.

What God desires to see in his kingdom is not just that immediate needs are taken care of, but that there is also social change. The "new heaven and the new earth" in Isaiah 65:17–25 are echoes of Revelation 21:1 and describes a world where God reigns. The passages point prophetically to a world where there would be no sorrow, weeping and crying because there would be no

---

7. Hall, *The Cross*, 28.

8. Skye Jethani, "Making the Invisble Kingdom Visible (part 1)," *Christianity Today*, 6 May 2013, accessed 13 May 2013, http://www.outofur.com/archives/2013/05/making_the_invi. html?utm_source=parse&utm_medium=Newsletter&utm_term=12502841&utm_content=174724452&utm_campaign=2013.

9. Deut 10:19; Lev 19:10, 23:22, 25:35–43; Deut 24:19–21; Num 35:15; Exod 22:22–24; Deut 10:18; 24:17–21.

injustice that robs people of their possession, homes, livelihood, and families. There would be neither child mortality nor premature deaths, and balance would be restored in the ecological system.

Therefore efforts at social change and transformation by the people of God are acts of prophetic witness that point to what the kingdom of God is like. But prophetic acts and symbols have little value unless they are explained. Their meaning needs to be understood. The unstated assumption among most Christian development professionals is that somehow their acts of compassions will be understood as reflecting their faith in Christ without having to explain anything. A commonly used quote attributed to St Francis of Assisi is, "Preach the gospel at all times. Use words if necessary." Unfortunately, there is no record by his disciples or his early biographers of St Francis having ever said this. The actual statement in chapter 17 of the Rule of 1221, 1–4 of his monastic order is, "Let none of the brothers preach contrary to the form and institution of the holy Roman Church, and unless this has been conceded to him by his minister . . . Nevertheless, let all the brothers preach by their works."[10] The rules in chapter 17 are guidelines about preaching and the exhortation is for there to be integrity between what the Friars preach and their lives.

At other times 1 Peter 3:15 is quoted. "But in your hearts revere Christ as Lord. Always be prepared to give an answer to everyone who asks you to give the reason for the hope that you have." The context of Peter's statement is his teaching on how to live in a world where there is opposition to Christians, persecution and suffering, and yet in the midst of that being a people who are compassionate and reaching out to those who are broken and living on the margins – the meaning of "doing good" (vs. 11). The next verse clarifies that in such a context, when one is maligned for being loving, sympathetic, compassionate and humble, one can then respond as to why they act the way they do. "But do this with gentleness and respect, keeping a clear conscience, so that those who speak maliciously against your good behavior in Christ may be ashamed of their slander." This verse does not speak about "doing good" and then hoping that someone will ask why I do what I do. Most beneficiaries of assistance are only too glad to receive the help and are not bothered about my motives. Research on humanitarian assistance shows that beneficiaries are often unable to differentiate between the various agencies that provide aid

---

10. St Francis of Assisi, *The Writings of St. Francis of Assisi,* translated by Father Paschal Robinson (1905) (Santa Cruz: Evinity Publishing Inc., 2009), 50.

in a disaster context.[11] What this means is that most beneficiaries of assistance would not necessarily understand the difference between what Christians do as an outcome of their faith in Christ, and what secular NGOs like Save the Children and Doctors without Borders (MSF) do.

Bearing witness in such a context does not necessarily mean sharing a gospel illustration, or telling them *at this point* that they are sinners who need forgiveness and need to be reconciled to God. They need to understand the larger narrative – that the way the world is now, is not what God created it to be or intends it to be. The world where God's reign is one of compassion for the poor and the broken, where God hates evil and injustice and is heartbroken when people are killed and driven from their homes, where God is concerned ("worries") that children not die from polluted water or malnutrition. As we explain that our acts of compassion reflect the reality of God's kingdom and display the character of God, there may be an appropriate time to introduce them to the King and how to enter his kingdom. The basic principle is stated in Colossians 3:17, "And whatever you do, whether in word or deed, do it all in the name of the Lord Jesus, giving thanks to God the Father through him." Truth is better explained and understood as relationships are built. However, none of these are guidelines or templates on when or how to share the gospel, as God often works in human hearts in ways that we don't understand or can plan for.

Jesus would often use the work he was doing and his miracles to explain profound spiritual truths. In doing so he would connect the physical, temporal world with eternal reality and the things of God. In John chapter 6 he feeds the five thousand and then to those who were wanting to know more he speaks about "food that endures to eternal life" (6:27), and then identifies himself as the Living Bread (6:51). In chapter 9, after healing the man who was born blind, Jesus reveals his identity as the Son of Man. In chapter 11 after he raises Lazarus from the dead, Jesus identifies himself as the resurrection and the life (11:25). In chapters 13 and 14, when his disciples experienced severe discouragement about what was about to happen, Jesus gives them hope for the future by identifying himself as the way, the truth and the life (14:6). At all other times, the healings and miracles he did were while he was teaching or on occasions where people clearly knew who he was. There was never a distinction between providing help, ministering to needs,

---

11. Samir Elhawary and M. M. M. Aheeyar, *Beneficiary Perceptions of Corruption in Humanitarian Assistance: A Sri Lanka Case Study, HPG Working Paper* (London: Overseas Development Institute, August 2008), *passim*.

and teaching spiritual truths, neither was there any conditionality in anything that he offered.

The early church understood this also. In Acts 3, when Peter heals a lame beggar, he does it in the name and power of Jesus Christ of Nazareth (3:6). He clearly identifies to the beggar and to those around him where the power for healing was from, so that there was no doubt that this was not just an act of compassion, but that Christ wanted his healing and wholeness. In Acts 2, Luke describes how the early community of the followers of Christ lived. They focused on the teaching of the apostles, on fellowship, prayer, and celebrating communion. It is in this context, where everyone was aware of the centrality of Christ that the apostles performed many wonders and miracles (2:43). The description does not end here. Luke describes how they were generous with their wealth and material possessions and gave "to anyone who had a need" (2:25). This is a remarkable statement, because as various biblical researchers have pointed out that about 80–85 percent of the population of Palestine either lived near the poverty line or below it.[12] This percentage would have been reflected in the early church in Palestine. The charity, compassion and assistance were clearly identified with being part of what it meant to follow Christ. The spiritual disciplines, the celebrations and worship as a community, and acts of charity and compassion were not in separate compartments, but were an integral part of communal life. Each one by itself is somewhat diminished; but taken together, they have an impact. Acts 2:47 describes this: "And the Lord added to their number daily those who were being saved."

John Howard Yoder, the Mennonite theologian and ethicist, wrote about what the community of Christ followers would look like:

> When he called his society together, Jesus gave its members a new way of life to live. He gave them a new ways to deal with offenders – by forgiving them. He gave them a new way to deal with violence – by suffering. He gave them a new way to deal with money – by sharing it. He gave them a new way to deal with the problems of leadership – by drawing upon the gift of every member even the most humble. He gave them a new way to deal with a corrupt society – by building a new order, not smashing the old. He gave them a new pattern of relationships between man and woman, between parent and child, between master and

---

12. Harland, "The Economy," 515.

slave, in which was made concrete a radical new vision of what it means to be a human person.[13]

It is this radical community, the kingdom of God, that the followers of Christ are witnesses of. By their lives together, they not only make the invisible kingdom visible, but they also speak about the King who reigns. David Bosch writes, "Those who know that God will one day wipe away all tears will not accept with resignation the tears of those who suffer and are oppressed *now*. Anyone who knows that one day there will be no more disease can and must actively anticipate the conquest of disease in individuals and society *now*. And anyone who believes the enemy of God and humans will be vanquished will already oppose him *now* in his machinations in family and society. For all of this has to do with *salvation*."[14] Being a prophetic witness means living and working in the present in the light of the future. It involves proclaiming salvation in both deeds and words that point to the reality of kingdom of God, which George Elton Ladd described as the *presence of the future*.[15]

The Challenge of Bearing Witness

There are a number of challenges in bearing witness to the work of God in this world and the reality of his kingdom. In combining the proclamation of the kingdom of God and the King in word and deed, the often-heard accusation is that it creates "rice Christians"[16] or that it manipulates people with assistance so that they would become Christians or members of a specific church. There are a number of issues involved.

Conditionality and the Misuse of Power

The first is that there should be *no conditionality* in the assistance that is provided. The assistance needs to be provided whether people want to hear

---

13. John Howard Yoder, *The Original Revolution: Essays on Christian Pacifism* (Scottsdale: Herald Press, 2003), 30.

14. Bosch, *Transforming Mission*, 400.

15. George Elton Ladd, *The Presence of the Future* (Grand Rapids: Zondervan, 1974).

16. The term originated in Asia and specifically in China and Japan where many missionaries and critics of the efforts of the missionaries expressed concern that people converted to Christianity because of the material benefits or opportunities that they received. The term "rice Christian" has come to mean that material benefits are used to manipulate and entice individuals to join a specific church or to "convert."

or not. Yet at the same time, *after* the assistance is provided the beneficiaries may be given the opportunity to hear about the kingdom of God and a God who is compassionate, if they want to. It is important to recognize that there is a power dynamic involved between the church or organization providing the assistance and the beneficiaries. The provider of the assistance is in a position of power because of the assistance that is being provided. Not being aware of this power dynamic can result in the use of the aid that is being provided to manipulate the beneficiaries. This is a very real danger. However, power dynamics are part of every human relationship, whether it is the relationship between parent and child, between husband and wife, between leaders of a community or a country and its citizen, or between an employer and employee. It is unrealistic and naïve to think that aid can be provided without any kind of power dynamic between the provider of assistance and the beneficiaries in any context. The only thing that can be done is to be aware of the power dynamics and to ensure that there is no manipulation or conditionality.

In many non-western cultures there is a social contract or a sense of obligation to reciprocate to any assistance that is provided. Abu Zayd 'Abd al-Rahman Ibn Muhammad Ibn Khaldun al-Hadhrami (known as Ibn Khaldun), the fourteenth-century North African historian and the father of sociology wrote, "Only tribes held together by group feelings can live in the desert . . ."[17] since the group ensured the survival and well-being of the individual. American biblical scholar Bruce Malina writing about collectivistic societies states, "Should a group member fall ill, the goal of an individual's healing is group well-being. Focus is on the ingroup, cooperation with ingroup members, maintenance of ascribed status, and group-centered values."[18] The member of the group who is assisted reciprocates with loyalty to the group. In societies that are based on honor and shame, being poor or in difficult circumstances and not being able to fulfill one's social obligations is shameful.[19] Receiving assistance in such a culture is not necessarily humiliating. After all, members of a group help each other. However, not being able to reciprocate in some way brings further shame.

---

17. Quoted in Ernest Gellner, *Muslim Society* (Cambridge: Cambridge University Press, 1981), x.

18. Bruce J. Malina, "Collectivism in Mediterranean Culture," in *Understanding the Social World of the New Testament*, ed. Richard E. DeMaris and Dietmar Neufeld (London: Routledge, 2010), 23.

19. Malina and Rohrbaugh, *Social Science Commentary*, 390–391, 400.

So, a beneficiary receiving assistance from Christians and then choosing to do something that was meaningful for the Christians who helped her, for example by deciding to come to a Christian meeting, is in a sense reciprocating for the compassion shown and the assistance provided. Their choice to come is not based on manipulation but on social obligation. They could have chosen a number of different ways to reciprocate, and their decision to attend a Christian meeting, is their choice. Fulfilling their social obligation by reciprocating provides beneficiaries a way to preserve their honor and dignity, and thus fulfill their part in a social contract.

The biblical basis of non-conditionality in the assistance that is provided is in understanding the grace of God. Grace means unmerited favor. There is nothing that a person can do to experience the favor of God. He blesses freely and unconditionally. The Apostle John describes the principle in 1 John 3:16–17, "We know love by this, that he laid down his life for us; and we ought to lay down our lives for the brethren. But whoever has the world's goods, and sees his brother in need and closes his heart against him, how does the love of God abide in him?" As God shows unconditional favor towards us, we are to do the same in assisting those in need.

On the issue of compassion and conditionality, John Stott provides an important distinction. Exploring the relationship between social action and evangelism, he asks what is the purpose of social action? Is it to facilitate evangelism? Or does showing love and compassion have value as a ministry in its own right? He writes, "If good works are visible preaching, then they are expecting a return; but if good works are visible loving, then they are "expecting nothing in return" (Luke 6:35)."[20]

The Issue of Forcing Conversions

The second challenge to bearing witness is directly connected with the issue of conditionality and has to do with conversion. In the field of relief and development, this is a highly controversial issue and the biblical perspective is probably least understood. The accusation is that provision of help to people who are vulnerable is used as an incentive to convert them. The term conversion is rarely used in the Bible. The root of the concept is the Greek word *epistrepho,* which means, "to turn." A dictionary defines conversion

---

20. Luke 6:35, "But love your enemies, do good to them, and lend to them without expecting to get anything back. Then your reward will be great, and you will be children of the Most High, because he is kind to the ungrateful and wicked."

as changing to another form. While conversion is not a biblical term, it is a contemporary theological concept that is understood as turning to or returning to God. It is used in the Old Testament to refer to God's people returning to him[21] or God returning to his people.[22] In the New Testament, the theological concept is understood as turning to God (away from the idols). In a few places, such as in Acts 3:19 and 26:20, the idea of repentance and turning appear together.

But the question is, how does conversion take place and can someone convert another person? A term outside of Scripture that is used for a Gentile to convert to Judaism is "proselyte." In the Greek Old Testament it refers to a stranger or a newcomer to Israel. To proselytize means to "induce someone to convert to one's faith." Unfortunately, the term conversion is used synonymously with proselytism and is most commonly understood to mean changing one's religious beliefs by leaving a particular lifestyle or faith and joining a new faith. Somehow the discussion on proselytism and conversion has a very poor view of human nature and an individual's ability to think rationally for themselves and make their own decisions. There is a certain arrogance to think that aid providers are rational human beings who have freedom of choice, but that the poor and vulnerable are unthinking individuals who can be easily manipulated. Each adult person chooses what he or she wants to believe, and those who are induced to change their religious and social affiliation, do so because of their own choice (whatever their reason) and not because of some kind of stimulus that they unconsciously and unknowingly respond to.

However, Scripture understands conversion differently. Conversion is an internal human dynamic and not merely a process of changing social and religious groups. It is God who draws a person to Christ. John 6:44, "No one can come to me unless the Father who sent me draws them, and I will raise them up at the last day." Then it is the Holy Spirit who convicts the individual of sin. John 16:8 (NASB), "And he, when he comes, will convict the world concerning sin and righteousness and judgment." Finally, it is God who seals the new believer with the Holy Spirit. Ephesians 1:13, "And you also were included in Christ when you heard the message of truth, the gospel of your salvation. When you believed, you were marked in him with a seal, the promised Holy Spirit." While the individual has a choice of whether to

---

21. Isa 6:10, 31:6; Jer 3:10, 3:12, 3:14, 3:22; Amos 4:6, 4:8, 4:10; Zech 1:2–4.
22. Isa 63:17; Amos 9:14.

believe God and accept the gift of new life, it is God who draws people to himself to make them citizens of his kingdom. Conversion as understood from Scripture is an experience[23] that is much deeper and more profound that impacts the whole individual and is not just about joining a different religious group.

So in effect, according to Scripture it is impossible for anyone to convert another person, especially through using incentives and arguments. However it is possible to proselytize and convince someone to change their social and religious groups. But it is only God who truly converts a person. So the caution when providing assistance and bearing witness to the love and compassion of God and the reality of his kingdom is to ensure that there is no conditionality and proselytism to force individuals to change their social group and religious affiliation. However, if there is evidence of true conversions brought about by the Spirit of God, then every effort must be made to ensure that the conversions are genuine and not the result of proselytism. It was for this very reason early Protestant missionaries would "instruct" converts for a while during which they discerned if the conversion was genuine before they baptized them publicly and allowed them to participate in the life of the local church.

Conversion is a change of conviction and not of changing one's religious or social group. It is always a profound experience that results in their convictions being transformed. While there may be many influences, including arguments and enticements, in the end it is personal choice. Human beings are not passive instruments who can be manipulated, but are responsible human beings.

Being a witness and proselytism is not the same thing. Proselytism has no place in the ministry of God's people. Being a witness means having a prophetic role and explaining reality – that God is present and at work in the midst of the problems, challenges, and injustices. Being a witness means speaking about the reality of the spiritual world and about the kingdom of God. It means being like the prophet Elisha in 2 Kings 6:15–17 who asks God to open the eyes of his fearful servant so that he could see the armies of God in the midst of a seemingly hopeless and desperate situation. Being a witness is never about conversion, because conversion is only something that God does in an individual's life.

---

23. It may be an instantaneous experience or a process over time.

10

The Face of Compassion

The discussion around compassion as a core ministry of the church is often described using terms such a community development, empowerment, disaster relief, human rights, and social and economic justice. While these are supposedly understood to be the means of compassion, for many in the church, as well as some theologians, missiologists and church leaders it would seem that these non-biblical terms are adding new dimensions to the ministry of the church, which were never intended by the writers of the New Testament. Without really understanding what these terms mean, they dismiss them as valid ministries of the church. Each of these terms also brings with them a particular way of doing ministry. For example, a community development project is designed in a particular way so that there are clear goals and objectives resulting in specific outcomes. They are time-bound initiatives using the tools of project design and management. Most churches find the technical language of development and project management to be too complex and intimidating and are only too happy for an NGO to do the work. There is a need to move beyond the terminology and understand what these terms mean.

The ministries of development, disaster relief, human rights and justice are very much part of the biblical mandate. The need to coordinate large-scale disaster responses or implement technical development projects in food security or microfinance requires specialized agencies and is beyond the capacity of local churches. Yet local churches need to find ways to respond to human needs and issues of injustice in the community with the limited capacities and resources that they have. There are more ways of responding to human need than just using the tools of project cycle management. New language has to be found to describe how the *pathos* of God is translated into his work of redemption and restoration.

Throughout this book we have traced how the compassion of God was revealed in the laws he gave and how a lack of justice and compassion destroyed ancient Israel. We saw how Christ embodied and lived out compassion through every aspect of his ministry. We looked at the fact that compassion was one of the key factors for the growth of the early church. This was also foundational throughout the history of missions, even though at times the compassion was limited to only the spiritual dimensions of life and was not concerned about life in the here and now. So how does compassion connect with the mission of God and what would it look like in today's world?

A critical question needs to be answered at this point: Is compassion a uniquely Christian virtue, that in the mere demonstration of it, there will be recognition that compassionate people are followers of Christ?

Every religious and non-religious tradition in the world values compassion and charity among their highest virtues. In a world where greed and self-centeredness are crippling realities and where the primary concern in most cultures is to only take care of one's own, there is a recognition that there is something noble, almost heroic, about being able to help those who are desperately poor or are victims of disasters or brutal conflicts. Our heroes are Mother Teresa, aid workers (organizations such as Doctors without Borders–MSF), and emergency response workers, and we idolize them in the media and honor them with Nobel prizes.

This is not surprising, because if compassion is a divine attribute, then remnants of it will still be visible throughout his creation in spite of the fall, because creation reflects the nature and character of who God is (Rom 1:20). God in his providence and intervention in time and history, and through common grace is active in and through all people, in all societies across the world whether they acknowledge him or not. The creator God is at work sustaining his creation as well as redeeming it. His will and objective is stated in Ephesians 1:9–10 (NLT). "God has now revealed to us his mysterious plan regarding Christ, a plan to fulfill his own good pleasure. And this is the plan: At the right time he will bring everything together under the authority of Christ – everything in heaven and on earth." As is evident throughout the biblical narrative, he uses his people, as well as those who do not acknowledge him to accomplish his purposes.

It is within this larger context of God sustaining and redeeming the world that he gives his people a mission and mandate. Jürgen Moltmann writes, "It is not the church that has a mission of salvation to fulfill in the world; it is the mission of the Son and the Spirit through the Father that includes the church."[1] This is a subtle but major change in understanding what is mission and what is the purpose of the church. While the identity of the church is to be the bride of Christ, whom he is preparing to be holy and blameless (Eph 5:27), her mission is to be sent (that is the meaning of the word mission). The purpose of being sent is to proclaim the kingdom of God. The apostle Paul understood this and that was his central message no matter where he went. Luke, recording Paul's final message to the elders of the church in Ephesus, quotes Paul, "I have gone about preaching the kingdom" (Acts 20:25). Later in Rome Luke writes, "He proclaimed the kingdom of God and taught about the Lord Jesus Christ – with all boldness and without hindrance!" (Acts 28: 31).

The concept of a kingdom is not well understood now days. The usual image is of a ruthless despotic king amassing great wealth for himself at the expense of the citizens of his kingdom. Such kingdoms are characterized by fear, torture, imprisonment and a lack of freedom. The other image that exists in the twenty-first century is of constitutional monarchs such as in the UK, Japan, the Netherlands, or Sweden, who are mere figureheads and have no real authority. Neither of these images does justice to the biblical revelation of the kingdom of God.

The kingdom and the rule and authority of God are based on the character of God himself. *God is love* (1 John 4:8); so the way he treats human beings is with love. He provides for all that they need and more. He is concerned for their well-being. He nurtures and treasures all that he has created. *God is holy* (Rev 4:8). While the meaning of the term holiness includes moral perfection and that there is no evil in who he is, it is more than that. It describes the very nature of who God is, that he is separate from his creation; it describes his transcendence and his magnificence. The rule of such a God in his kingdom is characterized by complete separation from anything that is evil, sinful or morally imperfect. *God is just* (2 Thess 1:6). Everyone in his kingdom is treated equitably and no one is above the law. Because he is just, he will judge wickedness. *God is compassionate* (Ps 103:8), *kind* (1 Pet 2:3 – MSG) and *gracious* (Ps 145:8). He cares for those who are broken and hurt, and does not treat us the way we deserve; he draws us to himself like a loving father and nurtures us liking a loving mother. Yet in the midst of all of this, "God is *magnificent*; he can never be praised enough. There are no boundaries to *his greatness*" (Ps 145:3 – MSG). He is *awesome and to be feared* (Ps 89:7). All

---

1. Jürgen Moltmann, *The Church in the Power of the Spirit: A Contribution to Messianic Ecclesiology* (London: SCM Press, 1977).

of this is displayed in the magnificence and splendor of his kingdom and the terrifying power in his creation.

Such is the kingdom that God wants human beings to experience. His divine attributes are present in the world he created, and it is through his creation that he seeks to bless human beings so that they could live out the potential that he created them with. In the beginning, in Genesis 1 and 2, God created the world and placed human beings within that creation, not only to be stewards but to also enjoy the blessings, the beauty and the pleasures of this creation. Not only did he breathe life into them but also he gave them the air he created to breathe and be sustained. The human creatures he created are a little less than the angels (Ps 8:5 and Heb 2:7) and the writer of Hebrews says God crowned them with glory. There is a grandeur to human beings that no human philosophy has ever been able to fully comprehend or describe.

It is only in understanding this does one begin to grasp what Jürgen Moltmann refers to as the *pathos* of God, when God is deeply disturbed and moved because of the suffering that human beings experience; when he see their actions, behavior and rebellion rob them of the blessings he intended for them. "He is affected by them because he is interested in his creation, his people . . ."[2] Douglas John Hall writes that the fallenness of human beings has been reduced to a list of sins rather than understanding the deterioration of the quality of the relationship with the creator God, to the point of it being broken.[3]

The biblical narrative describes in detail how God feels about this broken relationship and the rejection by human beings of the blessings he intended for them. The prophet Isaiah reveals the heart of God when he recorded (Isa 48:17–18), "Thus says the Lord, your Redeemer, the Holy One of Israel, "I am the Lord your God, who teaches you to profit, Who leads you in the way you should go. If only you had paid attention to my commandments! Then your well-being would have been like a river, And your righteousness like the waves of the sea." The parable of the prodigal son (Luke 15:11–32) shows a father who is distraught over a son who rejects the blessings of his father's household and fortune and leaves to live on his own terms. In the parable of the lost sheep (Luke 15: 1–7) Luke describes a shepherd who frantically goes looking for one single sheep from his flock who is lost and could suffer and die because it is not under the protection of the shepherd.

---

2. Moltmann, *The Crucified God*, 270.

3. Hall, *The Cross*, 104.

It is this *pathos*, the fact that God is deeply disturbed by what happens when people reject his kingdom and the blessings and life he intended for them, that is the wellspring of his compassion, his "gut-wrenching response." This then is his motivation for redemption; to restore a world and a people to the blessings, the life, the creativity, the unsullied pleasures of experiencing him and his creation that he always intended them to.

If God is concerned for all aspects of life, then there are three dimensions of compassion:

- First, God sees human beings struggle with the daily challenges of life and often sink into despair. They are unable to perceive and comprehend that he is a loving God; that he seeks to provide for their needs (Matt 6:25–34). They are unable to comprehend the magnificence of his creation (Ps 19:1–4); that he created all of this for human beings to marvel and enjoy (Ps 145:3–7). In the midst of their struggles in life, people miss the fact that *God seeks to bless human beings and his creation.* He wants them to be aware of and enjoy the richness of life and the grandeur, beauty and magnificence of his creation.

- Second, God hates evil because it destroys what he has created. *He defends and protects those who are the victims of evil.* He is their advocate and seeks to rescue them.

- And lastly, *God desires his creation to be restored to him.* He is a redeemer and he has given them a Savior. He offers forgiveness for their rebellion and rejection of him.

God demonstrates these three dimensions of his compassion through human beings who are willing to partner with him as he restores and establishes his kingdom here on earth.

Agents of Blessings

God speaking to Abraham declares in Genesis 12:3, "all peoples on earth will be blessed through you." This was literally fulfilled in Christ as Galatians 3:8–14 states. Salvation and knowing God was now no longer limited to the Jews, but through Christ anyone could be blessed and be part of the kingdom of God if they chose to do so (Eph 2:14–19). The concept of blessings in the Old Testament was very real materially, socially and politically for the people who belonged to him and obeyed his laws (Deut 28:1–14). The blessings promised to both Jews and Gentiles that have been fulfilled in Christ are comprehensive and encompass all of life and are not only limited to life after death.

Richard Bauckham, senior scholar at Ridley Hall, Cambridge, writes about the comprehensiveness of God's blessings:

> Blessings is the way God enables his creation to be fertile and fruitful, to grow and to flourish. It is in the most comprehensive sense God's purpose for his creation. Wherever human life enjoys the good things of creation and produces the good fruits of human activity, God is pouring out his blessing. Wherever people bless God for his blessings, to the extent God is known as the good Creator who provides for human flourishing. God's blessing is universal.[4]

William E. Brown writes, "God's intention and desire to bless humanity is a central focus of his covenant relationships. For this reason, the concept of blessing pervades the biblical record. Two distinct ideas are present. First, a blessing was a public declaration of a favored status with God. Second, the blessing endowed power for prosperity and success."[5] The word bless in the Old Testament is *barak* meaning literally "to kneel," which can be described as the act of praising, saluting or congratulating. To kneel before someone implied humbling oneself and acknowledging the worth of the other person. In the New Testament the word is *eulogeo*[6], which can also mean to consecrate something or to cause to prosper. So in effect, *to bless someone is not just to praise them, but also to give them something of ourselves that is of value, which enhances their well-being and worth.* When God blesses someone, he gives his presence to him or her so that they prosper (Ps 21:6).[7] When people bless God, they do not just mouth words of praise, but acknowledge him with their intellect, heart, will and emotions; they give of themselves.

In order to understand the nature of blessings it is important to go back and understand the character of God. Psalm 145:8–9 states, "The Lord is gracious and compassionate, slow to anger and rich in love. The Lord is good

---

4. Richard Bauckham, *Bible and Mission: Christian Mission in a Postmodern World* (Carlisle: Paternoster; Grand Rapids: Baker Academic, 2003), 34.

5. William E. Brown, "Blessings," in *Baker's Evangelical Dictionary of Biblical Theology,* 2014, accessed 18 November 2014, http://www.biblestudytools.com/dictionaries/bakers-evangelical-dictionary/blessing.html.

6. Strong's Number: 2127.

7. Not necessarily always financially, but that they are able to enjoy life and have favor with people.

to all; he has compassion on all he has made." This is what the prophet Jonah struggled with. Jonah lived in Israel at a time of great prosperity, which he interpreted as a sign of God's favor. He acknowledged that God was gracious and compassionate (4:2) but he could not accept the fact that God would show compassion and choose to bless and prosper any nation other than Israel (after all they were his people), and definitely not a nation as evil and degenerate as Nineveh (1:2). His attitude reflected a very fundamental understanding of how society was structured in the ancient Near East and in the Middle East today. Describing the structure of tribal and sectarian societies in the Middle East, the Arab historian Ibn Khaldun (as already mentioned previously) wrote, "Only tribes held together by group feelings can live in the desert . . ."[8] since the group ensured the survival and well-being of the individual. Tribes are very much inwards looking, safeguarding their wealth and taking pride in their heritage and identity. Compassion was only shown towards those who belonged to the tribe. Blessings and benefits were only for those who were part of the tribe. The tribal god was for their blessing and protection only and not to be shared with anyone else. Croatian theologian Miroslav Volf described such attitudes within the church as *Exclusion and Embrace* (also the name of his book). The inherent question is, whom are we excluding and whom should we be embracing?

Jesus counters such thinking when he teaches that one is not just to love their own family and community, exclude everyone else, and hate their enemies. In Matthew 5:45 he says that God "causes his sun to rise on the evil and the good, and sends rain on the righteous and the unrighteous." God never restricted his blessings to only the community of faith, to those who have chosen to follow Christ and be part of his kingdom. He is compassionate to all; because both the sun and the rain sustain life here on earth and without them people would die. In the parable of the Good Samaritan (Luke 10:25–37), Jesus does not identify the ethnic and religious identity of the victim and thus teaches that anyone in need is worthy or assistance.

Earlier in his discourse on the mountain in Galilee (Matt 5:13–16), Jesus described his followers as being *salt* and *light* as a way of demonstrating compassion and being a blessing. Salt in the ancient Near Eastern culture had a two-fold purpose. Because of the intense heat, foods such a meat and

---

8. Quoted in Gellner, *Muslim Society*, x.

fish would spoil very quickly. So, salt was used as a preservative.[9] Second, salt was used to flavor the food that was cooked. Thus salt was of such great value that Roman soldiers were sometimes paid in salt, which they could not only use but also trade for goods and services that they needed. Salt also had symbolic meanings. It symbolized permanence. The term "covenant of salt" implied the long lasting nature of agreements and covenants and was used when two parties signed an agreement or treaty (2 Chron 13:5) or in rituals of hospitality (symbolizing the lasting nature of the friendship). However, if a treaty was violated, the violator's land would be sprinkled and plowed with salt so that it's productivity would be diminished (Judg 9:45). Salt also symbolized cleansing and as a result protection from contamination (2 Kgs 2:20–22; Ezek 16:4).

While the concept of light is understood in many passages of Scripture as being the truth, describing God (John 8:12; 1 John 1:5) and showing the way (Ps 119:105; 1 John 1:7), Jesus, when referring to his followers as being light, clarifies in Matthew 5:16 what he meant. "Let your light shine before others, that they may see your good deeds and glorify your Father in heaven." The followers of Christ were to be compassionate and help others. Acts of charity, justice, mercy, and compassion are like lights – a breath of fresh air in a very dark and stifling world that is focused on itself and undermined by evil. These good deeds would shine in a way that would reveal God for who he really is.

So when Jesus described his followers as being salt and light, they are to act to prevent evil from decaying and destroying society. They are to be channels of compassion and advocates for justice. They are to be agents of cleansing in a community, and by their presence and actions be a protection from contamination by evil. They are to enhance the quality of life through who they are, the gifts and talents they have, and through their actions and behavior. They enable people to rise above the routines and limits of everyday life and stand in awe and wonder of God's creation. They flavor life through their talents. The presence of the followers of Jesus is also a visible symbol of God's everlasting covenant with his creation, speaking of the lasting nature of the relationship – God has not given up on human beings and his creation. Yet at the same time, their presence is also a condemnation of those who have broken his covenant.

---

9. Salt would drain the blood or any liquid and dry the flesh in order to inhibit the growth of bacteria.

We see examples of this right through out Scripture. Joseph came into a position of power and authority not only to save the family of Jacob, but also the nation of Egypt and the surrounding countries during the famine. Previously, his presence and skills were a blessing to the house of Potiphar and even the prison where he had been unjustly incarcerated. Later in Israel's history, Daniel became a close advisor to a number of the most powerful pagan kings of his time, and as result blesses them with wisdom from God and wise counsel. Elisha the prophet instructed Naaman, a Syrian general, on how to be healed. The basic principle is described in the letter that the prophet Jeremiah wrote to the Jewish exiles in Babylon. He speaks words from God (Jer 29: 7), "Also, seek the peace and prosperity of the city to which I have carried you into exile. Pray to the Lord for it, because *if it prospers, you too will prosper.*" The people of God do not live in isolation but are to be a blessing and seek the prosperity of the places where they live.

The church throughout history has understood the idea of being a blessing. The early church, by responding to the suffering of the huge influx of the poor that almost crushed the infrastructure of the cities of the eastern provinces of the Roman Empire, transformed the attitudes of Roman citizens towards the poor.[10] Robert Woodberry's research on Protestant missions highlighted their impact in the rise of liberal democracy in many parts of the majority world through providing access to education and healthcare, and promoting literacy.

The discussion as to whether the church should be involved in community development and efforts of social transformation is almost redundant and a non-issue.[11] The followers of Christ are supposed to be salt and light in the world and a blessing to others. So whether they are digging a well, ensuring food security, strengthening the livelihoods of families, providing access to education, helping a family in need, or even enabling an individual to overcome addiction, they are being a blessing and are preventing the further deterioration of the well-being of families and communities. When followers of Christ stand up against human trafficking and the exploitation of human beings, they are being a blessing; they are advocates for the victims, while seeking their protection and justice. God wants his creation to thrive and he will use his people and even those who don't know him for his purposes. So it does not matter whether it is a Christian or secular NGO that provides the

---

10. Brown, *Poverty*, 8.
11. What is not discussed throughout this book is what is meant by "church."

assistance or is involved in the empowerment of communities. God is at work in and through history, and through all that he has created.

The concept of blessing is much wider than just helping people. It is about enabling people to come alive to the reality of who God is. The impact of sin on all of God's creation darkens the ability of human beings to perceive God and fully comprehend the greatness and magnificence of his creation. *So God in his compassion seeks to enable all people to enjoy the gift of life and the world he has created.* He uses those involved in addressing poverty, those in the helping and healing professions, the civil administrators, the judges, the artists, the musicians, the writers, the naturalists, photographers, scientists, and those responding to humanitarian disasters, to give people a glimpse of what the kingdom of God is like. As a matter of fact he desires everyone to be a blessing with the gifts and talents he has given them.

Advocates for Justice

Those who are victims of evil cry out to God (Ps 82:3); "Defend the weak and the fatherless; uphold the cause of the poor and the oppressed." King Solomon,[12] recalling what his mother had taught him about the role of a king, writes (Prov 31:8–9), "Speak up for those who cannot speak for themselves, for the rights of all who are destitute. Speak up and judge fairly; defend the rights of the poor and needy." Later, God speaking through the prophet Jeremiah about what makes a good king, states in Jeremiah 22:15–16; "he did what was right and just, so all went well with him. He defended the cause of the poor and needy, and so all went well. Is that not what it means to know me?"

Those who have the power and ability to speak up and defend those who are the victims of injustice and violence and those who are destitute, have a sense of who God is and have a glimpse into his character. In the economy of God, each person is created with tremendous worth because they are created in the image of God. So anyone who desecrates the image of God in any of his treasured creations invokes the wrath of God. God speaking through the prophet Micah presents his case for judgment against the Northern Kingdom of Israel. Micah (6:8) states that they had no excuse because "he has shown you, O mortal, what is good. And what does the Lord require of you? To act justly and to love mercy and to walk humbly with your God." Israel through

---

12. The passage ascribes the sayings to King Lemuel, who is only mentioned in the Proverbs 31 passage, and is otherwise unknown. However *Strong's Concordance* and various Bible commentators state that it is the symbolic name of Solomon.

their injustices and exploitation of the poor had blasphemed and shown irreverence towards God. They had not understood that by doing so they had made God their enemy, as he would defend the poor and the needy. They had forgotten what God had told them in Exodus 22:21–24. "Do not mistreat or oppress a foreigner, for you were foreigners in Egypt. Do not take advantage of the widow or the fatherless. If you do and they cry out to me, I will certainly hear their cry. My anger will be aroused, and I will kill you with the sword; your wives will become widows and your children fatherless."

I remember that every time I would hear the stories of the Syrian refugees as they spoke of their terror and despair as they lost their homes and saw family members killed or maimed, and sensed the hopelessness as they looked at the future, my heart would break and I recall thinking that this is not the way God intended the world to be. It let me understand how compassion would drive God to defend the victims of a conflict, where they were mere pawns in the midst of the lust for power and greed.

In the ancient world, where widows, orphans and foreigners had no rights because they did not own property and therefore had no place in the community and were often abused, God was their advocate as he ensured that the laws of ancient Israel protected and provided for them. This continued throughout the New Testament, where in the book of Acts (6:1–7) the widows were taken care of. Later James, one of the key leaders of the church in Jerusalem, writes (1:27) that the evidence of one's faith in Christ is whether they have cared for the widows and orphans (the most vulnerable in society at the time). These were not just acts of compassion but acts of justice as they ensured that the most vulnerable in the community were not abandoned or abused but were protected.

The history of the church and of Christian missions is replete with examples of individuals and communities that followed Christ who stood against injustice and evil. Whether it was the abolition of slavery, the burning of widows in India (*sati*), or of foot binding of babies in China that often crippled them, or more recently, the civil rights movement in the US, the struggle against apartheid in South Africa, human trafficking and child labor, Christians have played key leadership roles in standing against what is evil in society.

Evil is the very opposite of everything that God is. Evil deprives God's creatures of life and destroys all that he has created. Evil is manifested through the injustices of society. So the second face of compassion and being salt in the world means being an advocate for justice, and thus becoming light and revealing and displaying the character of the God we worship.

Proclaiming God the Redeemer

The ultimate face of compassion is in understanding the lostness of human beings in their rebellion against the God who is their creator. The apostle Paul, writing about the frailty of human existence and waiting by faith for God's new creation with the awareness that judgment awaits (2 Cor 5:1–10), speaks of the ministry of reconciliation that the people of God have been entrusted with. "All this is from God, who reconciled us to himself through Christ and gave us the ministry of reconciliation: that God was reconciling the world to himself in Christ, not counting people's sins against them. And he has committed to us the message of reconciliation. We are therefore Christ's ambassadors, as though God were making his appeal through us. We implore you on Christ's behalf: Be reconciled to God." (2 Cor 5:18–20)

The motivation for evangelism and for the proclamation of the kingdom of God is not to conquer the world for Christ. Too often our image of Christ is based on Handel's oratorio *Judas Maccabeus* as the choir triumphantly proclaims, "See, the conquering hero comes!" The hymn, "Thine Be the Glory," inspired by Handel's oratorio, echoes these sentiments:

> *"Thine be the glory, risen conquering Son,*
> *Endless is the victory,*
> *Thou o'er death hast won."*

The absolutely stunning fact of Jesus' triumph over death and sin is turned into a triumphalism that in its arrogance is more destructive than it is life giving. Jesus' victory is somehow translated into a mandate for us to eradicate evil and any authority that is perceived to be against God. Douglas John Hall tells the story of French explorer Jacques Cartier who traveled up the St Lawrence River into Mohawk territory. At the village of Hochelaga, the site of present day Montreal, along with some of his sailors, Cartier planted a crude cross on the small mountain that dominates the landscape and declared, "All this land now belongs to the king of France."[13] Similar incidents were repeated right across the world during the great age of exploration in fifteenth to the eighteenth centuries. The natives who witnessed these

---

13. Hall, *The Cross*, 36.

incidents quickly associated the cross and the religion it symbolized with the brutality and exploitation of the conquerors. They understood the God of the cross as merely a more powerful tribal god who had vanquished their own tribal deities. Scott Sunquist at Fuller Theological Seminary writes poignantly, "Carrying the cross, the symbol of the suffering, gentle, and compliant Savior, had become an oppressive sign of military conquest: from passion to power and humility to hubris."[14]

The message of Easter Sunday *is* one of triumph and victory over evil, sin and death. It is a message to be proclaimed, because that is the only hope that we have for our existence. However, the astounding triumph of Easter Sunday is preceded by God humbling himself through the incarnation, demonstrating godliness in the mundane routines of life, enduring the unspeakable horrors of a crucifixion, and then the confusing silence of the Saturday before Easter Sunday. The method is as much the message as the message itself. Jesus described the method when he said (John 20:21), "As the Father has sent me, I am sending you." God the all powerful could have destroyed all opposition to him, but he would have won a pyrrhic victory and in the process destroyed all he had created. The apostle Paul writing to the church at Philippi instead describes God's method (Phil 2:5–8): "Your attitude should be the same as that of Christ Jesus: Who, being in very nature God, did not consider equality with God something to be grasped, but made himself nothing, taking the very nature of a servant, being made in human likeness. And being found in appearance as a man, he humbled himself and became obedient to death – even death on a cross!" God has built into nature his method of ministry, of how life comes into being. Jesus speaking about his impending death reveals this very fundamental law of life (John 12:24 RSV); "Unless a grain of wheat falls into the earth and dies, it remains alone; but if it dies, it bears much fruit."

The God we proclaim is a redeemer and not an earthly conqueror. Neither does he stand at a distance and in pity throw us a few coins or some morsels of food to meet our daily needs. Instead he buys back and redeems, for a price, what is rightfully his. It is a humiliating process, because as creator he could have forcefully taken back what he had created. However, redemption is the only process through which he could have demonstrated his compassion, the gut-wrenching agony he feels as he sees his creation decay, and human beings

---

14. Scott W. Sunquist, *Understanding Christian Mission: Participation in Suffering and Glory* (Grand Rapids: Baker Academic, 2013), 38.

try and live while being cut off from their source of life. The biblical narrative is of God restoring all of his creation to the glory he had planned at the very beginning of time. Only then will his kingdom have been restored.

Proclaiming God as redeemer is the third face of compassion. The proclamation is in word and in deed. Our actions and lives demonstrate the reality of the kingdom of God and complement the verbal proclamation of the gospel. People see and experience the goodness and compassion of God before they are able to understand how to be reconciled to this God. The Micah Declaration provides the balance between addressing the issues in the world that most people face and verbally proclaiming the way of reconciliation. It concludes: "If we ignore the world we betray the Word of God, which sends us out to serve the world. If we ignore the Word of God, we have nothing to bring to the world."[15]

Paul urges the people of God to embody compassion in their lives and ministry. To the church at Ephesus he wrote (4:32), "Be kind and compassionate to one another, forgiving each other, just as in Christ God forgave you." These qualities were to characterize who they were and how they dealt with people. To the church at Colossae he wrote (3:12), "Therefore, as God's chosen people, holy and dearly loved, clothe yourselves with compassion, kindness, humility, gentleness and patience." Through their lives they were to be the face of the compassion of God.

Compassion Is the Face of Discipleship

Discipleship today has been reduced to a set of activities. A discipleship class in most churches or in any campus ministry will focus on having a regular devotion in order to cultivate one's relationship with Christ, being in a small group Bible study, becoming a person of prayer, being involved in evangelism, discipling others, worshiping God, and giving generously. These are critical pieces in becoming rooted and grounded in one's faith. But somehow, the disciplines of the Christian life and the means of grace have become ends in themselves. The question, beyond being grounded in one's faith, is how do I follow this God I now worship? Where and how do I fit into his mission of redeeming and reconciling the world to himself? How do I reveal to people, in ways that they would understand, that the kingdom of the creator God is already here?

---

15. Micah Network, *Micah Network Declaration*, 1.

If compassion does not drive evangelism, disciple making, church planting, relief and development, then each of these activities that are meant to be life giving become egocentric means of manipulation. As the people of God demonstrate the compassion of God, these and other activities become the means of grace for people to encounter the living God.

11

Conclusion:
A God of Compassion

*Only where there is doxology is there any emergence of
compassion, for doxology cuts through the ideology that pretends
to be a given. Only where there is doxology can there be justice,
for such songs transfigure fear into energy.[1]*
Walter Brueggemann

Theology has to translate into personal reality, as much as personal and communal experiences raise theological questions. It is often hard to bring focus and an end to a discussion that has spanned the purposes of God through time – wondering who this God of eternity is, and struggling with trying to understand what it means to be his people. We started this book by asking *why* does God care for the poor and those who are broken? As we journeyed through the Bible, church history, and missions, we encountered a God who is compassionate. This is an uncomfortable journey because it challenges our lifestyle, our understanding of how society functions, and asks the question whether we live for ourselves or if we have obligations in the world we live in.

As I have traveled through countries and cultures, I have wondered how the poor, the refugees, those who are victims of human trafficking and abuse, and those who have survived catastrophic disasters, understand God. Is there a theology that makes sense to them? While I react with anger at the

---

1. Walter Brueggemann, *The Prophetic Imagination*, 2nd ed. (Minneapolis, MI: Fortress Press, 2001), 18.

injustices I see, and this is usually accompanied with a deep sense of sadness in realizing that this is not the way God intended this world to be, I have been at a loss on how to see the world through the eyes of those who are victims of evil, or to understand why they would even turn to a God who seemingly has betrayed them. Yet, they see a God who is compassionate.

Maybe the reason I don't understand why the poor and the victims of evil would even seek God, is because my theology focuses so much on a triumphant God. Does this exclusive focus on the victory of Christ set up expectations that his victory protects us from all evil and suffering here in the present? Maybe this is the reason for our challenges to God as to why he allows suffering in our lives when supposedly he has conquered sin, suffering and death? Our scientific and technological worldview expects instant solutions to every problem we face. So if Christ has won the battle over evil and suffering and we still suffer, then maybe his victory was not real, or maybe God and the spiritual world are not relevant to our daily lives. The God we believed in did not live up to our expectations.

When we don't experience this triumphant reality in the "in-between times" that we live in, when the kingdom of God has come but is not yet manifested in all its fullness, we are at a loss as to what to believe about this present world and the reality of evil. Our theology has missed the importance of the darkness and disillusionment that the disciples experienced in the "in-between time," – the Saturday between Good Friday and Easter Sunday.[2]

On that first Good Friday the disciples had no knowledge that there was going to be an Easter Sunday. Their teacher, whom they had come to realize was God himself, had died on the cross. With his death, the promises of a better world and of the kingdom coming were shattered by the events at the Garden of Gethsemane and all that followed, culminating with the horrors and despair of the crucifixion. The darkness, the confusion, and the death of the dreams as they woke up on Saturday morning are hard to imagine, and can only be understood by those who have faced a sudden, horrifying and tragic death of a loved one. It was only later that they understood the meaning of the cross as being the means of forgiveness of sins and redemption. However, what unfolded on that Easter Sunday morning, would forever transform the disciples. The resurrection was so completely unexpected, stunning, and unbelievable. The realization that death had been conquered, that the dreams

---

2. With due credit to Jürgen Moltmann, *The Crucified God*; Douglas John Hall, *The Cross in Our Context*; and Alan E. Lewis, *Between Cross and Resurrection*.

of a new world were not dead, and that evil did not have to enslave people, sent a thrill through the disciples. The sense of desolation that the Saturday of the salvation narrative speaks so eloquently about through its silence is not the end of the story. There is a resurrection, with God reappearing.

Unlike the disciples who did not know that there would be an Easter Sunday, we know that there is a future because of the resurrection. The promises of Easter Sunday for new life and a new beginning come into focus. One day in the social, economic and political order of society there will be justice and peace – the promise of the kingdom of God. We look forward to the day when, "the kingdom of the world has become the kingdom of our Lord and of his Messiah, and he will reign for ever and ever" (Rev 11:15).

Yet, so much of life is lived in the Saturdays of the salvation narrative, when dreams, hopes and parts of our being may have died, when there is a sense of abandonment and of being alone. It was to a disciple like Matthew that God reveals the identity of Christ. Even though he was reasonably wealthy, Matthew lived on the margins of Jewish society hated by most people because he worked for the Roman occupiers as a tax collector. He was a Jew who did not belong. Matthew the outcast, now the gospel writer, identifies Christ as *Immanuel* – as God who would dwell with his people, even with somebody like him. This then is the image of a compassionate God – one who dwells with his flawed people, and in the process, transforms them.

Moses understood the significance of God dwelling with his people. On one occasion when the people of God had rebelled and he sought to destroy them completely, Moses reminded God that they were his people: "If your presence will not go with me, do not bring us up from here. For how shall it be known that I have found favor in your sight, I and your people? *Is it not in your going with us, so that we are distinct, I and your people, from every other people on the face of the earth?*" (Exod 33:15–16, ESV). It was the presence of God that was central in Moses' theology. Through all of human history, it has been the presence of God in the midst of his people that distinguished them from all the other people on the face of the earth. This then is foundational in how the church is to minister. It is by enabling people to encounter the living God, one who is compassionate and cares for them deeply. Do they understand what it means that Christ is Savior (that he is able to save them) and that he is Lord (that he is greater than the circumstances that enslave them)?

The people we minister to – the poor, those who live on the margins of society, the refugees, the migrant workers, the abused and abandoned women and children, the single mothers – understand the good news as the fact that God is compassionate and that he will hear them if they call. The gospel that Christ has conquered sin and death, and offers forgiveness, and that they need to repent, has little meaning for them, when in fact they feel that they are the ones who have been sinned against and experience the full brunt of evil in society. Most are not seeking revenge, or a political and social revolution. They know the full impact of evil only too well and they feel that they are powerless to change things in society.[3] Neither can they relate to a message of a triumphant God, when their reality seems to speak about a God who is absent.

Instead they want help in the here and now; they want to know that someone cares and that they haven't been abandoned; they want justice and what is rightfully theirs. They want to know that there is something greater than the struggles of their present lives. So when they encounter a compassionate God, the experience is radical for them.

I am often ashamed that I have forgotten how life giving the reality of the presence of Christ is. When I see desperate refugees, who have experienced unspeakable horrors, hear about a God of who cares for them and that he hears their prayers because of Christ, I wonder how deep is my understanding of the God I worship. The transformation and awe is so visible in their faces when they speak about the God they have encountered. The strange paradox on this side of eternity is that the victory of God is not that the church is triumphant, but that God enters into the darkness and walks with his people without the darkness overcoming him.

If the poor and the broken are seeking a God who is compassionate, how do we as the people of God then live? Jesus in John 10:10 says, "The thief comes only to steal and kill and destroy; I have come that they may have life, and have it to the full." Jesus talks about two value systems, one of death and one of life. In my sojourn through many cultures as an outsider looking in, I see life and death co-existing side by side. In most non-western cultures life is not sanitized and children are not protected from the realities of death and dying. Death is very much part of the fabric and vocabulary of everyday living. Yet in the midst of death and decay the routines of life continue.

It is this imagery that illustrates what the mission of God is. Because of his compassion, he seeks to bring life where there is death and decay, till one day the eternal kingdom will break through and all of creation will

---

3. It is this sense of powerlessness among the poor that militant groups tap into and use to find recruits to foment revolutions. They try to translate the powerlessness into anger that is directed at social and political structures.

be filled with life, as God had intended at creation. The Russian novelist Fyodor Dostoyevsky tells the story of Prince Lev Nikolayevich Myshkin, a descendant of an old Russian noble family, who supposedly suffered from epilepsy and other mental weaknesses. As he returns home from his treatment in Switzerland, he is immersed into a society that is obsessed with power, greed and sexual conquest. Relationships are destructive and are scarred by manipulation and the abuse of power in every way possible. Maybe because of his mental challenges, Myshkin is a simple soul, in a sense naïve, and as a result trusting. His goodness and his ability to extend grace to various people have no place in the midst of the ugliness of such a society, and he is labeled an "idiot."

> Myshkin's inclination is to help rather than to harm, to give mercy rather than malice, forgiving again and again, though surrounded by people who do not. In fact, it is this group who tirelessly labels Myshkin the "idiot" because he refuses to participate in the disparaging and destructive ugliness of their own ways but instead takes what is cruel and repulsive in them and dispels it.[4]

Such a life is countercultural and demonstrates an alternative to ugliness, manipulation, cruelty, revenge, and death. The theologian Walter Brueggemann writes that what is needed is a prophetic imagination that is able to present and live out an alternative value system and worldview to that of the society in which we live. He writes, "The task of prophetic ministry is to nurture, nourish, and evoke a consciousness and perception alternative to the consciousness and perception of the dominant culture around us."[5] The ministries of compassion and social justice are in effect prophetic ministries because they embody the values at the core of the kingdom of God. Most people encounter the invisible kingdom for the first time through these ministries and realize that maybe there is an alternative to the realities of the world they live in. This opens them to the possibility of a God who is compassionate.

---

4. Jill Carattini, "The True and Beautiful," RZIM website, 4 July 2011, accessed 4 August 2011, http://www.rzim.org/a-slice-of-infinity/the-true-and-the-beautiful/.

5. Brueggemann, The Prophetic Imagination, 3.

Dostoyevsky summarized the central moral of the story: "Compassion was the most important, perhaps the sole law of human existence."[6] The story of Myshkin is a parable and such compassion is not humanly possible. It requires a transformed life for love to not be egocentric but be driven by grace and compassion. Douglas John Hall writes, "Trust in God then frees us sufficiently from *self* to make us cognizant of and compassionate in relation towards the other – in particular, the other who suffers, who is hungry and thirsty, who is imprisoned; the other who 'fell among thieves'; the other who knocks at our door at midnight in need."[7]

To be compassionate in the midst of a culture which robs people of life is what it means to be the people of God in the world that we live in. Such a life reflects the very nature and character of the God we worship.

"He will have compassion on the poor and needy,
And the lives of the needy he will save." (Ps 72:13 NASB)

---

6. Fyodor Dostoevsky, *The Idiot*, trans. Alan Myers (Oxford: Oxford University Press, 1998), 242.

7. Hall, *The Cross*, 152.

Bibliography

Abraham, K. C. ed. *Third World Theologies: Commonalities and Divergence.* Maryknoll: Orbis, 1990.

Allis, Oswald T. *Prophecy and the Church.* Phillipsburg: P & R Publishing, 1945.

Anderson, Gerald H. "The American Protestants in Pursuit of Missions: 1886–1986." *International Bulletin of Missionary Research* 12 (1988): 98–118.

Aristides. "The Apology of Aristides." *Early Church Fathers – Additional Texts.* Edited by Roger Pearse. 21 November 2003. Accessed 23 June 2013, http://www.tertullian.org/fathers/aristides_02_trans.htm.

Atkins, Margaret, and Robin Osborne. *Poverty in the Roman World.* Cambridge: Cambridge University Press, 2006.

Badr, Habib. "American Protestant Missionary Beginnings in Beirut and Istanbul: Politics, Practice and Response." In *New Faiths in Ancient Lands,* edited by Heleen Murre-van den Berg, 211–239. Leiden: Brill, 2006.

Bailey, Kenneth E. *Jesus through Middle Eastern Eyes: Cultural Studies in the Gospel.* Downers Grove: IVP Academic, 2008.

Baker, Ash. *Slum Life Rising: How to Enflesh Hope within a New Urban World.* Amazon Digital Services Inc. 24 May 2012.

Ball, Philip. "Few Had Wealth in Ancient Egypt." *Nature: International Weekly Journal of Science.* 29 November 2002. Accessed 8 December 2012. http://www.nature.com/news/2002/021129/full/news021125-8.html

Barth, Karl. *God in Action.* Edinburgh: T & T. Clark, 1936.

Barth, Karl and Thomas Forsyth Torrance. *Church Dogmatics: The Doctrine of Reconciliation, Volume 4, Part 3.2: Jesus Christ, the True Witness.* New York: T&T Clark International, 2004.

Bartholomew, Craig G. and Michael W. Goheen. *The Drama of Scripture: Finding Our Place in the Biblical Story.* Grand Rapids: Baker Academics, 2004.

Bassham, Rodger C. *Mission Theology 1948–1975: Years of Worldwide Creative Tension, Ecumenical, Evangelical, and Roman Catholic.* Pasadena: William Carey Library, 1979.

Batten, Alicia. "Brokerage: Jesus as Social Entrepreneur." In *Understanding the Social World of the New Testament*, edited by Dietmar Neufed and Richard E. DeMaris, 167–177. London: Routledge, 2010.

Bauckham, Richard. *Bible and Mission: Christian Mission in a Postmodern World*. Carlisle: Paternoster; Grand Rapids: Baker Academic, 2003.

Bayat, Asef. *Life as Politics: How Ordinary People Change the Middle East*. Stanford: Stanford University Press, 2010.

Bell, Jr, Daniel. *Liberation Theology after the End of History*. London: Routledge, 2001.

Bennett, Harold V. *Injustice Made Legal: Deuteronomic Law and the Plight of Widows, Strangers and Orphans in Ancient Israel*. Grand Rapids: William B. Eerdmanns Publishing Company, 2002.

Bird, Phyllis. *Missing Persons and Mistaken Identities: Women and Gender in Ancient Israel*. Minneapolis: Fortress Press, 1997.

Birnbaum, Philip, trans. *Mishneh Torah: Maimonides' Code of Law and Ethics*. New York: Hebrew Publishing Company, 1974.

Blasi, Anthony J. *Early Christianity as a Social Movement*. New York: Peter Lang, 1989.

Boesak, A. A. *Farewell to Innocence: A Socio-Ethical Study on Black Theology and Black Power*. Maryknoll: Orbis Books, 1977.

Boff, Leonardo, and Clodovis Boff. *Introducing Liberation Theology*. Maryknoll: Orbis Books, 2008.

Borden, Paul. "Is There Really One Big Idea in That Story?" In *The Big Idea of Biblical Preaching*, edited by Keith Willhite and Scott M. Gibson, 67–80. Grand Rapids: Baker Books, 1998.

Bosch, David J. *Transforming Mission*. New York: Orbis Books, 2008.

Brackney, William H. *Human Rights and the World's Religion, Revised and Updated*. Westport: Praeger Publishers, 2013.

Bradshaw, Richard I. "Exile." Bible Society website. 1999. Accessed 18 January 2013. http://www.biblestudies.org.uk/article_exile.html.

Bremner, Robert H. *Giving: Charity and Philanthropy in History*. London: Transaction Publishers, 1996.

Brown, Peter. *Poverty and Leadership in the Later Roman Empire*. Hanover: University Press of New England, 2002.

———. *Through the Eye of a Needle: Wealth, the Fall of Rome and the Making of Christianity in the West 350–550 A.D.* Princeton: Princeton University Press, 2012.

Brown, William E. "Blessings." In *Baker's Evangelical Dictionary of Biblical Theology*. 2014. Accessed 18 November 2014. http://www. biblestudytools.com/dictionaries/bakers-evangelical-dictionary/ blessing.html.

Brueggemann, Walter. *The Prophetic Imagination*. 2nd edition. Minneapolis, MI: Fortress Press, 2001.

———. "How the Early Church Practiced Charity." *The Christian Century* (June 2003): 30–31.

Burggraff, David L. "Determining Our Place in Our World or Social Responsibility versus Irresponsibility." *A Dispensationalist Fundamentalist Ponders the Difficult Charge of Social Irresponsibility*. 1 September 2010. Accessed 8 December 2010. http://bobbixby. wordpress.com/2010/09/01/a-dispensationalist-fundamentalist- ponders-the-difficult-charge-of-social-irresponsibility/.

Brunner, Emil. *The Christian Doctrine of Creation and Redemption, Dogmatics ii*. Philadelphia: Westminster Press, 1952.

Buber, Martin. *I and Thou*. New York: Scribner, 1958.

Carter, G. *Anglican Evangelicals: Protestant Secessions from Via Media, c. 1800–1850 (Oxford Theological Monographs)*. Oxford: Oxford University Press, 2001.

Catechism of the Catholic Church. 2nd edition. Washington DC: United Sates Catholic Conference, 1994, # 2446.

Carattini, Jill. "The True and Beautiful." RZIM website. 4 July 2011. Accessed 4 August 2011. http://www.rzim.org/a-slice-of-infinity/the- true-and-the-beautiful/

Chaney, Charles L. *The Birth of Missions in America*. Pasadena: William Carey Library, 1976.

Chester, Tim, ed. *Justice, Mercy and Humility: Integral Mission and the Poor*. Milton Keynes: Paternoster Press, 2002.

Christian History. "William Booth." *Christianity Today*, 8 August 2008. Accessed 9 December 2013. http://www.christianitytoday.com/ ch/131christians/activists/williambooth.html.

Christian, Jayakumar. *God of the Empty-Handed: Poverty, Power and the Kingdom of God*. Monrovia: MARC, 1999.

Christianity Today. "Personal But Never Private." *ChristianityToday. com, 13 September 2010*, accessed 14 September 2010, http://www. christianitytoday.com/le/2010/summer/personalneverprivate.html.

Cohen, Mark. *Poverty and Charity in the Jewish Community of Medieval Egypt*. Princeton: Princeton University Press, 2005.

Corbett, Steve, and Brian Fikkert. *When Helping Hurts: How to Alleviate Poverty without Hurting the Poor and Yourself*. Chicago: Moody Publishers, 2009.

Cragg, Kenneth. *The Arab Christian: A History of the Middle East*. Louisville: Westminster John Knox Press, 1991.

Culver, Robert Duncan. *Systematic Theology: Biblical and Historical*. Fearn, Scotland: Christian Focus Publications, 2005.

Curzon, Robert. *Visits to Monasteries in the Levant*. London: John Murray, 1849.

Cyril of Jerusalem. "*Catechesis* V, 12." In *Opera quae supersunt omnia*, edited by W. C. Reischl. Munich: Keck, 1849.

Daley, Brian E. *Gregory of Nazianzus*. London: Routledge, 2006.

Dever, William A. *Who Were the Early Israelites and Where Did They Come From?* Grand Rapids: William B. Eerdmans Publishing Company, 2003.

Domeris, William. *Touching the Heart of God: The Social Reconstruction of Poverty among Biblical Peasants*. New York: T&T Clark, 2007.

Donovan, Vincent J. *Christianity Rediscovered*. New York: Orbis Books, 2003.

Dostoevsky, Fyodor. *The Idiot*. Translated by Alan Myers. Oxford: Oxford University Press, 1998.

Dunn, James D. G. *The Theology of Paul the Apostle*. Grand Rapids: William B. Eerdmans Publishing Company, 1998.

Easterly, William. "IMF and World Bank Structural Adjustment Programs and Poverty." In *Managing Currency Crises in Emerging Markets*, edited by Michael P. Dooley and Jeffrey A. Frankel. Chicago: Chicago University Press, 2003.

Elhawary, Samir, and M. M. M. Aheeyar. *Beneficiary Perceptions of Corruption in Humanitarian Assistance: A Sri Lanka Case Study, HPG Working Paper*. London: Overseas Development Institute, August 2008.

Ellsberg, Robert, ed. *Modern Spiritual Masters: Writings on Contemplation and Compassion*. Maryknoll: Orbis Books, 2009.

Farquhar, John Nicol. *The Crown of Hinduism*. New Delhi: Oriental Books Reprints Corp., 1971 [1913].

Fensham, F. Charles. "Widow, Orphans and the Poor in Ancient Near Eastern Legal and Wisdom Literature." In *Essential Papers on Israel and the Ancient Near East*, edited by Fredreick E. Greenspan, 176–192. New York: New York University Press, 2000.

Fiensy, David A. "Ancient Economy and The New Testament." In *Understanding the Social World of the New Testament*, edited by Dietmar Neufeld and Richard E. DeMaris, 194–206. London: Routledge, 2010.

Finger, Thomas N. *A Contemporary Anabaptist Theology: Biblical, Historical, Constructive*. Downers Grove: InterVarsity Press, 2004.

Fleischmann, Ellen. "Evangelization or Education: American Protestant Missinaries, The American Board, and the Girls and Women of Syria (1830–1910)." In *New Faiths in Ancient Lands*, edited by Heleen Mutrevan den Berg, 263–280. Leiden: Brill, 2006.

Frank, Arthur W. *Letting Stories Breathe: A Socio-Narratology*. Chicago: The University of Chicago Press, 2010.

Freedman, David Noel. *Poor, Poverty*. Vol. 5. In *The Anchor Bible Dictionary*, 402. New York: Doubleday, 1996.

Frei, Hans W. *Types of Christian Theology*. Edited by George Hunsinger and William C. Plancher. New Haven: Yale University Press, 1992.

Freire, Paulo. *Pedagogy of the Oppressed*. New York: The Seabury Press, 1970.

Frenkel, Mariam, and Yaacov Lev. *Charity and Giving in Monotheistic Religions*. New York: Walter de Gruyter, 2009.

Gellner, Ernest. *Muslim Society*. Cambridge: Cambridge University Press, 1981.

Gilbert, Peter, ed. "St. Basil's Sermon to the Rich," *De Unione Ecclessiarum*, 2008. Accessed 28 June 2013. http://bekkos.wordpress.com/st-basils-sermon-to-the-rich/.

Glasser, Arthur. *Announcing the Kingdom: The Story of God's Mission in the Bible*. Grand Rapids: Baker Academic, 2003.

Gutiérrez, Gustavo. *A Theology of Liberation*. Maryknoll: Orbis Books, 2009.

Haggerty, Donald. *Contemplative Provocations*. San Francisco: Ignatius Press, 2013.

Hall, Douglas John. *The Cross in Our Context: Jesus and the Suffering World*. Minneapolis: Fortress Press, 2003.

Halsall, Paul. "Code of Hammurabi." March 1998. Accessed 9 December 2012. http://www.fordham.edu/halsall/ancient/hamcode.asp#text .

Hamel, Gildas. *Poverty and Charity in Roman Palestine: First Three Centries CE*. Berkeley: University of California Press, 1990.

Hanks, Thomas D. *God So Loved the Third World: The Biblical Vocabulary of Oppression*. Maryknoll: Orbis Books, 1983.

Harland, Philip A. "The Economy of First-Century Palestine: State of the Scholarly Discussion." In *Handbook of Early Christianity: Social Science Approaches*, edited by Anthony J. Blasi, Jean Duhaime and Philip-Andre Turcotte, 511–527. Walnut Creek: Alta Mira Press, 2002.

Harnack, Adolf von. *The Mission and Expansion of Christianity in the First Three Centuries*. translated by J. Moffat. New York: Harper & Brothers, 1961.

Harris, R. Laird, Gleason L. Archer, Jr., and Bruce K. Waltke. *Theological Workbook of the Old Testament*. Chicago: Moody Publishers, 1980.

Hartnett, Daniel. "Remembering the Poor: An Interview with Gustavo Gutiérrez." *America, the National Catholic Weekly.* 3 February 2003. Accessed 14 December 2010. http://www.americamagazine.org/content/article.cfm?article_id=2755.

Hassan, Fekri. "Fall of the Egyptian Old Kingdom." 17 February 2011. Accessed 9 December 2012. http://www.bbc.co.uk/history/ancients/egyptians/apocalypse_egypt_01.shtml.

Hiebert, Paul. *Anthropological Reflections on Missiological Issues*. Grand Rapids: Baker, 1994.

Henry, Carl F. H. *The Uneasy Conscience of Modern Fundamentalism*. Grand Rapids: William B. Eerdmans Publishing Company, 1947.

Henry, Matthew. *Matthew Henry's Concise Bible Commentary*. Nashville: Thomas Nelson, 2003.

Hill, Craig C. *In God's Time: The Bible and the Future*. Grand Rapids: Eerdmans, 2002.

Holman, Susan R. "Healing the World with Righteousness? The Language of Social Justice in Early Christian Homilies." In *Charity and Giving in Monotheistic Religions*, edited by Mariam Frenkel and Yaacov Lev, 89–110. New York: Walter de Gruyter, 2009.

Hoppe, Leslie J. *There Shall Be No Poor among You: Poverty in the Bible*. Nashville: Abingdon Press, 2004.

Horsley, Richard. *Jesus and the Powers: Conflict, Covenant and the Hope of the Poor*. Minneapolis: Fortress Press, 2011.

Houston, Tom. "The Story of the Lausanne Covenant: Case Study in Cooperation." 2013. Accessed 23 July 2013. http://www.lausanne.org/en/gatherings/global-congress/lausanne-1974/story-of-the-covenant.html.

Houston, Walter J. *Contending for Justice*. London: T & T Clark, 2008.

Hughes, Dewi. *God of the Poor: A Biblical Vision Of God's Present Rule.* Milton Keynes: Authentic Media, 2006.

Jethani, Skye. "Making the Invisble Kingdom Visible (part 1)." *Christianity Today*, 6 May 2013. Accessed 13 May 2013. http://www.outofur.com/archives/2013/05/making_the_invi.html?utm_source=parse&utm_medium=Newsletter&utm_term=12502841&utm_content=174724452&utm_campaign=2013.

Knight, Douglas A. *Law, Power, and Justice in Ancient Israel.* Louisville: Westminster John Knox Press, 2011.

Ladd, George Elton. *The Presence of the Future.* Grand Rapids: Zondervan, 1974.

Lampe, Peter. *From Paul to Valentius: Christians in Rome in The First Two Centuries.* Minneapolis: Fortress Press, 2003.

Laniak, Timothy S. *Finding the Lost Images of God.* Grand Rapids: Zondervan, 2010.

Levinson, Bernard M. "The Reconceptualization of Kingship in Deutronomy and the Deutronomistic History's Transformation Torah." *Vetus Testamentum* 51, no. 4 (2001): 511–534.

Lewis, Alan E. *Between Cross and Resurrection: A Theology of Holy Saturday.* Grand Rapids: William B. Eerdmans Publishing Company, 2001.

Lewis, David. "Anthropology and Development: The Uneasy Relationship." In *A Handbook of Economic Anthropology,* edited by James D. Carrier. Cheltenham: Edward Elgar, 2005.

Lindsay, Thomas M. "The Church and the Ministry in Early Centuries." Christian Classics Etherel Library. 9 July 2000. Accessed 12 June 2012. http://www.ccel.org/ccel/lindsay/early_church.html.

Little, Christopher. "Christian Mission Today: Are We on a Slippery Slope? What Makes Mission Christian?" *International Journal of Frontier Missiology* 25, no. 2 (Summer 2008): 65–72.

Loffler, Paul. "Conversion in an Ecumenical Context." *The Ecumenical Review* 19, no. 3 (1967): 252–260.

Lohfink, Norbert. "Poverty in the Laws of the Ancient Near East and the Bible." *Theological Studies* 52 (1991): 34–50.

Longenecker, Bruce W. *Remember the Poor: Paul, Poverty and the Greco-Roman World.* Grand Rapids: William B. Eerdmans Publishing Company, 2010.

Longman III, Tremper, and Raymond B. Dillard. *An Introduction to the Old Testament.* Nottingham: Inter-Varsity Press, 2007.

Malina, Bruce J. *The Social World of Jesus and the Gospels.* London: Routledge, 1996.

———. "Collectivism in Mediterranean Culture." In *Understanding the Social World of the New Testament,* edited by Richard E. DeMaris and Dietmar Neufeld, 17–28. London: Routledge, 2010.

Malina, Bruce J., and Richard L. Rohrbaugh. *Social Science Commentary on the Synoptic Gospels.* Minneapolis: Fortress Press, 2003.

Matthews, Victor H. *Social World of the Hebrew Prophets.* Peabody: Hendrickson Publishers Inc., 2001.

Matthews, Victor H., and Don C. Benjamin. *Old Testament Parallels: Law and Stories from the Ancient Near East.* Mahwah: Paulist Press, 2006.

McClendon, James. *Doctrine: Systematic Theology, Vol. II.* Nashville: Abingdon Press, 1994.

———. *Ethics: Systematic Theology.* Vol. 1. Nashville: Abingdon Press, 2002.

McGavran, Donald. "Will Uppsala Betray the Two Billion." *Church Growth Bulletin: Special Uppsala Issue* IV, no. 5 (May 1968).

———., ed. *Eye of the Storm: The Great Debate in Mission.* Waco: Word Books, 1972.

———. "Salvation Today." In *The Evangelical Response to Bangkok,* edited by Ralph Winter, 27–32. Pasadena: Wlliam Carey Library, 1973.

McGrath, Alister E. *The Christian Theology Reader.* Oxford: Blackwell Publishing, 2001.

———. *Christian Theology: An Introduction.* 5th. Chichester: Wiley-Blackwell, 2011.

McKnight, Scott. "Jesus vs. Paul." *Christianity Today.* 3 December 2010. Accessed 5 December 2010. http://www.christianitytoday.com/ct/2010/december/9.25.html.

Meeks, Wayne A. *The First Urban Christians: The Social World of the Apostle Paul.* New Haven: Yale University Press, 1983.

———. *The Origins of Christian Morality: The First Two Centuries.* New Haven: Yale University Press, 1993.

Micah Network. *Micah Network Declaration on Integral Mission.* Oxford: Micah Network, 2001.

Migliore, Daniel L. *Faith Seeking Understanding: An Introduction to Christian Theology.* Grand Rapids: William B. Eerdmans Publishing Company, 2004.

Miranda, Jose Porfirio. *Marx and the Bible: A Critique of the Philosophy of Oppression.* English Translation. London: SCM Press, 1977.

Moltmann, Jürgen. *The Crucified God,* London: SCM Press Ltd., 1974.

————. *The Church in the Power of the Spirit: A Contribution to Messianic Ecclesiology.* London: SCM Press, 1977.

————. *History and the Triune God.* New York: Crossroad, 1992.

————. *A Broad Place: An Autobiography.* London: SCM Press, 2007.

Morphew, Derek J. *Breakthrough: Discovering the Kingdom.* Cape Town: Vineyard International Publishing, 1991.

Mother Teresa. *In My Own Words,* comp. Jose Luis Gonzalez-Balado. Linguori: Linguori Publications, 1996.

Myers, Bryant L. *Walking with the Poor: Principles and Practices of Transformational Development.* Maryknoll: Orbis Books, 2006.

Nelson, Gary. *Borderland Churches: A Congregation's Introduction to Missional Living.* St Louis: Chalice Press, 2008.

Nelson, Gary, Gordon W. King, and Terry G. Smith. *Going Global: A Congregation's Introduction to Missions Beyond Our Borders.* St Louis: Chalice Press, 2011.

Newbigin, Lesslie. *The Open Secret: Sketches for a Missionary Theology.* Revised. Grand Rapids: Eerdmans, 1995.

Neyrey, Jerome H. "Loss of Wealth, Loss of Family and Loss of Honour: The Cultural Context of the Original Makarisms in Q." In *Modelling Early Christianity: Social Scientific Studies of the New Testament in its Context,* edited by Philip F. Esler, 139–158. London: Routledge, 1995.

Niebuhr, H. Richard. *Christ and Culture.* New York: Harper, 1951.

Niebuhr, Reinhold. *Moral Man and Immoral Society: A Study of Ethics and Politics.* New York: Scribner's, 1932.

Niles, D. Preman. *From East and West: Rethinking Christian Mission.* St Louis: Chalice Press, 2004.

Noll, Mark A. *Turning Points: Decisive Moments in the History of Christianity.* Grand Rapids: Baker Academic, 2000.

Oord, Thomas Jay, "Pannenberg Dies; An Interview," 8 September 2014, accessed 13 September 2014, http://thomasjayoord.com/index.php/blog/archives/pannenberg_dies_an_interview/

Padilla, C. René, and Tetsunao Yamamori. *The Local Church, Agent of Transformation: An Ecclesiology for Integral Mission.* Buenos Aires: Kairos Ediciones, 2004.

Pahlitzsch, Johannes. "Christian Pious Foundations as an Element of Continuity between Late Antiquity and Islam." In *Charity and Giving in Monotheistic Religions*, edited by Miriam Frenkel and Yaacov Lev, 125–151. New York: Walter D. Gruyter, 2009.

Patterson, Richard D. "The Widow, Orphan, and the Poor in the Old Testament and the Extra-Biblical Literature." *Bibliotheca Sacra*, July 1973: 223–234.

Pinker, Steven. *The Better Angels of Our Nature: Why Violence Has Declined.* New York: Allen Lane, 2011.

Pleins, J. David. *The Social Visions of the Hebrew Bible: A Theological Introduction.* Louisville: Westminster John Knox Press, 2001.

Pocock, Michael. "The Destiny of the World and the Work of Missions." *Bibliotheca Sacra* 145 (1988): 436–451.

Polkinghorne, J. *Serious Talk, Science and Religion in Dialogue.* Valley Forge: Trinity Press International, 1995.

Powell, Mark Allan. "The Forgotten Famine: Personal Responsibility in Luke's parable of 'The Prodigal Son.'" In *Literary Encouters with the Reign of God*, edited by Sharon H. Ringe and H. C. Paul Kim, 265–287. London: T & T Clark International, 2004.

Premnath, D. N. *Eighth Century Prophets: A Social Analysis,* St Louis: Chalice Press, 2003.

Pritchard, James B., ed. *Ancient Near Eastern Texts Relating to the Old Testament.* 3rd edition. Princeton: Princeton University Press, 1969.

Ramsey, Boniface. *Ambrose.* London: Routledge, 1997.

Ratzinger, Cardinal Joseph. "Liberation Theology: Preliminary Notes," in *The Ratzinger Report.* Reprinted in: *The Essential Pope Benedict XVI,* edited by J. F. Thornton and S. B. Varenne. New York: Harper, 2007.

Rauschenbusch, Walter. *A Theology for the Social Gospel.* New York: The Macmillan Company, 1917.

Richards, E. Randolph, and Brandon J. O'Brien. *Misreading Scripture with Western Eyes: Removing Cutural Blinders to Better Understand the Bible.* Downers Grove: IVP Books, 2012.

Rohrbaugh, Richard L. "Ethnocentrism and Historical Questions about Jesus." In *The Social Setting of Jesus and the Gospels*, edited by Wolfgang Stegemann, Bruce J. Malina and Gerd Theissen, 27–43. Minneapolis: Fortress, 2002.

———. "Honor: Core Value in the Biblical World." In *Understanding the Social World of the New Testament*, edited by Dietmar Neufeld and Richard E. DeMaris, 109–125. London: Routledge, 2010.

Rostovtzeff, Michael. *The Social and Economic History of the Roman Empire.* Edited by P. M. Fraser. Oxford: Clarendon Press, 1957 [1926].

Samosata, Lucian (of). "The Passing of Peregrinus." Transcribed by Roger Pearse. 21 August 2001. Accessed 25 June 2013. http://www.tertullian.org/rpearse/lucian/peregrinus.htm .

Sanneh, Lamin. *Encountering the West: Christianity and the Global Cultural Process.* London: Orbis Books, 1993.

———. *Translating the Message: The Missionary Impact on Culture.* London: Orbis Books, 2009.

Schaff, Philip. *Ante-Nicene Fathers: Fathers of The Second Century.* Vol. II. Grand Rapids: Christian Classics Ethereal Library, 2001 [1885].

———. *Nicene and Post Nicene Fathers, Series II.* Vol. 8. Grand Rapids: William B. Eerdmans Publishing Company, 2001 [1885].

———. *The Apostolic Fathers with Justin Martyr and Irenaeus.* Grand Rapids: Christian Classics Ethereal Library, 2001 [1885].

Sider, Ron. Lecture, Acadia Divinity College, Acadia University, Wolfville, NS, 27th May 2013.

Sider, Ronald J. "An Evangelical Theology of Liberation." *Christian Century* (March 1980): 314.

———. *Good News and Good Works: A Theology for the Whole Gospel.* Grand Rapids: Baker Books, 1993.

———. *Rich Christians in an Age of Hunger: Moving from Affluence To Generosity.* Nashville: Thomas Nelson, 2005.

Simon, Wolfgang. *The Starfish Manifesto.* Antioch: Asteroidea Books, 2009.

Smith, Eugene L. *Mandate for Mission.* New York: Friendship Press, 1968.

Snodgrass, Klyne. *Stories with Intent: A Comprehensive Guide to the Parables of Jesus.* Grand Rapids: Eerdmans, 2009.

Sobrino, Jon. *Spirituality of Liberation: Toward Political Holiness.* Maryknoll: Orbis Books, 1988.

St Francis of Assisi. *The Writings of St Francis of Assisi.* Translated by Father Paschal Robinson (1905). Santa Cruz: Evinity Publishing Inc., 2009.

Stassen, Glen H., and David P. Gushee. *Kingdom Ethics: Following Jesus in Contemporary Context.* Downers Grove: IVP Academic, 2003.

Stott, John. *Christian Mission in the Modern World.* Downers Grove: IVP Press, 1975.

———. *Issues Facing Christians Today.* Bombay: Gospel Literature Service, 1984.

Sunquist, Scott W. *Understanding Christian Mission: Participation in Suffering and Glory.* Grand Rapids: Baker Academic. 2013.

Sweet, Leonard and Frank Viola. *Jesus Manifesto: Restoring the Supremacy and Sovereignty of Jesus Christ.* Nashville: Thomas Nelson, 2010.

Taleb, Nassim Nicholas. *The Black Swan: The Impact of the Highly Improbable.* New York: Random House Trade Paperbacks, 2010.

Tertullian. *The Apology of Tertullian.* Translated by William Reeves. Vol. 31. London: Griffith, Farran, Okeden & Welsh, 1889.

The Lausanne Movement. "The Lausanne Covenant." 2013. Accessed 23 July 2013. http://www.lausanne.org/en/documents/lausanne-covenant.html.

"The Reforms of Urukagina." World History Project. 2007. Accessed 10 December 2012. http://world-history.org/reforms_of_urukagina.htm.

Tizon, Al. *Transformation after Lausanne: Radical Evangelical Mission in Global-Local Perspective.* Eugene: Wipf and Stock Publishers, 2008.

UNESCO. "Statement of Commitment for Action to Eradicate Poverty Adopted by Administrative Committee on Coordination." 1998. Accessed 6 July 2012. http://www.unesco.org/most/acc4pov.htm.

Vaux, Roland (de). *Ancient Israel: Its life and Institutions.* London: Darton, Longman & Todd, 1965.

Vicedom, Georg F. *The Mission of God.* St Louis: Concordia, 1965.

Volf, Miroslav. *Exclusion and Embrace: A Theological Exploration Of Identity, Otherness, and Reconciliation.* Nashville: Abingdon Press, 1996.

Wagner, C. Peter. *Latin American Theology: Radical or Evangelical.* Grand Rapids: William B. Eerdmans Publishing Company, 1970.

Walker, Percy. in *Conversations with Walker Percy,* edited by Peggy Whitman Prenshaw. Jackson: University of Mississippi Press, 1985.

Walls, Andrew. *The Missionary Movement in Christian History: Studies in the Transmission of Faith.* Maryknoll: Orbis, 1996.

Walsh, William, and John Langan. "Patristic Social Consciousness – The Church and the Poor." In *The Faith That Does Justice,* edited by John Haughey, 113–151. Mahwah: Paulist, 1977.

Walton, John H. *Ancient Near Eastern Thought and the Old Testament.* Grand Rapids: Baker Academics, 2006.

Webb, Clement C. J., ed. *The Devotions of St Anselm Archbishop of Canterbury.* London: Methuen & Co., 1903.

Weber, Robert E. *The Younger Evangelicals: Facing the Challenges of the New World.* Grand Rapids: Baker Books, 2002

Weber, Timothy. *Living in the Shadow of the Second Coming.* 2nd. Grand Rapids: Zondervan, 1983.

Weber, Max. *The Protestant Ethic and the Spirit of Capitalism.* New York: Scribner, 1901.

———. *Theory of Social and Economic Organizations.* Edited by Talcot Parsons. New York: Free Press, 1947.

Wenham, David. *Paul: Follower of Jesus or Founder of Christianity.* Grand Rapids: William E. Eerdmans Publishing Company, 1995.

Wicker, Brian. *The Story-Shaped World: Fiction and Metaphysics: Some Variations on a Theme.* Notre Dame: University Press, 1975.

Wilson, Godfrey. *An Essay on the Economics of Detribalization in Northern Rhodesia, Part II,* Rhodes-Livingstone Papers, no. 6. Livingstone, Rhodesia: Rhodes-Livingstone Institute, 1942.

Wink, Walter. *Engaging the Powers: Discernment and Resistance in a World of Domination.* Minneapolis: Fortress Press, 1992.

Wolterstorff, Nicholas. *Justice: Rights and Wrong.* Princeton: Princeton University Press, 2008.

Woodberry, Robert, D. "The Missionary Roots of Liberal Democracy," *American Political Science Review* 106, no. 2 (May 2012).

World Council of Churches. *The Church for Others and the Church for the World.* Geneva: World Council of Churches, 1967.

Wright, Christopher J. H. *Living as the People of God.* Nottingham: Inter-Varsity Press, 1983.

———. *The Mission of God's People: A Biblical Theology of The Church's Mission.* Grand Rapids: Zondervan, 2010.

Wright, N. T. *The New Testament and the People of God.* Vol. 1. Minneapolis: Fortress Press, 1992.

———. "Paul's Gospel and Caesar's Empire." In *Paul and Politics,* edited by R. A. Hosley, 160–183. Harrisburg: Trinity, 2000.

———. *Paul for Everyone: Galatians and Thessalonians.* London: SPCK, 2002.

———. *Evil and the Justice of God.* London: Society for Promoting Christian Knowledge, 2006.

———. *Surprised by Hope.* London: SPCK, 2007.

———. *How God Became King: The Forgotten Story of the Gospels.* New York: Harper Collins Publishers, 2011.

Wright, N. T., and M. Borg. *The Meaning of Jesus.* London: SPCK, 1999.

Yancey, Philip. *Finding God in Unexpected Places*. London: Authentic
   Books, 1997.
Yoder, John Howard. *The Politics of Jesus: Vicit Agnus Noster*. 2nd ed. Grand
   Rapids: Eerdmans, 1994.
———. *The Royal Priesthood: Essays Ecclesiological and Ecumenical*. Edited
   by Michael G. Cartwright. Scottsdale: Herald Press, 1998.
———. *The Original Revolution: Essays on Christian Pacifism*. Scottsdale:
   Herald Press, 2003.

Langham Literature and its imprints are a ministry of Langham Partnership.

Langham Partnership is a global fellowship working in pursuit of the vision God entrusted to its founder John Stott –

to facilitate the growth of the church in maturity and Christ-likeness through raising the standards of biblical preaching and teaching.

Our vision is to see churches in the majority world equipped for mission and growing to maturity in Christ through the ministry of pastors and leaders who believe, teach and live by the Word of God.

Our mission is to strengthen the ministry of the Word of God through:
- nurturing national movements for biblical preaching
- fostering the creation and distribution of evangelical literature
- enhancing evangelical theological education

especially in countries where churches are under-resourced.

Our ministry

Langham Preaching partners with national leaders to nurture indigenous biblical preaching movements for pastors and lay preachers all around the world. With the support of a team of trainers from many countries, a multi-level programme of seminars provides practical training, and is followed by a programme for training local facilitators. Local preachers' groups and national and regional networks ensure continuity and ongoing development, seeking to build vigorous movements committed to Bible exposition.

Langham Literature provides majority world preachers, scholars and seminary libraries with evangelical books and electronic resources through publishing and distribution, grants and discounts. The programme also fosters the creation of indigenous evangelical books in many languages, through writer's grants, strengthening local evangelical publishing houses, and investment in major regional literature projects, such as one volume Bible commentaries like *The Africa Bible Commentary* and *The South Asia Bible Commentary*.

Langham Scholars provides financial support for evangelical doctoral students from the majority world so that, when they return home, they may train pastors and other Christian leaders with sound, biblical and theological teaching. This programme equips those who equip others. Langham Scholars also works in partnership with majority world seminaries in strengthening evangelical theological education. A growing number of Langham Scholars study in high quality doctoral programmes in the majority world itself. As well as teaching the next generation of pastors, graduated Langham Scholars exercise significant influence through their writing and leadership.

To learn more about Langham Partnership and the work we do visit **langham.org**

CPSIA information can be obtained
at www.ICGtesting.com
Printed in the USA
LVHW010639060919
630126LV00005B/32